CW00321458

Michael's
NEW YORK

THE NEW GUIDE
Michael's
NEW YORK

Managing Editor
Michael Shichor

Series Editor
Amir Shichor

INBAL TRAVEL INFORMATION LTD.

Inbal Travel Information Ltd.
P.O.Box 1870 Ramat Gan 52117
Israel

Intl. ISBN 965-288-121-X

Text: Michael Shichor, Aaron Young
Graphic design: Michel Opatowski
Cover design: Bill Stone
Photography: Shahar Azran
Photo editor: Sharon Bentov
Editorial: Sharona Johan, Or Rinat, Lisa Stone
D.T.P.: Michael Michelson, Irit Bahalul
Maps: Roni Kinderman, Itzik Hazan, Rina Waserman
Printed by Havatzelet Press Ltd.

**Sales in the UK
and Europe:**
Kuperard (London) Ltd.
9 Hampstead West
224 Iverson Road
London NW6 2HL

**Distribution in the UK
and Europe:**
Bailey Distribution Ltd.
Learoyd Road
New Romney
Kent TN28 8X

U.K. ISBN 1-85733-108-7

CONTENTS

TABLE OF MAPS

The idea of producing a guide to New York City occurred to us almost by chance over 12 years ago. Two factors were decisive in our decision to go through with it: our thorough familiarity with, and our affection for, this overwhelming city. Aaron is a born-and-bred New Yorker, and I am a frequent visitor from abroad; as a team, we considered ourselves fit for the task. As veteran "explorers", accustomed to the tourist experience and fully at home with its ins and outs, we wished to share our acquaintance with the city – its sights, scenes and special nature – with newer arrivals. This is the 6th edition of Michael's Guide New York in English; the guide was published in 6 other languages as well.

Aaron is a successful art dealer who lives and breathes New York, knows the city's layout, geographical as well as emotional; and, as a visitor who knows the (unjustified) sense of alienation with which New York greets newcomers, I felt a need to try and ease the tourist's encounter with the metropolis and lead him on a route which ensures not only a smoother landing but also an enjoyable, fascinating visit – a wonderful and mind-broadening experience.

In this guide, we aimed at meeting the needs of the discriminating tourist who yearns for the special, who seeks the root of things and the stories behind them. We directed the visitor's attention to all those elements which make New York unique and captivating, charming and welcoming. The feeling of "too much" which the mammoth metropolis imposes on visitors often blunts their ability to tell things apart and blinds them to the city's genuine luminescence. From beginning to end we worked with these guidelines, neutralizing the impact of the city's dimensions as best as we could and trying to present our subject in the manner most easily and comfortably grasped.

Production of this book engaged many people for many months; we haven't the space to thank them all. Nevertheless, I would like to express my gratitude to the entire staff of Inbal Travel Information Ltd.

The New York we present is ours: yours and mine. For New York belongs to no one, and no one is really a stranger here. We aimed that during your visit to New York you would ingest the largest possible slice of the city's limitless spectrum, the inexhaustible wealth of its resources; and our final, most important goal is that when you take off for home, you'll feel for New York what we feel.

Michael Shichor

Using this Guide

In order to reap maximum benefit from the information in this guide, we advise the traveler to carefully read the following passage. The facts contained in this book were compiled to help the tourist find his or her way around and to ensure that he enjoys his stay to the upmost.

The "Introduction" provides details which will help you make the early decisions and arrangements for your trip. We suggest that you carefully review the material, so that you will be more organized and set for your visit. Upon arrival in New York, you will feel familiar and comfortable with the city.

The tour routes, laid out geographically, lead the visitor up and down the city's streets, providing a survey of the sites and calling attention to all those details which deepen one's familiarity with New York, and make a visit there so much more enjoyable.

The reader will notice that certain facts tend to recur. This is deliberate; it enables the tourist who starts out from a point other than the one we choose to be no less informed. The result is a flexibility in personal planning.

The rich collection of maps covers the tour routes in great detail. Especially prepared for this book, they will certainly add to the efficiency and pleasure of your exploration of New York.

A concise list of "Musts" follows, describing those sites without which your visit is not complete.

Since New York is highly esteemed for its cuisine, shopping and entertainment, a special chapter is devoted to "Making the Most of Your Stay" in the city. Here you will find a broad range of possibilities to suit your budget, needs and tastes.

To further facilitate the use of this guide, we have included a detailed index. It includes all the major sites mentioned throughout the book. Consult the index to find something by name and it will refer you to the place where it is mentioned in greatest detail.

During your visit you will have many fascinating experiences. We have therefore left a couple of blank pages at the end of the guide. These are for you to jot down your observations, thoughts, and reactions along the way.

Because times and cities are dynamic, an important rule of thumb when traveling, and especially when visiting a vibrant city like New York, should be to consult local sources of information. Tourists are liable to encounter certain inaccuracies in this guide, and for this, we apologize.

In this guide we have tried to present updated information in a way which allows for an easy, safe and economical visit. For this purpose, we have included a short questionnaire and will be most grateful for those who will take the time to complete it and send it to us.

Have a pleasant and exciting trip – Bon Voyage!

PART ONE –
A TASTE OF WHAT'S TO COME

History in a Nutshell

Long before the first European explorer sailed into New York Harbor, the area that is New York City today was controlled by Indian tribes: The north was shared by the Rechgawawanc and Weckquaesgeek tribes, while the Canarsee dominated the area in the south of today's Manhattan. In fact, the name Manhattan or "Minna-atn" comes from their language and means "Island of Hills".

Italian navigator Giovanni da Verrazano is the first European known to have entered New York. In 1524, he anchored his ship *La Dauphine* on the shores of New York, and named it Angouleme, after a town in France. The Verrazano-Narrows Bridge, built in 1964, to cross the bay between Brooklyn and Staten Island, bears his name in recognition of his discovery.

Verrazano's visit was short, and the next important expedition to New York wasn't until 1609, when Henry Hudson's *Half-Moon* sailed into lower New York Bay. An Englishman in service of the Dutch East India Co., Hudson took the *Half-Moon* upstream as far as today's Albany, the capital of New York State, in search of the Northwest Passage from Europe to the Orient. Hudson didn't find the northwest passage, but he did bring home a cargo of valuable furs to the Netherlands, which inspired the Dutch to send out further expeditions.

In 1621 the Dutch authorities granted the Dutch West India Co. a 24 year trade monopoly in the area, including colonizing and governmental powers. The first permanent settlement took root in 1624 with the arrival of a group of pioneers, chiefly Protestant Walloons fleeing Spanish-ruled, Inquisition-ridden Belgium in search of religious freedom (all but eight of these pioneers continued on to Albany). More families arrived in 1625. They settled together with an engineer and some livestock, at Manhattan's lower tip and named their hamlet Nieuw Amsterdam.

Although the Dutch West India Company's initial interest was purely commercial, it decided to establish a fort and ten adjoining farms in April, 1625. The colony's first Director-General, Peter Minuit, arrived the following year to supervise the community of 300 people. It was

A view of Manhattan's skyline from Brooklyn Bridge

Minuit who purchased Manhattan Island later that year in a deal now famous as one of history's greatest bargains – 60 Dutch guilders' worth of goods for property currently worth some 600 billion dollars (though all the Dutch wanted was better farmland than Manhattan's rocky, non-arable southern tip). Shrewd though they were, the Dutch mistakenly negotiated the deal with the Canarsee, whom they thought governed the entire island. Once the deal was settled, the Canarsee relocated to Brooklyn and the Dutch moved northward into what was Weckquaesgeek land, a move which precipitated in the Dutch-Indian wars. The imposition of a trade tax on the Indians fuelled the hostilities, and in 1643 the massacre of over 100 Indians triggered two years of war. In 1647, believing that a change of leadership would lead to peace, the Company replaced Director-General Kieft with peg-legged Peter Stuyvesant as the Director-General of the 500-strong colony.

For 17 years Stuyvesant administered Nieuw Amsterdam, until the British seized the colony in the war of 1664-67. Though Stuyvesant initially refused to surrender, Fort Amsterdam was in poor condition and the burghers' council would not defend the settlement. Taking over on Sept. 8, 1664, the British renamed the colony "New York", after the Duke of York, who not only bestowed his name on the colony, but also owned and ruled it in the manner of a king. Though they retained many Dutch legal practices, the British introduced their language as the official tongue. When a Dutch fleet entered the harbor in 1673 and demanded the colony back, the British surrendered – though for only one year. The Treaty of Westminster (1867) resulted in a colony swap: New York to the English and the South American colony of Surinam to the Dutch.

Britain wanted New York for several reasons: to thwart trade competition, to close the last gap in its coastal holdings in the area, and to obtain the eastern seaboard's finest natural harbor. This harbor is large, deep and accessible from two directions, making New York a particularly valuable property. Long Island and Staten Island, in the lower bay, shield the harbor against ocean turbulence and keep the water ice-free, particularly important in an era of wooden ships. The Hudson River, along Manhattan's western shore, offers a trade passage inland.

While under Dutch rule, Nieuw Amsterdam, as it was walled off at its northern extremity against Indian attacks in 1653, never really expanded. Until 1699 when the wall was removed (the first street outside the old boundaries was aptly named Wall Street) the colony consisted of a few streets on the southeastern shore. The bank of the Hudson was completely vacant since the colonists, who were unwilling to move west or north, purchased "water lots" along the East River and extended the shoreline with landfills of earth and trash. The "Water Street" they built on the original bank of the East River runs two blocks inland today.

Despite the colony's maritime economy, Nieuw Amsterdam did not prosper as one might have expected. One reason may have been competition from British colonies, as well as a lack of

A Hundred Years Ago...

How did Sheep Meadow get its name?

exportable goods other than furs. Even when under British domination colonial shipping opened to a larger market, trade grew slowly because of the strife between England and Holland, and because Britain's restrictive Navigation Acts of the late 1600's confined British trade to British-built or British-manned vessels.

The answer to the problem was "a trade triangle": While continuing to ship furs to England for manufactured goods, New York also traded agricultural products for rum, limes, coffee and sugar grown in the West Indies, where these crops were so lucrative that no one bothered to grow food and were, therefore, dependent on imports.

Though New York City finally began to prosper, Boston and Philadelphia still dominated the Eastern seaboard in population and culture. The first newspaper, the *New York Gazette*, was established in 1725; the competing *Weekly Journal* appeared in 1733. Its founder, John Peter Zenger, fought off libel charges for having criticized the government in a landmark 1735 court battle, the echoes of which – with regard to freedom of the press – later surfaced in the First Amendment to the United States Constitution. Kings College, the colony's first institute of higher learning (1754), became one of

*Taking a lunch break
on Park Avenue*

America's foremost universities; it was renamed Columbia University at the end of the American Revolution.

The seeds of the American Revolution were sown in 1754-5, with the tension between France and Britain over domination of the North American colonies, and 1756-63 (the Seven Years War); heavy taxes imposed by the British to help finance their wars against the French created great resentment among the colonists. The 1765 Stamp Act was the last straw; a Stamp Act Congress of delegates from nine colonies met in Lower Manhattan and drafted a Declaration of Rights that petitioned against "taxation without representation." The Stamp Act was repealed but the taxation policy remained. New York was wallowing in a ten-year economic depression at the time and, despite its magnificent harbor, the port was not favored because its few wharves were so shabby. Economic stagnation, coupled with stiff taxation, made NYC a hotbed for revolution.

In 1775 the colonies revolted and New Yorkers built forts in the highlands of today's Central Park. Following the capture of New York City in 1776, the British succeeded in holding the port throughout the war. However, in 1783 General George Washington, with his out-manned, under-supplied army of volunteers somehow defeated the British who withdrew from the city, leaving it in shambles. New York quickly recovered, and was chosen as seat of the first national government, and remained so until 1790. The special Government bonds issued during those years to cover war debts became so popular that a special market for their trade came into being, later encompassing other securities and commodities. Thus, in 1792, the New York Stock Exchange was born.

The early 19th century found NYC in an economic boom, spurred by innovations in industry and transportation. Robert Fulton's steamship *Clermont* chugged up the Hudson towards Albany in 1807 in the first steam-powered voyage of considerable length. The Erie Canal (1825) brought domestic and foreign commerce further inland at a time when highways were nonexistent and railroads were not extensive. NYC's superior harbor was the gateway to the Canal, and its shipbuilding yards were the best in the nation. Businessmen began amassing fortunes from trade and commerce. By 1860 more than 50% of the nation's exports and 70% of its imports flowed through New York City.

The Civil War (1861-1865) found New Yorkers split in their loyalties, with the majority siding with the North, actually favoring the city's secession as a free port.

Technological feats accompanied and fuelled New York's growth. NYC featured the world's first elevators (1853) and apartment building (1869). The first "El" (elevated railroad) began to rumble over 9th Ave. in 1870, followed by three others. The last of these, the 3rd Ave. El, closed down only in 1955. Grand Central Terminal opened in 1871, and the Brooklyn Bridge was completed in 1883.

The city grew vertically as well as horizontally. Above ground, high speed elevators and steel skeletons made skyscrapers feasible, while underground, the first subway opened in 1904. The Statue of Liberty was unveiled in 1886, greeting millions of immigrants (five million during the late 1880s alone). The first neon light, forever identified with Broadway and Times Square, was installed in New York City in 1923.

Administratively, present-day NYC began to crystallize first with a partial (1874) and then a total (1895) union with The Bronx; the separate boroughs of Brooklyn, Queens and Staten Island (Richmond) joined the City in 1898.

NYC today, with its approx. 7.3

Central Park, surrounded by NYC's massive skyscrapers

million residents, is a world center of finance, culture, advertising, fashion, art and entertainment, and much of what we associate with today's NYC (e.g., the UN; diplomatic home to over 180 nations, which opened in 1952) began to take shape in the early to middle 20th century.

NYC Topography

NYC rests on metamorphic rock formed during the archeozoic era, the earliest geological epoch. This bedrock, called Manhattan Schist and Inwood Dolomite, provides a foundation strong enough to support the weighty skyscrapers of the city. During the Ice Age, the entire area, with the exception of the southern edge of Brooklyn, was covered with glaciers.

New York Harbor is comprised of a Lower Bay off the Atlantic Ocean to the south, and a naturally protected Upper Bay. Manhattan owes its development into a center of trade and finance to the advantages

NEW YORK CITY

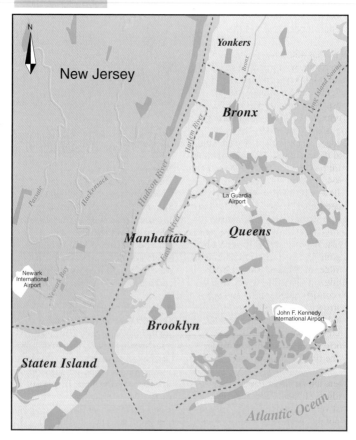

of a calm harbor and deep rivers on either side – the Hudson on the west and the East River on the east. The latter is not a true river at all, but rather a sixteen-mile-long (approx. 25 km) strait connecting Long Island to the north with Upper New York Bay to the south. The Hudson leads inland, joined to the great Lakes and the St. Lawrence Seaway by means of the New York State Barge Canal System, the outgrowth of the Erie Canal.

Three Government-owned islands rest in the Upper Bay: Governors Island (a U.S. Coast Guard Station), Ellis Island (the former immigration facility) and Liberty Island (home to the Statue of Liberty, the famed national monument donated by France).

NYC has 450 miles (720 km) of waterfront, with an additional 300 miles (480 km) of waterfront in neighboring New Jersey to the west. With the exception of The Bronx, all of New York's boroughs are islands and are linked by bridges and tunnels with each other and the mainland. The bridges were built between the years 1883 and 1964; the first was Brooklyn Bridge followed by Williamsburg and Queensboro Bridges in 1903, Manhattan Bridge in 1905, Goethals Bridge and Outerbridge Crossing in 1928, Bayonne and George Washington Bridges in 1931, Triborough Bridge in 1936 and Throgs Neck Bridge in 1961. The last bridge to be constructed was the Verrazano-Narrows Bridge, completed in 1964. It is interesting to note that each of these bridges was the world's longest suspension bridge at the time of construction.

There are far fewer tunnels than bridges. Holland Tunnel, the city's first vehicular tunnel (1927), which is not part of the city's mass transit system, connects Manhattan and New Jersey, as does Lincoln Tunnel, which was opened in 1937. Queens-Midtown Tunnel (1940) runs from Queens into Manhattan and Brooklyn-Battery Tunnel (1950) connects Manhattan with Brooklyn.

Climate

New York experiences all four seasons, with all the attendant advantages and disadvantages. Summer (June-September) presents a temperature range from the mid-70's to the high 90's F. (25°-35°C) often accompanied by oppressive humidity (dress accordingly) and a strong sun, requiring the necessary precautions.

Autumn (October through mid-December) is a beautiful time to see the city. Temperatures drop from approximately 60°F (15°C) in October to around 50°F (10°C) in November, plunging seriously only around mid-December. The crisp air and the splendor of autumn leaves make this an ideal time to tour NYC on foot.

Winter (late December through March) is harsh: the temperature hovers near or below freezing (27°-32°F, 0°C) with a wind-chill factor that often brings it down another 20°-30°F. Bring a heavy overcoat, but don't dress too warmly since Americans tend to overheat their homes and public buildings. Dressing in too many layers – a good idea in Europe – tends to be counterproductive here. Winter is full blast in January and February, when snowstorms are common. March, as the saying goes, "comes in like a lion and goes out like a lamb."

Spring (mid-April through May) replays autumn's temperature range. It's ideal sweater weather, and you will find New Yorkers out in force walking and bicycle riding through the parks. Rain is liable to fall at any time of the year.

New York City – A Melting Pot or Not?

New York is often referred to as a "melting pot" where people from around the world are forged, as it were, into a homogenous entity. This is only half-true. It is true that NYC is largely a city of immigrants or descendants of immigrants. However, not everyone has "melted" in; neither is everyone equally welcome to "melt", despite the fact that the right to do so is anchored in the citizenship laws.

Though NYC has always been a refuge for people from many different countries, the greatest waves of immigration occurred between 1820 and the 1920s; of the more than 33 million newcomers who reached the United States during those years, two-thirds arrived at New York Harbor, passing through the Ellis Island Immigration Center which opened in 1892.

Demographically, 1880 was the watershed year. A vast majority of pre-1880 immigrants had come from Ireland and Germany; most of the successors hailed from Italy, Russia and Austria-Hungary. By 1910, an astonishing 78% of all New Yorkers were first- or second-generation immigrants. They changed the face of NYC forever, contributing to the fabric of dreams and talent that make New York the cosmopolitan city it is today.

The Irish were the first to arrive in

20 million immigrants passed through the Ellis Island Immigration Center

great numbers – in the 1820s because of the booming canal and railroad construction job market, and in the 1840s to escape the potato famine back home. Being the first newcomers, and adherents to the Catholic faith (as opposed to the native Protestants), the Irish did not always get red carpet treatment.

The Germans began arriving in the 1830s in the wake of political and economic upheaval. While most settled in the Midwest, those who remained in New York were more readily accepted than the Irish. Despite their language barrier, they were mostly Protestant and exhibited business skills that could be incorporated into the city's growing economy.

The first German and Irish immigrants to settle in New York City moved into the Lower East Side, a neighborhood abandoned by established New Yorkers for more exclusive districts. Over the next sixty years the Irish moved into the area known as Hell's Kitchen in the West Forties and Fifties, and farther north into The Bronx. The Germans relocated on the East Side between Houston and 14th Street (Little Germany), and farther north to Yorkville in the East Eighties and sections of Brooklyn.

The Lower East Side became the first rung in the American socio-economic ladder for one immigrant group after another – Italians, Russian and Hungarians. In 1880 it was home to approximately half the city's population, a million "green-horns" who often found work in factories near their tenement homes. Italians inhabited an area nicknamed "New Italy" (today's Little Italy). Of the Russian immigrants, 90% were Jewish. From the Lower East Side they moved on to Little Germany and thence, in great numbers, to Brooklyn and The Bronx. The Jewish immigrants, many of them talented merchants, prospered and advanced more quickly than other groups.

The "melting pot," in the meantime, was not on the high burner. Neighborhoods were quite clearly demarcated and NYC was more like a patchwork quilt than a "melting pot."

Most immigrant parents were well aware of the hardships of life in a new country: they took jobs nobody else wanted, labored for wages nobody else would accept, and dreamed of a better life for their children. But social advancement required education, and the New York Public School System became perhaps the single greatest contributor to the "melting pot" theory. Language, often a great barrier, became the great unifier of the second generation as one and all "pledged allegiance to the flag" in English every morning in the class-

room. Teachers used the common
language to teach American
customs which the children took
home.

Modern NYC – Manhattan in particular – is perhaps less of a
"melting pot" than ever, with vast
wealth and extreme poverty, with
little in between. Hard work helps,
but no longer guarantees a high
standard of living. The wealth of
Wall St., Midtown and Madison
Ave. is professional wealth, not
sweatshop labor. Land in Manhattan is far too valuable and rent too
high to use for light industry. The
business districts are reserved for
doctors, lawyers and advertising
executives.

NYC is currently enjoying its greatest surge of immigration since the
1940s. More than 2.5 million
of its approx. 7.3 million residents
are foreign-born. There are more
Greeks in New York than in any
other city outside Athens; the vegetable markets seem to be owned
and operated by Koreans only. Less-
established arrivals endure hardships because it is still better here
than where they were. They retain

hope that life can always improve.
Furthermore, NYC is in itself a
goal, a destination. There is almost
a romantic desire to join the history
of human tides washing ashore
here.

But one minority group remains
conspicuously "out": American-
born Blacks, who watch newly-
arrived Hispanics and Asians
advance much more rapidly than
themselves. Perhaps part of the
reason is the history of Blacks in
America, a litany of slavery and
racial prejudice. Harlem, New
York's most famous black neighborhood, is a depressed shadow of
the jazz capital it was in the 1930s
and 1940s.

Hence today's NYC is not an
evolving melting pot but rather a
non-ethnic "mainstream" coexisting
with pockets of ethnic culture. The
continued existence of Chinatown,
Harlem, Spanish Harlem, the
Lower East Side, etc., disproves the
image of a melting pot. And yet, it
is the retainment of ethnic neighborhoods, culture and cuisine
which makes the city interesting
and fun.

The Big Apple – the World's Pre-eminent Metropolis

New York City, affectionately called "The Big Apple," is the world's pre-eminent metropolis and the financial center of the nation, if not of the world. It is a leading force in the world of culture and art, and as the home of the UN, NYC also plays a unique role in world politics.

The New York Stock Exchange (NYSE) is the most important marketplace in the United States, where brokers handle shares of national companies on its floor. The country's economic and political stability is immeasurably determined by its ups and downs. From the NYSE Observation Deck – a sight every visitor should see – what looks like chaos is really a complex, hectic, well-organized series of sales and purchases by a hierarchy of participants.

The twin towers of the World Trade Center, built just north of the NYSE near the Port Authority of New York and New Jersey, provides all services necessary for international trade: the U.S. Customs House, trade agencies and associations, international banks, manufacturers, importers and exporters, under two roofs.

While most manufacturing has left NYC, the corporate headquarters remain. Of America's 500 largest industrial corporations, 68 are based here and at least 46 others in nearby suburbs. Their executives require banking and financial services, and indeed find them close by: 12 of the 100 largest commercial banking companies plus 12

of the 100 largest diversified financial companies (as ranked by assets) are headquartered in NYC. Behind these figures is a phenomenal concentration of the country's financial power and resources.

Turning to culture, we find modern NYC to be one of the world centers of music, art, theater and less conventional entertainment. It was not always that way. Sneered at by Bostonians and Philadelphians, New Yorkers in 1775 were considered ill-mannered, poorly-schooled and blind to the arts and sciences. However, by the mid-1800s a publishing industry had transplanted from Boston, together with its attendant writers and illustrators, awarding NYC intellectual and cultural supremacy. Toward the end of that century, new tycoons began to satisfy philanthropic impulses by supporting artists and founding museums. Massive immigration brought a variety of talents to NYC's shores.

Today, NYC is the capital of the music world both in excellence and abundance, from the opulent Lincoln Center, to informal jazz clubs and avant-garde lofts. One must credit immigration for much of this diversity; NYC's ethnic mix creates a demand for a wide variety of musical styles – performers can always find an audience. Musicians seek out NYC for fame (it's the world's media center) and fortune (performances pay better here than anywhere else).

Though the Broadway theater is legendary (especially for great musicals), theaters exist throughout the city though not all of them offer luxurious surroundings. Discovering a wonderful production put on by a little-known company is half the fun and half the ticket price.

Art is everywhere: on walls of buildings, in galleries, at the Metropolitan Museum and other museums. Shopping and dining possibilities are similarly endless.

Immigrants, with no access to other fields, often find the restaurant business more easily penetrated. As a result, NYC's streets are lined with restaurants serving every imaginable cuisine. NYC also offers the widest selection of wines in the world (wine prices are now set mostly in New York, not in France). Fashion is created here, from haute-couture to bargain-basement "finds".

This city of immigrants, where almost anything goes, is a natural home for the United Nations, whose member countries represent billions of people around the world. More important for what it represents than what it actually accomplishes, the UN's chief goal – maintenance of international peace and security – is admirable and vital to striving toward global stability. Above all, the UN provides its members with a forum for discussion of the problems they share in the complex world.

Part of Manhattan's skyline, with the Twin Towers of the World Trade Center in the middle

PART TWO – SETTING OUT

Helpful Hints

New York is so different from other cities worldwide; both Americans and tourists from outside the city, will feel alien and at home all at once in New York City.

New York is a tough town which moves at a dizzy pace. It is very expensive, full of temptations and rich in possibilities. It has its perils. **Always** keep your eyes open – for your property, for your physical safety – against willful and accidental misfortunes alike. The first rule is caution.

When planning a visit to New York, study the destination thoroughly in advance; arrive in New York prepared, and start touring immediately. Every day here is valuable. Even if you avoid luxury hotels, or stay with a friend or relative willing to put you up, you'll find that New York has a voracious appetite for your money. Considering this, and the wealth of sights and destinations you'll want to visit, correct use of time is important here.

If you planned your visit to coincide with the holiday season or the peak summer tourist season, it is advisable to reserve accommodation. With hotels almost totally booked at those times, prices tend to skyrocket.

New York is usually a captivating city with a mind-boggling variety of things to do. To get the most out of your visit, be careful, plan ahead, and give efficiency and good organization top priority. As effective as

these precautions are anywhere, they are particularly vital here.

How to Get There

BY AIR
Scores of airlines and hundreds of flights connect New York with the rest of the world and every major city in the US. Choosing among the many competing airlines is primarily a matter of comparing service and price. If you are departing from a preferred take off point in Europe – Frankfurt, Brussels, Paris or London, for example – you may reasonably expect to cross the Atlantic for a very attractive price. Stand-by service from London is especially inexpensive, and the chances of getting stuck are negligible.

Combination travel and accommodation packages to New York – usually at attractive prices – are regularly available from various cities in the United States. Depending on time of year and point of departure, airfare itself can be very expensive (from unpopular take off points or minor cities) or ridiculously low-priced (from especially popular points or places where inter-airline competition is tough at the moment). Therefore, do some thorough comparison shopping before you buy a ticket.

If you intend to visit other cities, consider the possibility of purchasing a VUSA ticket which is good for flights between a number of cities in the United States (sometimes including Hawaii), and at times, Canada and Mexico. VUSA tickets are sold **only** outside the United States and **only** to non-Americans who hold round-trip airline tickets. VUSA prices and conditions vary according to airline and season, so check your itinerary, make inquiries and compare.

Here are a few of the airlines which have branches in Manhattan:

Air Canada: Tel. (800) 776-3000.
American Airlines: Tel. (800) 433-7300.
British Airways: Tel. (800) 247-9297.
Northwest: Tel. (800) 225-2525.
Olympic: Tel. (800) 838-3600.
United: Tel. (800) 241-6522.

BY LAND
Bus: Major bus lines connect Manhattan with the rest of North America, with arrivals and departures from Port Authority Bus Terminal, 42nd St. and 9th Ave., Tel. 330-1234. For destinations, timetables and prices, contact bus companies such as *Greyhound*, *Trailways*, etc.

Though getting to New York by bus is rather convenient and Port Authority Terminal offers many services, such as information, baggage check, etc., keep in mind that the Terminal area itself is rather unwelcoming, especially at night.

For those planning to tour the US by bus, note that the large companies offer unlimited-travel passes. Inquire at travel agencies.

Buying a ticket at the Grand Central Terminal

Rail: *Amtrak* provides extensive service from NYC to points throughout North America. Trains arrive at either Grand Central Station, 42nd St. and Park Ave., or Pennsylvania Station, 33rd St. and 7th Ave.

Car: It is generally not recommended to drive in NYC. For further information see "In-town Transportation."

BY SEA
Sea cruise lines dock on the Hudson River Piers, along 12th Ave. between 40th and 60th Sts.

Before Leaving

DOCUMENTS AND CUSTOMS REGULATIONS
Everyone arriving in NYC from abroad is required to fill out a Customs declaration in which he must answer general questions and declare the amount of money being brought into the U.S.

American Customs laws allow you to bring in personal gear and belongings without duty. "Personal" means just that: gifts in a modest quantity and of reasonable monetary value, limited amounts of cigarettes and alcohol (essentially for personal use). Even so, most customs officers are usually generous and sympathetic, unless you've really gone overboard.

At the airport, citizens of the United States, as opposed to all others, have their own passport inspection lanes. Tourists from abroad, by contrast, usually require **entry visas**, obtained from any United States consulate. Visa requirements vary from one country to another.

U.S. immigration authorities are tough when it comes to entry visas. Even if a visa is stamped into your passport there is no guarantee of entry, and it may have no bearing on the length of stay allowed. The decision to permit you entry is in the hands of the

Immigration Officer. He will generally ask the purpose of the visit, intended duration, and may occasionally ask to see proof of financial means and a return ticket. Unless his suspicions have been aroused, however, he will not place too many obstacles in your way.

If you wish to stay in the United States beyond the period stamped in your passport upon entry into the country, you must obtain a permit from the Immigration Authority.

Another document worth getting before entering the United States is an **International Driver's License**. It is good for the first three months of your stay; afterwards you must take out a local driver's license. A valid **International Student Card** with the bearer's picture, professional certificates, and any other documents in your possession, often prove very useful.

Passport Information: Tel. 399-5290.

INSURANCE

Health care in the United States is private, and is run as a profit-making enterprise in every sense. Accordingly, no illness or injury gets treated by private physicians or by medical institutions, unless payment is assured. Since medical costs in the United States are very high, the idea of setting out on a tour of this country without a valid health insurance policy is inconceivable. While insuring yourself, attach a luggage clause to your health coverage. This addition to the premium will protect you against loss or theft of your belongings.

WHEN TO COME

NYC is most "touristy" during the summer and holiday seasons, particularly late November through January. If you plan to visit at these times, be absolutely sure to book flights and hotels weeks in advance.

The best time to visit New York is during the "off-season", from April to June, or between Labor Day (1st Monday in September) and Thanksgiving (last Thursday in November). This is in order to avoid the unbearable heat and crowdedness which plague the city from Memorial Day (end of May) until the

Labor Day weekend. During this peak season it is difficult to find accommodationand many shows are booked up in advance. The shops, museums and entertainment spots are extremely crowded. December through January sees a new influx of visitors to the city, Americans and foreigners alike. In addition to this, from December to February the temperature drops to below freezing and it is often difficult to get around in the snowed-under city.

NATIONAL HOLIDAYS

Holidays in the United States generally differ from those of other nations. As the population evolved from different immigrant groups, many holidays have a secular basis (except for Christmas), which symbolize particularly American values. Most holidays fall on a Monday, creating a long weekend. Few Americans still celebrate these occasions in traditional ways, and prefer to go away for the weekend or take advantage of the many sales which coincide with the different holidays.

Banks, government offices and some sites, such as museums and shops, are closed on the following legal holidays. Hotels and transportation operate as usual. Certain holidays are big sale days for retail shops.

New Year's Day – January 1.
Martin Luther King's Birthday – January 16.
Presidents Day – the Monday between Lincoln's Birthday (February 12) and Washington's Birthday (February 22).
Memorial Day – last Monday in May.
Fourth of July/ Independence Day – July 4.
Labor Day – first Monday in September

Parading on 5th Avenue

Columbus Day – second Monday in October.
Veterans' Day – second Monday in November.
Thanksgiving – last Thursday in November.
Christmas Day – December 25.

HOW LONG TO STAY

Stay in NYC as long as possible, for as long as you can afford. There is much to do – you cannot exhaust all the possibilities New York has to offer. Nonetheless, you can see many things and get a real feel for the city in several days. You are the best judge of how much walking and exploring you can withstand in how short a time. A fair amount of time to spend in NYC is one to two weeks.

One of New York's huge Subway's smaller passengers

HOW MUCH WILL IT COST

A thrifty student, or the young at heart, should expect to need about $70-$100 per day; for the more mature traveler, we recommend a budget of about $250 per day. A businessman would find $350 per day an average for his expenses. These estimates include accommodation, food, transportation, admission fees, etc. Please remember that your choice of dining and entertainment will radically determine how far your budget goes. For example, an evening at a Broadway theater, including a light pre-theater meal, full-price tickets and a cab fare back to your hotel (an absolute must) can easily reach a high of $200 per couple.

CLOTHING

Regardless of the season, men should bring a suit or sports jacket and tie, and women a dress; some restaurants require such attire. Apart from this, dress for comfort. Think of NYC's street life and pack comfortable footwear. Remember the city's oppressive summer, its occasional chill of spring and fall, and the snow, slush and genuine cold of winter. There is a chance of rain at any time of the year, so it's best to have an umbrella ready.

At Times Square – the city's theater center

PART THREE – GETTING AROUND

New York Airports

JFK INTERNATIONAL AIRPORT, QUEENS

After passport control, you will arrive in a hall where your luggage is awaiting you. It is a good idea to have some change in dollars and cents ready for a cab and public telephones. Money exchange is only open during the day.

The *Carrey* bus service pick up around all JFK terminals, one route leads to La Guardia Airport, the other to Manhattan. The first stop in Manhattan is by Port Authority on the West side, the second, at Grand Central Station.

Taxis are available at the curb outside most terminals; Limousines and rental car service can be arranged at booths inside. Finally, there's public transit: subway, bus or helicopter. The JFK express subway is a one-hour trip with stops at Wall St., the World Trade Center, Greenwich Village, 34th St., 42nd St., Rockefeller Center and 57th St. at 6th Ave. It runs every 20 min. from 5am to midnight. It has stops at all major hotels (a shuttle bus service will take you from the terminal to the first subway station). Express buses depart from JFK every half-hour from early morning until midnight. The 60-minute trip ends at the East Side Airlines Terminal, 1st Ave. and 37th St., Tel. (718) 244-4444. The helicopter ride, from JFK's *TWA* terminal to the East 34th st. Heliport, is 20 minutes long and expensive, Tel. (800) 889-0986.

JFK Airport (General Information): Tel. (718) 244-4015.

LA GUARDIA AIRPORT, QUEENS

A free shuttle bus connects all terminals every 15 minutes from 5am to 2am. Taxis stand at designated locations outside most terminals; limousine and car rental service is arranged at booths inside. There are

JFK Airport in Queens

In front of the Port Authority Bus Terminal

a few public transit possibilities: the *Grey Line Air Shuttle*, 1740 Broadway, Tel. (800) 451-0455, a minibus to Manhattan hotels. Fare: $13; *MTA Transit* operates frequent buses Q48 or Q47 service between Marine Air Terminal, Main Terminal and subway connections. Fare: $1.25; the *New York Helicopter* service from the *American Airlines* Terminal to the East 34th St. Heliport. The flight is 6 minutes long and rather expensive, Tel. (800) 889-0986.

La Guardia Airport (General Information): Tel. (718) 476-5072.

NEWARK AIRPORT, NEWARK, NEW JERSEY

Although not part of New York City, or the State of New York for that matter, Newark Airport is only a 30-minute ride from mid-Manhattan, and it is considered one of the most modern and convenient airports in the country. It is comprised of four terminals: A, B, C, and the North Terminal which is located 3.5 miles (approx. 5.5 km) away from the central terminal area. International flights requiring federal clearance arrive at the North Terminal. A free shuttle bus connects the terminals and also serves the long-term parking areas. Taxis stand at designated locations outside most terminals; limousine and car rental service is arranged at booths inside the airport's main terminals.

Other public transit possibilities are available. *Share and Save* taxi service is good for up to four passengers with Manhattan destinations. The group rates are in effect from 8am-midnight and the passengers share the taxi fare among them. *NJ Transit* Tel. 564-8484, a bus service to the Port Authority Bus Terminal at 41st St. and 8th Ave. operates daily, departing every 15 minutes, 24-hours a day. A convenient mini-bus connects the airport with mid-Manhattan hotels. It departs every 30 minutes, from 7-1am on weekdays, less frequently on weekends and late at night, Tel. 564-1114. For train connections, *Airlink* mini-coach buses shuttle between the airport and Newark's Penn Station, where train and bus service is available to suburban New Jersey and NYC. The shuttle departs every 20-30 minutes during day and evening hours. Note that the only direct service to NYC's Financial District, i.e., the World Trade Center, is the *PATH* rail transit service. For information on *PATH*: Tel. (201) 216-2677, *Amtrak*: Tel. 582-6875 and *NJ Transit*: Tel. 564-8484.

Newark Airport (General Information): Tel. (201) 961-2000.

In-Town Transportation

In light of New York's vast dimensions and the volume of in-town travel, public transportation is the city's life line. The slightest disruption in its flow can cause extended, nerve-wracking delays within this strange city where "time is money."

You can get around New York by foot, bicycle, bus, taxi, even a luxury limousine with uniformed chauffeur. Do as the natives do: make a special effort to adjust your in-town travel with the city's own rhythm and to pace your schedule to "New York time." Spare yourself endless tedium by staying put during the famous rush hour. During peak hours – 7:30-9:30am and 4:30-6pm – the streets are clogged, taxis are hard to flag down, and the crowding and pressure in tunnels, buses and subways is literally insufferable. You will see it at its worst during New York's sweltering summer.

Never forget, by the way, that New York's subway is not a place to be at night (and that's putting it mildly). When returning from a night out, call a cab and consider the fare a necessary expense.

In general, however, public transportation in New York is convenient and efficient and despite its flaws, it serves the public faithfully.

PRIVATE CAR

Driving a car is neither the easiest nor the most convenient way to get around Manhattan. Parking is a headache. Using indoor parking facilities is expensive and on the street you risk: 1) alternative side-of-the-road parking, depending on the day of the week; 2) specific regulations on each street which are difficult to decipher; 3) parking meters; 4) theft. If you violate 1-3, the police will tow your car away; you can only retrieve it after paying the towing charges plus a stiff fine. In case 4, you probably won't see your car again.

If you've decided to drive anyway, try to avoid the rush hour traffic jams which clog the city entrances, early morning and late afternoon. Make sure not to park in concealed areas and never leave anything of value in your car.

All in all, driving a car into Manhattan is more trouble than it's worth. If you can avoid it, do. If you must drive, remember that New York State enforces the mandatory seat-belt law, with a fine for not wearing one.

CAR RENTAL FACILITIES

For out-of-town excursions, this is certainly the most convenient way to go. Dozens of rent-a-car companies are active in New York; most offer attractive deals for periods of several days, especially at weekends.

The large companies:
Avis: Tel. (800) 831-2847;
Tel. (914) 356-7272.

Traveling in slumber through Soho

Hertz: Tel. (800) 654-3131.
Budget: Tel. (800) 527-0700.
National: Tel. (800) 227-7368.
Dollar: Tel. (800) 800-4000.
Thrifty: Tel. (708) 252-1777.

Always compare prices, even those of small, little-known companies. Generally, you must be over 21 years old and carry a credit card to rent a car.

LIMOUSINE SERVICE

Visitors to New York will notice the elongated Cadillacs with tinted windows, enabling the occupant to observe the outside world while maintaining privacy. They cruise down stately avenues, park in front of luxury hotels and prestige shops and protrude from the parking lots of elegant office buildings. These vehicles, with their uniformed chauffeurs, are New York's limousines. Anyone who's anyone, or thinks he's anyone and can afford it, travels around in one.

It's unquestionably a prestige service and it's also an extremely comfortable, easy and fast way to get around town. A chauffeured car which lets you out at a shop entrance, waits there until you're done and whisks you off to your next destination is undoubtedly a luxury which makes life in New York easier and more efficient; but you pay for the pleasure.

A number of companies rent limousines by the hour or the day, with experienced, reliable drivers. Don't trust the *Yellow Pages* in this matter; ask the concierge in your hotel and compare prices.

Here are a few reliable companies:

Allstate Car & Limousine:
Tel. 741-7440.

City Ride Car & Limo:
Tel. 861-1000.
Romantique Limousines Inc.:
Tel. 921-9444.

TAXIS

Taxis or "cabs," come in two varieties: licensed medallion cabs (the bright yellow ones) and unlicensed gypsy cabs. Medallion cabs are recommended because they use fare meters which are based on rates printed on the door. The amount indicated on the meter is shared by ALL occupants, up to a maximum of 4 or 5, and is NOT paid by each rider individually.

The yellow taxi cabs cannot be ordered by phone, and can only be hailed on the street. If you want to order a taxi to meet you on your doorstep, there are a number of car service firms offering this service at only a slightly higher cost to the regular taxis:

All city: Tel. (718) 402-4747.
XYZ Taxi: (718) 499-2007.
UTOG: Tel. (718) 361-7270.

There's an extra charge for large baggage and a 50 cent surcharge after 8pm and on Sundays. Passengers must pay all bridge and tunnel tolls. When taking a cab from the airport, it is advisable to ask the driver how much the trip will cost before you get in.

In Manhattan, hail a cab at the curb side by signaling with your arm, don't try whistling, it doesn't work! A cab is available only when its roof light is illuminated, which is almost never during rush hours and in the rain. Add 15% to the meter fare as a tip for the driver. The likelihood of being overcharged decreases if you know where you are going and the shortest way to get there.

A taxi driver cannot refuse to take you to your destination once you're in the cab. In case of problems, get the driver's identification number from the dashboard plaque and contact the NYC Taxi Commission, Tel. 840-4734. This number will also assist you in the case of articles left inside a cab.

BUSES

Buses run round-the-clock on most major avenues (north-south) and streets (east-west). For route information, call Tel. (718) 330-1234. Bus stops are marked by curb side shelters. Route numbers (posted on shelters as well as on the bus dashboards) are preceded by letters which indicate the bus' destination:

BX – Bronx
B – Brooklyn
M – Manhattan
Q – Queens
S – Staten Island

Buses don't stop at every marked bus stop, you have to pull the cord or press the signal tape as you approach your stop. Exit the bus by the rear door. Be sure to have exact change or subway tokens, for bus drivers carry neither and give no change if you over-pay (Bear in mind that shopkeepers do not like to give change without making a sale). Bus fare is the same as subway fare.

Transfers from line to line are free, but you must ask the driver for a transfer stub to give the second driver.

Buses are generally safer though slower than the subways. A few of the major bus companies that operate in the city: *Greyhound:* Tel. (800) 231-2222. *NY Bus Service:* Tel. (718) 994-5500.

SUBWAYS

To ride any subway, descend the station steps and purchase tokens from the booth. Deposit one token per person at the turnstile. Children under six ride free of charge. If you need directions or a map, you can usually ask the token seller. Depending on his or her patience and the line of people behind you, you will get an answer; generally they are helpful. It is recommended to buy more than one token at a time; they are available in packs of 10. You will not only avoid lines; it will spare you the distress of finding some token booths closed at night.

INTRODUCTION

The entrance to a subway station in Chinatown

Many tourists are wary of using the subway, which has acquired a rather dubious reputation. The dirty stations with the many homeless seeking shelter and the endless throngs of travelers, all make the New York subway system rather daunting. However, for those who master the system, the subway can provide a speedy and relatively inexpensive method of transportation throughout the city. This allows freedom of movement as well as a concentrated sampling of the different inhabitants of the city, from smartly dressed businessmen in three-piece suits to downcast beggars. Of course, the subways should always be used with great caution and must be avoided after midnight or in unsavory neighborhoods.

In recent years the trains themselves have been improved, and many have been installed with air-conditioning. A number of policemen patrol the trains, to secure the safety of the passengers and keep the carriages clean, particularly of graffiti.

Although the network itself is confusing with over 20 different lines, you will probably need to use only two or three different lines. Manhattan is long and narrow, divided into the east side and the west side.

Each side has a local train and two express trains running from north to south and vice versa. On the east side, the expresses are the trains numbered 4 and 5, the local is numbered 6. On the west side, the expresses are numbered 2 and 3, the local is numbered 1.

Express trains are faster but don't stop at all stations. Local trains are slower since they do stop at all stations on their respective lines. You can transfer from local to express trains and vice versa, or from one local train to another, free of charge, at most stations at which the express trains stop. To transfer, you usually just walk to the other side of the platform. However, sometimes you must go up a flight of stairs, cross over the tracks, and then down on the other side. If you wish to transfer from one train to another, you must not leave the station area, but rather use the tunnels which lead to the train you are seeking. If you exit the station, you will have to use another token to re-enter and continue your journey. The directional signs use the terms "Uptown" (trains going to the north of the city, Queens and The Bronx) and "Downtown" (trains going to the south of the city and Brooklyn).

The signs above the subway tracks explain which trains run on those tracks. There are many more lines other than the 1, 2, 3, 4, 5 and 6. Consult the map we have provided and follow the directions in the tour of each neighborhood.

Grand Central Station (General Information): Tel. 532-4900.

For bus and subway information: call NY Transit Authority daily, between 6am and 9pm. Tel. 330-1234.

Tourist Services

New York Convention & Visitors Bureau provides free up-to-date information of all kinds. At the entrance you will find many maps and brochures, with information on tourist attractions in New York. At the Bureau they speak many languages (also on the phone). You can also get the *Quarterly Calendar of Events*, in which you will find details about all the main events.

The main office is at 2 Columbus Circle, next to the subway station, Tel. 397-8222, open Mon.-Fri., 9am-6pm; weekends and holidays 10am-3pm. There is also a branch at Times Square on 42nd St., between Broadway and 7th Ave.

The *Big Apple Greeter* Program invites visitors to share "the apple" with a "volunteer friend". Call 48 to 72 hours in advance for an appointment. Language requirements can be met. Tel. 669-2896.

Members of the AAA, the *American Automobile Association*, will be able to get more information, including maps of New York and anywhere else in the US.

The Manhattan branches are at 1881 Broadway, near 63rd St., a short walk from the municipal tourist office, and at the corner of Madison Ave. and 78th St. The Brooklyn branch is at 1781 Flatbush Ave. Tel. 586-1166; open Mon.-Sat. 8:45am-5:30pm.

You will find the best information about events in New York in the *New York Sunday Times*, in the "Arts and Leisure" section, which gives information about theater shows, dances, films, music, galleries, etc.

You can also find it in the weekly magazine *Village Voice*, published every Wednesday, with up-to-date information.

Maps of the city with details of bus and subway lines are given out at stands around Time Square.

The "Yellow Pages" is an excellent source of information; it offers maps, telephone numbers, etc. and is sometimes found in hotel rooms.

Accommodation

Manhattan offers virtually no inexpensive places to stay which are clean and safe; the short-term rental rooms which are available are usually in run-down and dangerous areas. For less expensive accommodation, you can try the suburbs (Long Island, for example) and take the train into the city. In Manhattan, the best and safest places to stay are the midtown hotels, most located in the 50's. Their price range: relatively inexpensive to deluxe. Inquire in each case whether the stated fee includes tax, extra charges, breakfast, etc.

The *Hotel Reservation Network* offers discounts at many good NY

Vacationers in a New York hotel

hotels with rates as low as $60 per night (Tel. 800-96-HOTEL).

It is worthwhile to note that, usually, even the most inexpensive hotel will have a bathroom attached and a television.

The following is a brief list of hotels according to their respective price categories, as per double room with a bathroom.

ULTRA-DELUXE – FROM $400

The Plaza: 5th Ave. and 59th St, Central Park South. A stylish Edwardian-French building with an illustrious past, its list of guests making it a legend in its own time. It flies the flags of its important foreign guests. 900 rooms, five restaurants, including *Trader Vic's*. Tel. 759-3000, fax 759-3167.

New York Palace: 455 Madison Ave. and 50th. Two restaurants,

The grand façade of the Plaza Hotel

four cocktail lounges, efficient business services. 1,050 rooms soaring above the Villard Houses, Tel. 888-7000.

Park Lane: 36 Central Park South. 640 rooms, Tel. 371-4000.

Plaza Athenée: 37 E 64th St. Home of the acclaimed *Le Regence* restaurant. 122 rooms decorated with Swiss fabric, Irish carpeting and rose aurora marble, Tel. 606-4647.

The Stanhope: 995 5th Ave. at 81st St. Conveniently close to Museum Mile, Tel. 288-5800.

St. Regis-Sheraton: 2 E 55th St. and 5th Ave. Convenient to 5th Ave. shopping. Built by John Jacob Astor in 1904. 521 rooms, Tel. 753-4500.

The Pierre: 5th Ave. and 61st St. Overlooking Central Park. 235 rooms, Tel. 838-8000, fax 758-1615.

DELUXE – FROM $300

Omni Berkshire Place: Madison Ave. and 52nd St. Concierge service. Special packages available. 414 rooms, Tel. 753-5800 or 800-THE-OMNI, fax 355-7646.

Omni Park Central: 7th Ave. and 56th St. Conveniently close to Central Park and Carnegie Hall. Special packages available. Tel. 247-8000.

The Grand Hyatt: Park Ave. just east of Grand Central Terminal. Multilingual staff. 1,407 rooms, Tel. 883-1234 or 800-228-9000.

UN Plaza Hotel: 1st Ave. and 44th St. Glittery, new. 24-hour room service, health club, Tel. 758-1234.

Essex House: 160 Central Park South, 722 rooms, Tel. 247-0700, fax 484-4635.

Hotel Inter-Continental: 111 E. 48th St. and Park Ave. 24-hour room service. Home of the fancy *La Recolte* restaurant. The *Barclay* restaurant serves afternoon tea. 691 rooms, Tel. 755-5900, fax 644-0079.

Marriot Marquis: 1535 Broadway. Nice hotel with some beautiful views, Tel. 398-1900 or 800-228-9290, fax 704-8930.

Parker-Meridien: 118 W 57th St. Health club, home of the nouvelle cuisine restaurant, *Maurice*. 600 rooms, Tel. 245-5000, fax 708-7477.

Waldorf Astoria: 301 Park Ave. and 50th St. Six restaurants, 1,800 rooms, Tel. 355-3000, fax 758-9209.

EXPENSIVE – FROM $250
Golden Tulip Barbizon: 140 E 63rd St, 340 rooms. Recommended, Tel. 838-5700.

NY Penta: 7th Ave. and 33rd St. Convenient to midtown shopping and Theater District, Tel. 736-5000.

Halloran House: 525 Lexington Ave. at 49th St. Concierge service, Tel. 755-4000.

Algonquin: 59 W 44th St. Conveniently located midtown near 5th Ave. shopping. 200 rooms, Tel. 840-6800, fax 944-1419.

Dorset: 30 W 54th St., convenient midtown location, Tel. 247-7300, fax 581-0153.

Loew's Summit: 569 Lexington

Ave. and 51st St. Features a health club, Tel. 752-7000, fax 758-6311.

Madison Towers: 22 E 38th St. Conveniently located to Madison Ave. shops, Tel. 685-3700.

Sheraton City Squire: 790 7th Ave. and 51st St., close to Theater District, Tel. 581-3300, fax 541-9219.

Hotel Lexington: 511 Lexington Ave. and 48th St. 800 rooms, traditional, Tel. 755-4400 or 800-448-4471, fax 751-4091.

NY Hilton: 1335 Ave. of the Americas (6th Ave.) at 53rd St. Four restaurants, concierge service, private lounge in the Executive Tower. The staff speak 35 languages, Tel. 586-7000, fax 315-1374.

Warwick Hotel: 65 W 54th St. and Ave. of the Americas (6th Ave.). 500 rooms. One can enjoy some good views, Tel. 247-2700, fax 957-8915.

MODERATE/ EXPENSIVE – FROM $250
Best Western Skyline Motor Inn: 10th Ave. and 49th St. Slightly out-of-the-way but convenient to Theater District. Suburban-type accommodation, indoor pool. 240 rooms, Tel. 586-3400.

Service with a smile

Salisbury Hotel: 123 W 57th St., convenient to shopping and art galleries. 320 rooms, Tel. 246-1300, fax 977-7752.

The Shoreham: 33 W 55th St., convenient to 5th Ave. shopping. Trilingual (English-French-Spanish) staff, Tel. 247-6700, fax 765-9741.

Gramercy Park Hotel: 2 Lexington Ave. and 21st St. Lovely hotel in a lovely location. Recommended. Packages available, Tel. 475-4320, fax 505-0535.

Ramada Inn: 798 8th Ave. and 48th St. Convenient to Theater District. Packages available. Tel. 581-7000.

Roger Smith: Lexington Ave. and 47th St. Packages available. Tel. 755-1400, fax 319-9130.

The Roosevelt: Madison Ave. and 45th St. Convenient to 5th Ave. shops. Tel. 661-9600, fax 661-4475.

MODERATE – FROM $100
Consulate Hotel: 224 W 49th St. Close to Theater District, Tel. 246-5252, fax 245-2305.

Pickwick Arms: 230 E 51st St. 400 rooms, Tel. 355-0300, fax 755-5029.

Century Paramount: 235 W 46th St. Close to the Theater District. 650 rooms, Tel. 764-5500, fax 575-4892.

Gorham Hotel: 136 W 55th St. One block from *NY Hilton*. 173 rooms, Tel. 245-1800, fax 582-8332.

Wellington Hotel: 55th St. and 7th Ave., convenient to shops and Theater District. 700 rooms, Tel. 247-3900 or 800-652-1212, fax 581-1719.

Wentworth Hotel: 59 W 46th St., close to shops and Theater District. Tel. 719-2300 or 800-223-1900, fax 768-3477.

Chelsea: 222 W 23rd St. A place where many artists have lived on the way to fame, e.g., Arthur Miller, Janis Joplin. Leonard Cohen wrote a song called *Chelsea Hotel*. Book in advance, Tel. 243-3700.

Excelsior: 45 W 32nd St., alongside the museum of the History of Nature and Central Park, Tel. 362-9200, fax 721-2494.

Stanford: 43 W 32nd St. Friendly and comfortable, Tel. 563-1480, fax 629-0043.

St. Marks Hotel: 2nd St. Marks Place, Tel. 674-2192.

INEXPENSIVE – FROM $50
Aberdeen Hotel: 17 W 32nd St., near Madison Square Garden. Tel. 736-1600, fax 695-1813.

Collingwood Hotel: 45 W 35th St. 10001. Very central. Group discounts in summer, Tel. 947-2500.

Narragansett Hotel: 2508

Broadway. Attractive dormitory rooms available for summer students and tourists, Tel. 749-5100.

Arlington: 18 W 25th St. Friendly, Tel. 645-3990.

Malibu Studios Hotel: 2688 Broadway. Good for a long stay. Good rates for two weeks or two months, Tel. 222-2954, fax 678-6842.

McBurney Branch of the Y.M.C.A.: 206 W 23rd St., Tel. 741-9210.

Sloane House Branch of the Y.M.C.A.: 356 W. 34th St. A good students' hostel. You should book a few weeks in advance. It's a good place to find traveling partners. Reservations, Tel. 630-9600.

Vanderbilt Branch of the Y.M.C.A.: 224 E. 47th St. A good and central students' hostel. An excellent cafe-

teria. Should be booked in advance, Tel. 308-2899, fax 752-0210.

West Side Branch of the Y.M.C.A.: 5 W. 63rd St. Should be booked in advance, Tel. 787-4400, fax 580-0441.

Urban Venture: Tel. 594-5650. This is not a hotel but an apartment-rental agency. There are 400 rooms; 400 apartments. Bed & Breakfast accommodation. In Manhattan, this alternative is a veritable life saver, or should we say, budget saver? The hosts, of the approximately 500 rooms, have been carefully screened and range from older people with room to spare to young artists who need a little help with the rent. Some apartments are even available for two nights to two months without hosts.

STAYING IN THE SUBURBS

While most of the hotels are situated in Manhattan, there are many hotels and motels in the four other boroughs of NYC, Long Island and the New Jersey side of the Hudson River. If you have decided to stay there, you can still enjoy what New York City has to offer. While the shopping and restaurants are perhaps not as glamorous or sophisticated as in Manhattan, they are, very often, much less expensive. Furthermore, the transportation network is efficient and thorough and there is usually no problem to get to and from Manhattan.

Practical Tips

Business Hours

Offices are open from Monday to Friday 9am-5pm; stores and shops 10am-7pm and sometimes later.

Many shops and department stores are open on Saturday and Sunday, with Sunday hours generally reduced from noon-5pm. Many galleries are closed on Sunday and Monday, most of the museums are closed on Monday. During the holiday season, just before Christmas, the opening hours lengthen considerably to accommodate the crowds of shoppers. During a sale, each store determines its own hours.

Government offices are closed on Saturday and Sunday. Banks are open from Monday to Friday, 9am-3pm; telephone banking is sometimes possible until 5pm.

Mail
Post offices are open from Monday to Saturday, 8:30am-5:30pm, closed Sunday and all legal holidays. Most post offices sell stamps, post letters and packages in a variety of methods, insure the articles sent, and offer overnight express mail service. Mailboxes (blue in color) are located on the curb side at intervals of a few blocks. Be careful not to mail a regular letter in an express mailbox.

U.S. Postal Service:
Express Mail: Tel. 967-8585.
Main Post Office: Tel. 967-8585.
Zip Code Info.: Tel. 967-8585.
Federal Express Courier Service: Tel. 777-6500.

Telephones
Information: to ascertain the phone number or address of any business or person with a listed number, dial 411 – not the operator!

Operator: dialling zero is to help you make phone calls you cannot make on your own.

Police/Emergency: dial 911 or Operator (0).

800 numbers: Numbers which have "800" listed as their area code mean that the call is automatically charged to the **receiver** of the call. Businesses such as hotels, airlines etc., usually have such numbers for the convenience of their customers. To use it dial 1 + 800 and then the number you require.

Public telephones are usually situated at one of the four corners of a street intersection. You will need 25 cents coins ("quarter"). A convenient way of making long-distance phone calls is by using a telephone code. Prior to departure, open an international credit account through a telephone or credit company in

charged. Information calls from a
public phone are free of charge.

In order to make a collect call dial
800 and then 1.

AREA CODES
New York City is divided into two
area codes: 212 for Manhattan, 718
for Brooklyn, Bronx, Queens and
Staten Island. An area code must be
dialled only from outside its jurisdiction.

The area code of nearby Long
Island is 516; Westchester County
is 914.

Currency Exchange
Foreign currency is not widely
accepted in the United States, therefore it's best to arrive in New York
already possessing American
currency (the more the better, of
course). Although bank branches
greet you on every streetcorner,
only a few major ones exchange
foreign currency. Airports and
railroad terminals provide this
service, as do several money
changers' offices around town and
most large hotels. Exchange rates
among these do not differ much,
though hotels' rates are tradition-
ally much lower. Most facilities
charge a commission, which is
worth verifying when large sums
are involved.

The *Cheque Point* company
operates a few branches in which
you can change foreign currency
(traveler's checks and cash) – in the
J.F.K. airport and downtown. There
is a central branch at 551 Madison
Ave. corner 55th St. Tel. 869-6281.

The following banks make cash
advances against Master Cards or
Visa Cards:
Citibank: Tel. 627-3999.
Chemical Banks: Tel. 809-4952.

The following offers banking
services exclusively for foreign
visitors: *Citibank World Wide*:
Tel. 307-8100.

For information regarding current
exchange rate, call: *American
Express Customer Helpline*: Tel.
(800) 528-4800. *Citicorp Foreign
Currency Exchange*: Tel. 308-7863.

For lost or stolen Credit Cards:
Visa: Tel. (800) 336-8472.
Master Card: Tel. (800) 826-2181.
Diners Club: Tel. (800) 525-9135.
AT&T: Tel. (800) 423-4343.
American Express: Tel.
(800) 528-4800.

Thrifty Spending
In New York it seems as if any sum
of money which you bring will
vanish between the many tempting
restaurants, shops, theaters, etc.
Here are some tips that will let you
pay less and get more:

Food: As the New Yorkers rarely
eat breakfast out, restaurants try to
attract customers by offering very
cheap meals. Breakfast is usually
served between 6am-10am; it costs
around $5 and includes orange
juice, toast, eggs, baked potatoes
and coffee or tea. Lunch is served
between 11am-3pm, at $10-20. In
the evening the same meal will cost

your country. When calling from
the U.S.A., dial your telephone
code and your account will be

three times that much or more. Bars try to attract business in the afternoon with "Happy Hour" (usually 4-7pm), when drinks are served at half the usual price.

Free Shows and Entrance:
There are many free shows, about which you can find details in the "Art and Leisure" supplement to the *New York Times* or in the *Village Voice* which has a special section listing free events and shows. Among them you can find classic concerts in the park, dance performances, pop, shows, etc.

Most of the museums allow free entrance once a week.

Tipping
In most of the restaurants, it is accepted to tip 15% of the bill . Since sales tax is 8.25%, many people compute the tip by doubling the tax. At better restaurants you should tip 20% to the captain and 15% to the waiter.

Drinking
The legal drinking age in NYC is 21 years old. Many bars and restaurants offer a Happy Hour, generally from 4-7pm, where the cost of drinks is reduced or even half-price.

Cover and Minimum Charges
Many nightclubs charge a cover and a minimum. A cover charge is merely an admission fee. A minimum requires that you spend a certain amount of money **in addition** to the cover charge. The minimum can usually be satisfied with a purchase of either drinks or food. Even though you may not spend the minimum required, you will be charged this minimum amount.

Measurements
The American measurement system is not a decimal one. Following are

several conversion tables and "instant" tricks. Notice that U.S. measurements are the same as Imperial but measures of volume and capacity are smaller and the fluid ounce is larger.

TEMPERATURE
To convert Fahrenheit degrees to Centigrade (Celsius) subtract 32 from the Fahrenheit degree, multiply it by 5 and divide the total by 9.

WEIGHT
28.349 grams – 1 ounce
453 grams – 1 pound
1 kilogram – 2.2 pounds

CAPACITY
0.473 litres – 1 pint
3.785 litres – 1 gallon

DISTANCES
2.540 cm – 1 inch
30.480 cm – 1 foot
0.914 meter – 1 yard
1.609 km – 1 mile

TIME
NYC is within what is called in the Unites States the Eastern Time Zone (G.M.T. -5). Daylight Saving Time is usually from the end of April until the last week in October.

ELECTRIC CURRENT
110-115 a.c. 60 Hz. For those planning to buy American appliances, bear in mind that the American plugs are two flat pins which will require adapters. Foreign appliances brought to the United States generally require a transformer as well as an adapter.

Total bliss – lying in the sun at Central Park

NEW YORK

Before you Start

Most of Manhattan is a grid of numbered streets (in ascending order south to north) and avenues (east to west). This is the general and convenient rule, to which there are many confusing exceptions.

South of Houston St., for example, streets are named rather than numbered. In Lower Manhattan there is no grid at all because the colonists built their houses before paving their streets. West Village streets are a melange of names and numbers that defy all rules (a section of West 10th St. somehow lies south of West 4th St.). But generally, Manhattan is easy to follow from a map.

Buildings are numbered east and west of 5th Ave. West side addresses occur at intervals of 100 between each avenue; addresses on the east side are numbered at intervals of 50 until 3rd ave, where the interval becomes 100. Odd-number addresses are always on the north side of the street, with even numbers on the south side. Addresses along the avenues are slightly more difficult to locate. It is helpful to know what street is nearby. For Midtown Manhattan there is a fairly accurate mathematical system for predicting the nearby street: cancel the last figure of the address, divide the result by two, and add or subtract the number indicated below:

Avenues A, B, C, D	Add 3
First Avenue	Add 3
Second Avenue	Add 3
Third Avenue	Add 10
Fourth Avenue	Add 8
Fifth Avenue:	
63 to 108	Add 11
109 to 200	Add 13
202 to 500	Add 17

510 to 770	Add 19
776 to 1283	Subtract 18
1310 to 1494	For 1310 subtract 20, and

for every additional
20 street numbers increase deduction by 1, e.g.
1330-22 etc.

| Avenue of the Americas | Subtract 12 |

Seventh Avenue:
1 to 800	Add 12
1800 and above	Add 20
Eighth Avenue	Add 9
Ninth Avenue	Add 13
Tenth Avenue	Add 14
Eleventh Avenue	Add 15
Amsterdam Avenue	Add 59
Audubon Avenue	Add 165
Broadway	Anything below 754 is south of 8th St. hence a named street
756 to 846	Subtract 29
847 to 953	Subtract 25
Above 953	Subtract 31
Central Park West	Cancel last figure and add 60
Columbus Avenue	Add 59 or 60
Convent Avenue	Add 127
Fort Washington	Add 158
Lenox Avenue	Add 110
Lexington Avenue	Add 22
Madison Avenue	Add 27
Manhattan Avenue	Add 100
Park Avenue	Add 34
Riverside Drive	Up to No. 567 cancel last figure and add 72. Beyond 568 add 78
St. Nicholas Avenue	Add 110
West End Avenue	Add 59

Manhattan consists of many neighborhoods. There are few clearly defined boundaries between the neighborhoods. Even if we say 14th Street divides the West Village from Chelsea, you will not notice a remarkable difference between W. 13th and W. 15th streets.

A final note: 6th Ave. is officially named Ave. of the Americas; its street lights are marked with medallions representing all the countries of the American continents. Most New Yorkers, however, continue to call it "6th Ave.". For simplicity's sake, so shall we.

The concrete mass at Upper East Side, New York City

GETTING TO KNOW THE CITY

NYC offers diverse sightseeing services: group tours on boats, buses, helicopters or more individualized programs tailored to your own particular interests. The helicopter tours, perhaps the most breathtaking, are also the most expensive. We shall list a variety of touring possibilities, describing each in brief.

Sightseeing Boats

Circle Line: 3 hr. cruises around Manhattan, including views of the Statue of Liberty, World Trade Center, the UN and more. Leaves from Pier 83, West 43rd St. and 12th Ave., Spring and summer daily at 9:35am and 1:15pm, Tel. 563-3200. About $15 for adults, $7.5 for children.

Statue of Liberty Ferry Service: the ferry to the Monument and Museum of Immigration leaves from Battery Park hourly from 9am to 5:15pm, daily. There is a 1 hour cruise (Right waiting line), and a 3 hour cruise which includes Ellis Island (Left waiting line). Tel. 269-5755. Adults – about $6, children – about $1.50.

World Yacht Enterprise Ltd.: catering services also available. Daily luncheon, dinner, late-night cruises. Leaves from Pier on the Hudson 81 W. 41st St., Tel. 630-8800.

Bacon Yacht Charters: private sail on 45 feet yacht, including dinner. At Boat Basin, 79 W. St. Tel. 873-7558.

"All aboard" for a cruise around Manhattan

Port Imperial Ferry: Tel. (800) 533-3779.

Staten Island Ferry: Tel. (718) 390-5253.

Sightseeing Helicopters
Island Helicopter Corp: leaves from the foot of 34th St. on the East River. Daily (except winter) 9am-9pm. Tours start at $30 per person, minimum requirement of two passengers. No reservations necessary, Tel. 683-4575.

Sightseeing Buses
Campus Coach Lines: groups only. 545 5th Ave., Tel. 682-1050.

Carey/Gray Line: selection of nine different tours, plus trips to Atlantic City, New Jersey, for casino gambling. Terminal at 900 8th Ave. near 54th St., Tel. 397-2600.

Short Line-American: Ten tours daily on glass-roofed buses. 166 W 46th St., Tel. 354-5122.

Greyhound: Tel. (800) 231-2222.

Specialized and Individualized Programs
Of the numerous possibilities available, here are a select group. We have chosen a diverse selection of opportunities to suit everyone's needs.

Acoustiguide: cassette tours of major museums, including the Metropolitan, Intrepid, Guggenheim and others. 210 E 86th St., or inquire at each museum's information desk, Tel. 996-2121.

Allied Tours: Multilingual guides. 165 W 46th St., Tel. 869-5100.

Around Town, Inc.: individual area tours. 240 E 27th St., Tel. 532-6877.

Backstage on Broadway: behind the scenes at Broadway shows. 228 W 47th St., Tel. 575-8065.

Bilingual Interpreters: Rennert

Bilingual: Sightseeing, shopping tours, interpreters for business meetings. 2 W 45th St., Tel. 819-1776.

Brooklyn Bridge Tours: brownstones, churches, etc., Tel. 718-643-2046, 6am-9pm.

Campus Coach Lines: multilingual guides, trips to Atlantic City and elsewhere. 545 5th Ave., Tel. 682-1050.

Carey/Gray Line: multilingual guides for groups. 254 W 54th St., Tel. 397-2600.

Doorway to Design: visits to interior and fashion design trade showrooms. 1441 Broadway, Suite 338, Tel. 221-1111.

Field Studies Center of NY: student tours and seminars. 228 W 47th St. Call 575-8065 collect.

Harlem Spiritual, Inc.: different tours including gospel, soul food and jazz. Groups only. 1697 Broadway, Tel. 757-0425.

Looking for souvenirs

MANHATTAN – AREA BY AREA

The best way to get to know NYC is by walking through each neighborhood. We'll take you through NYC area by area, from one site to the next, pointing out entertainment spots, cultural institutions, shops, restaurants, architectural wonders and historic landmarks.

We have divided Manhattan into about 20 distinct tour areas from south to north. Our judgment in drawing the geographic borders is formed first and foremost by the thematic distinctions between one tour and another. These might reflect history, gastronomy, art, architecture, etc. The areas are so divided because of New York's historical development, and we think it best to highlight and emphasize these differences.

Lower Manhattan at night, with the long Brooklyn Bridge to the right

Lower Manhattan – Where it all Began

Much of our tour of Lower Manhattan is historical. We'll explore the remnants of Colonial New York, including government buildings, most of which are open only weekdays 9am-5pm. Plan accordingly. Certain highlights of this neighborhood are not to be missed: the Statue of Liberty, the World Trade Center, the NY Stock Exchange, the South Street Seaport and Chinatown. The entire historical tour requires a full day. Begin early; have lunch at the World Trade Center or the South Street Seaport. Combine the historical tour, or parts of it, with a visit to nearby Chinatown or Tribeca (following sections) for dinner and late-night dancing.

We shall start out where the European colonization of New York began: Manhattan's southernmost tip, known as **The Battery**. Steeped in history, the Battery served as the headquarters of the Dutch and British colonial regimes, as well as the United States' first capital. Here was the first permanent settlement (1624), populated mostly by Protestant Walloons fleeing the effects of Spanish Inquisition on their home country, Belgium. More settlers arrived in 1625, and by 1626 their number had reached 300.

Expanded by means of landfill, The Battery is a park at Manhattan's southern tip. By subway, take the R to Whitehall St. (walk south) or take the 1 or 9 to South Ferry, just beside the park. Another alternative is the Subway 4 or 5 to Bowling Green (walk south along State St.).

Following State St. to its end along the fringe of the park, we reach the **Staten Island Ferry**. The ferry ride (approx. 20 min. each way) affords a romantic view of the harbor at sunset or twilight. There is no fare charged to Staten Island but the return cruise costs 50 cents. The ferry gives you a new and beautiful view of Manhattan, and it is a good alternative to the tiring and expensive *Circle Line* tour (see "Getting to Know the City").

Battery Park, at Manhattan's southern tip

Continue southeast past South Ferry, crossing New York Plaza and passing the Coast Guard offices. Enter Admiral George Dewey Promenade, viewing the **Statue of Liberty** straight ahead. With a torch in

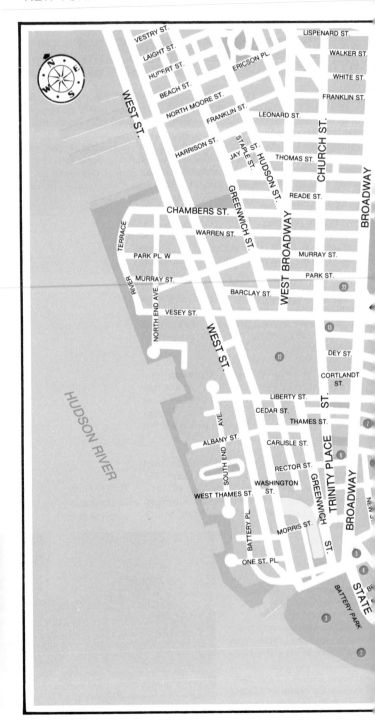

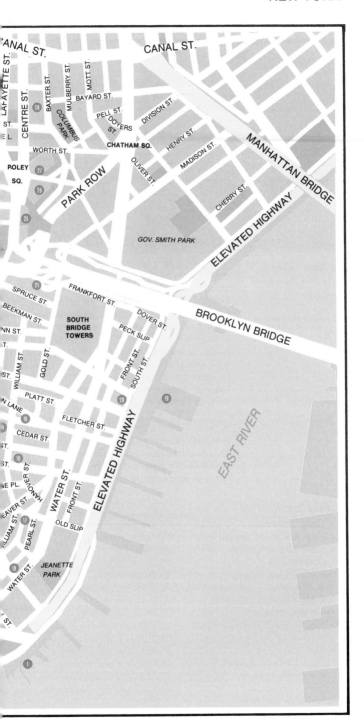

The Staten Island Ferry cruising around Manhattan

her right hand and a law book in her left, the 225-ton bronze Liberty (the exterior designed by Frederic Auguste Bartholdi, the framework by Gustave Eiffel) gazes down upon the harbor as a symbol of freedom to arriving immigrants. The statue, built in Paris and funded in part by the French in honor of America's 100th anniversary, was disassembled, shipped to New York and reassembled on her pedestal in 1886. Emma Lazarus' famous poem, added in 1903, greeted some ten million immigrants:

"Give me your tired, your poor,
Your huddled masses yearning to breathe free,
The wretched refuse of your teeming shore,
Send these, the homeless, the tempest-tossed, to me:
I lift my lamp beside the golden door!"

LOWER MANHATTAN   (see previous pages)

1. Staten Island Ferry
2. Ferry to Statue of Liberty
3. Castle Clinton National Monument
4. Old U.S. Custom House
5. Bowling Green
6. Trinity Church and Cemetery
7. Equitable Building
8. New York Stock Exchange
9. Federal Hall National Memorial
10. Bank of New York
11. Chase Manhattan Bank Plaza
12. World Trade Center
13. St. Paul's Chapel
14. Federal Reserve Bank
15. Chamber of Commerce
16. Louise Nevelson Plaza
17. India House
18. Fraunces Tavern
19. Fulton Market
20. South St. Seaport Museum
21. Pace University
22. Woolworth Building
23. City Hall
24. Tweed Courthouse
25. NYC Municipal Building
26. U.S. Federal Courthouse
27. N.Y. County Courthouse
28. Criminal Courts Building and Prison

For her 100th birthday in 1986, the statue under-went extensive rejuvenation to repair the ravages of time and nature. Repairs were focused on Liberty's face, arm, torch and 1,350 supporting ribs. The cosmetic surgery returned the torch to Frederic Auguste Bartholdi's original plan which called for a solid flame. Also in accordance with the original model, outside illumination has been added. Visitors will be glad to know that, although not part of the original plan, a modern ventilation system has also been added.

The United States began a massive campaign to collect contributions and donations to fund the ren-ovations, which, along with the restorations at Ellis Island, were estimated to reach over 200 million dollars. The campaign, swept across America bringing with it a spirit of national pride and generosity, reaching its peak in a gala unveil-ing of the restored Lady of Liberty on Independence Day, 1986.

Visit **Liberty Island** (the Statue and the Museum of Immigration) Wed.-Sun. 9am-4pm daily. The ferry ride costs about $6 adults, $5 senior citizens, $3 children 17 years and under. Boats leave 7 days a week every half hour 9:30am-3:30pm; Tel. 269-5755. Information on the Statue at Tel. 363-3200.

One of New York's most famous symbols – the Statue of Liberty

There is a lift to the top of the statue (worthwhile checking if it's in working order), for those who prefer a good steep climb there are 350 steps up to the lady's head. A cruise to the Statue of Liberty National Monument includes **Ellis Island**, the nation's principal immigration center from 1892 to 1943. The island south of Liberty Island, named for Samuel Ellis (its owner in the 18th century), underwent restoration and today screens movies depicting its history free of charge. One must pick up a ticket at the information stall at the entrance. There are two cruises to the island: the left queue for a 3 hr. cruise and the right queue for an hour's cruise.

The Museum of Immigration has permanent and changing exhibits about U.S. immigration history, including oral-history tapes, pho-tographs, prints and clothing. Open daily, 9am-5pm; July and Aug. until 6pm.

A recommended evening activity

is to board the *Circle Line's* "Harbor Lights Cruise". The cruise operates Wednesday, Thursday and Sunday only from the last weekend in May through the first weekend in September 9:30am-5:15pm. A special, more expensive, cruise leaves at 7pm. Reservations are not necessary. The breathtaking view consists of a two-and-a-half hour cruise around the New York Harbor. Admire the world's most impressive skyline and the Statue of Liberty.

Continuing along Dewey Promenade, we come upon eight upright stone blocks on our right, a memorial to U.S. Navy, Army and Air Force casualties in World War II and one of several memorials to servicemen throughout the park. The blocks frame a path to a large, powerful, sculpted American Eagle clutching olive branches. A left turn (facing the eagle) takes you to a statue of the Italian navigator Verrazano, the first European known to have entered New York Bay (1524). The Narrows between Brooklyn and Staten Island, as well as the suspension bridge spanning them, 4,260ft. (approx. 1,298 m) long, built 1964, bear his name.

Directly ahead of you is a red stone structure; the **Castle Clinton National Monument**. This is the last (const. 1808) of a series of forts which defended lower Manhattan during its Nieuw Amsterdam days. Admission charge. For opening hours, call Tel. 344-7220. Tours available upon request; groups and schools welcome. Make reservations.

A monument to Manhattan's defenders at Castle Clinton in Battery Park

The first fort in this area was Fort Amsterdam, erected against Indians and other European colonists in 1622 just north of Battery Park. The Southwest Battery, as Castle Clinton was originally known, was built by the young United States of America for strategic purposes. Renamed in honor of NYC Mayor and NY State Governor De Witt Clinton, the Southwest Battery served as headquarters of the U.S. Third Military District between 1815 and 1821, whereupon the headquarters relocated to Governors Island and the Castle was ceded to NYC. Reconstituted as Castle Garden in 1824, it served as a public center and theater until 1855: the gun rooms became a promenade, the officers' quarters a bar. Receptions for Presidents Jackson, Polk and Tyler were held here.

From 1855 to 1890 the Castle was the nation's principal immigration depot. Here more than eight million newcomers sought board and travel information, bought travel tickets, changed money and received medical attention. The sheer volume of immigration after 1880 forced the depot to relocate to Ellis Island in 1892.

The Twin Towers of the World Trade Center

The Castle's next tenant, from 1896 to 1941, was the NY Aquarium, the largest aquarium in the world (subsequently rebuilt in even larger quarters in Coney Island, Brooklyn). Since 1946, when Congress declared it a national monument, the Castle has been restored to its fortress-like appearance. Standing in the open air center and observing the different architectural styles of the modern NYC skyline above, it is quite hard to imagine the farmland that once was here.

Leave the castle and walk straight along the mall, noting the Twin Towers of the World Trade Center in the distance to your left. A flagpole at the park's exit commemorates the establishment of Fort Amsterdam in Dutch and English.

From the park exit at the corner of Battery and State Sts., cross State St. and find the old **U.S. Custom House** (Tel. 825-6700). The **National Museum of the American Indian** opened here with the world's largest collection of Indian art and artifacts from North, South and Central America. Well worth a visit, Tel. 283-2420. Directly to your right, at No. 8 State St. is the Watson House, a Federal-style landmark, constructed in 1800 and once part of a fashionable residential district and currently home of the **Church of Our Lady of the Rosary** (Roman Catholic). Of particular architectural interest is the colonnade, which follows the curve of the street. Next door is a chapel built on the site of the home of Elizabeth Ann Seton, the first American-born

Saint (canonized Sept. 14, 1975). Mass: Sun. at 8am and noon.

Returning to the Custom House, we find an exhibit opposite the façade which tells the building's story. The building, dating from 1907, is the work of architect Cass Gilbert, who also designed the Woolworth Building, the U.S. Federal Courthouse and the George Washington Bridge. Its location is the original site of Fort Amsterdam (barracks, storehouses, a church and the Governor's residence) with its entrance opening onto Bowling Green Park. The Custom House was built in an age when the U.S. was becoming a world power, fortunes were being amassed and the Customs Service was the Federal Government's greatest source of revenue in the pre-income tax era. The large beaux arts palace is adorned with granite columns crowned with busts of Mercury, god of commerce. The four sculptures at the base, crafted by Daniel Chester French – an American sculptor best known for the Lincoln Memorial – symbolically depict America (liberty, industriousness, optimism), Europe (imperialism, culture, religious supremacy), Africa (mystery, the unknown) and Asia (downtrodden masses, enslaved by ignorance and superstition). In 1936, artist Reginald Marsh was commissioned to paint a cycle of murals in the rotunda depicting the activity of NY Harbor. These masterpieces have been preserved. The Customs Service moved in 1971 to the World Trade Center.

A serene statue standing outside the Trinity Church

Across the way is **Bowling Green**, venue of Peter Minuit's purchase of Manhattan in 1626 and NYC's first park, since 1732, when three New Yorkers leased the tract for use as a bowling green, for one peppercorn per annum. After the Declaration of Independence was read here in 1776, a statue of King George III which had graced the park was toppled and melted into bullets for the rebel army.

When NYC was designated the nation's first capital, an elegant mansion was erected in 1790, atop the former Fort Amsterdam, as home of the US President. Never used as such, it later became the residence of New York Governors Clinton and Jay. Sold by New York State to NYC in 1813, the property was resold for double the original price within two years. The mansion was razed and the area subdivided into seven parcels upon which elegant row-houses were built. By the mid-1800s the area had become a commercial district known

The adorned interior of the Trinity Church

as Steamship Row. The first skyscrapers were erected here in the 1870s.

Walk along Bowling Green, heading north on the left side of Broadway. Crossing Rector St., we come upon **Trinity Church and Cemetery**, facing Wall St. on the left. Services at Trinity are held daily, tours gather at the pulpit at 2pm and the church often offers music recitals. For details call Tel. 602-0800. A museum inside is open Mon.-Fri. 9-11:45am and 1-3:45pm, Sat. 10am-3:45pm, Sun. 1-3:45pm (closed during concerts). Trinity, an active Episcopal parish on this site since 1698, is actually the third Trinity Church on this site. The edifice, a classic example of Gothic Revival architecture and a registered landmark, was Manhattan's tallest building in 1846. The interior features the Chapel of All Saints, stained glass windows, a beautifully carved organ loft and bronze doors by Richard Morris Hunt. In the

The Trinity Cemetery

cemetery are the graves of Alexander Hamilton (the first US Secretary of the Treasury, killed by Aaron Burr in a pistol duel), Robert Fulton (the famed steamship inventor) and Richard Churcher (whose tombstone, dated 1681, is the oldest in NY).

After exiting the church, note the mammoth 40-story **Equitable Building**, constructed in 1915 across Broadway at No.

120. Having robbed the street of light and air, it provoked a zoning regulation against future offenses of its type. This explains why so many of NYC's skyscrapers narrow-in from their base and climb heavenward in steps.

Inside are two galleries which are off-shoots off the Whitney Museum and feature some very nice works of art. Free catalogue available.

Straight ahead is **Wall Street** (if you're coming from elsewhere, take Subway 2, 3, 4 or 5). The **New York Stock Exchange (NYSE)** is two blocks down on your right. The NYSE actually came into being outdoors, on Wall St. itself, in 1792, in response to the need for a formal marketplace to handle the 1789 Congressional issue of 80 million dollars worth of stock to pay off Revolutionary War debts. Now, of course, it handles somewhat larger volumes. Enter from the corner at 20 Broad St., take the elevator to the 3rd-floor Visitors' Center (open Mon.-Fri., 9:15am-4pm; the admission is free, but it is recommended to pick up an entrance ticket in the morning – after 9am – before they run out, as they tend to, rather quickly) and walk through to the observation deck overlooking the trading floor. Though the Visitors' Center is informative in itself – slide shows, TV and computer displays on matters related to stocks and bonds are presented. An hour's tour free of charge is available. For details, call Tel. 656-5162. The most exciting part of the visit is undoubtedly the view of the chaotic trading floor, a pressure cooker of financial deals.

Pensive successful young men around Wall St.

Exit the Exchange and turn left, crossing Wall St. Immediately on your right, at 28 Wall St. (corner of Nassau St.) is the **Federal Hall National Memorial**, located on the site of NYC's second City Hall (1699-1788). From 1776-1783, delegates from nine colonies met here in the Stamp Act Congress, drafted a Declaration of Rights and petitioned against "taxation without representation". Just as King George III's statue was toppled in Bowling Green in 1776, his Coat of Arms was ripped from the wall here that same night.

After the Revolutionary War, New York raised

over $65,000 to renovate the former City Hall into Federal Hall, which served the young United States of America from 1789-1812. Here, on April 30, 1789, George Washington was sworn in as the first President. After the nation's capital moved out of New York, President John Adams transferred the building back to city ownership. It fell into disrepair and was purchased for 425 dollars for demolition salvage. The current structure, built in 1842 in Greek Revival style, served as the Custom House until 1862 (import trade went on beneath the rotunda) and as the U.S. Sub-Treasury, forerunner of the Federal Reserve, from then until 1920.

The entrance to the Federal Hall National Memorial

Though the Memorial houses several modest historical exhibits, the edifice itself – a lovely structure with a white rotunda, marble floor and stately columns – is the true reason for the visit. Occasional recitals are presented here. Open Mon.-Fri. 11am-3pm, admission free.

Exit Federal Hall and turn east onto Wall St. The street derives its name from a wall built by the Dutch in 1653 against Indian attack. The wall, probably more effective in inhibiting the colony's expansion than in enhancing its defense, remained standing until 1699.

At the corner of Wall St. and William St. is the **Bank of New York**. Established in 1784, NYC's oldest bank helped to rebuild the city after the Revolution, and now occupies its third building – const. 1928 – on this site alone. The bank's State

Aspiring high – the famous Twin Towers of the World Trade Center

Charter, drafted by Alexander Hamilton, set a standard for future banking rules nationwide. The interior is an ornate hall with eight wall murals depicting NY's commercial and industrial development during the 18th and 19th centuries.

Exit the Bank, turn north on William St. and head west on Pine St. On your right is the **Chase Manhattan Bank Plaza**, adorned with *Four Trees*, a giant black-and-white sculpture by Jean Dubuffet, and a sunken circular sculpture garden designed in 1963 by Isamo Noguchi.

It's time for the World Trade Center (WTC). Follow Pine St. back to Broadway. Cross Broadway, head north and turn west on Cortlandt St. Cross Church St. and bear right, walking through the sculpture plaza with works by Nagare, Rosati and Koenig. If you're coming from elsewhere, take Subway 4 or 5 to Wall St., R to Cortlandt St. or Subway 1 to the World Trade Center.

The **World Trade Center** is just that: everything necessary for international trade in a single complex. Admission charges only for the Observation Deck and restaurants. During its seven years of construction (1966-1973) 1.2 million cubic yds. (900,000 sq. m) of earth and rock were deposited in the Hudson River, as landfill, on top of which the residential Battery Park City was built. Famous for its Twin Towers, the World Trade Center actually consists of six buildings connected by an underground concourse lined with shops, banks and restaurants. Commodities trading takes place at 4 WTC, open Mon.-Fri. 10am-6pm; weekends 10am-5pm, admission free. **The US Custom House**, center for all customs and collection activities in the New York-New Jersey Port area, resides at 6 WTC, which also houses an exhibition gallery. Open Mon.-Fri. 9am-4:30pm, admission free.

The **Twin Towers** are at 1 and 2 WTC, with the observation deck, History of Trade exhibit, snack bar and gift shop on the 107th floor of 2 WTC. As advertised, it's "the closest some of us will ever get to heaven." On a clear day the view is breathtaking. Be sure to check visibility prior to purchasing tickets at the ticket counter on the Mezzanine level. Open weekdays 10am-6pm, weekends 10am-5pm. It may close for private parties, so phone first. In a February 1993 terrorist act, considered the most severe in the history of the United States, a bomb exploded in the center. As a result, six people were killed, and many others injured. The Twin Towers were also seriously damaged – but quickly restored.

Two excellent restaurants are located at 1 WTC. *Windows on the World*, on the 107th floor offers a spectacular view. Jacket and tie required, **no jeans allowed!** Open Mon.-Fri. 3pm-1am, Sat. noon-1am and Sun. noon-midnight. Reservations: Tel. 938-1100. *Cellar in the Sky*, also upstairs, serves a seven-course dinner with five wines, Tel. 234-6376; Mon.-Sat. 7:30pm.

On the Mezzanine level of 2 WTC is a *TKTS* booth (similar to the one in Times Square): half-price, same-day tickets to Broadway and off-Broadway shows. The booth, by the way, is adorned with a wall tapestry, by Spanish artist Joan Miro, weighing three tons. The *TKTS* booth closes at 6pm and sometimes beforehand.

Exit the Plaza on Church St., cross one block north at Fulton St. and head east on Fulton. On your left is the oldest public building in continuous use in Manhattan, **St. Paul's Chapel** (Tel. 602-0873), originally built in 1766 in a field outside the city. The attractive chapel is graced with 14 original cut-glass chandeliers handmade in Waterford, Ireland. The ornamental design of the "Glory" over the altar is by French-born architect Pierre L'Enfant who, after having volunteered to fight for American independence, was appointed by George Washington to design the nation's permanent capital. Washington himself worshipped here immediately following his inauguration (a special service is held each year on April 30th to commemorate the event) and con-

The tower of St. Paul's Chapel

The Federal Reserve Bank

tinued to do so far as long as NYC remained the capital.

Continue along Fulton St. to Broadway. Turn south on Broadway and east onto Liberty St. On your left, at the corner of Liberty and Nassau, are the Federal Reserve Bank and the NY Chamber of Commerce. The **Federal Reserve Bank** (1923-24), decorated with 200 tons of iron, is one of 12 area banks that carry out the functions of the "Fed," including bank regulation of credit and cash flow. Admission is free; tours must be arranged at least one week in advance, Tel. 264-8711. Closed Sat., Sun. The **Chamber of Commerce** (est. 1768, present building const. 1901) shares the Beaux Arts style invoked in the Custom House at Bowling Green.

Continue east along Liberty St. The triangle where Liberty and William Sts. meet Maiden Lane is site of **Louise Nevelson Plaza**, another lovely outdoor sculpture park with several large reproductions of the artist's work. Share the park with executives enjoying an outdoor lunch and local street musicians.

At Hanover Square

Continuing east (Liberty becomes Maiden Lane), turn south onto Pearl St., which marked the edge of Manhattan prior to the landfill. After crossing Wall St. you will arrive at Hanover Square. Named for King George I of the House of Hanover, the plaza was also known in colonial New York as Printing House Square because NYC's first printing press (1693) was located at 81 Pearl St. This is where Dutch settlement began. The streets around Hanover Square are among NYC's oldest; their winding character typifies early settlements laid out by the location of houses rather than in planned pattern.

A great fire in 1835 destroyed the last remnants of the old Dutch city and since then, most of their brownstone successors have also perished. **India House** (1851), at the corner of Pearl St. and Hanover Square, is one of the few exceptions.

Once the home of the Hanover Bank, the NY Cotton Exchange and W.R. Grace and Co., it is now a private club.

Continuing south along Pearl St. to Coenties Alley, you will come upon a modern building with a plaza embellished with excavations and markers. Here was the **Stadt Huys Block**, the location of NYC's first City Hall. Its foundations, uncovered during the recent construction, have been encased in thick glass at sidewalk level; a fine example of modern growth and historic preservation.

Continue south on Pearl St. to Broad St. On your left at the corner is **Fraunces Tavern**, a museum/restaurant owned and operated by the *Sons of the Revolution*. The museum, at 54 Pearl St., houses changing exhibits of American history. Open Mon.-Fri. 10am-4:45pm; Sat. noon-4pm, closed on Sunday. Admission charge; Tel. 425-1778. The restaurant, an elegant reconstruction of the tavern where Washington bade farewell to his troops, specializes in Yankee Pot Roast. Open for breakfast 7:30am-10.30am, for lunch and dinner (jacket required) Mon.-Fri. noon-9pm, closed Sat.-Sun., Tel. 269-0144.

Turn left from Pearl onto Broad St. and then left onto South St. At the base of Broad St. you can see *Governors Island Ferry Port* (U.S. Coast Guard Station) and Battery Marine Terminal. The latter, a huge steel structure, is painted green to resemble weathered copper.

A northward turn onto South St. gives you a clear view across the East River of Brooklyn and the Brooklyn Navy Yards. With the Manhattan Bridge directly behind, ahead of you is the **Brooklyn Bridge**. Its main span stretches 1,585 ft. (483 m) between two massive granite towers 271 ft. high (approx. 83 m) with the two side spans covering 930 ft. each (283 m). Its designer, John A. Roebling, died in 1869 in an accident while supervising the final surveys of his 1867 plan. The bridge, which cost nine million dollars, opened in 1883. We recommend a brisk morning walk on the bridge in either direction.

The next section of South St., a heavy construction zone under elevated FDR Drive (named after US

President Franklin D. Roosevelt) affords a perfect opportunity to witness the vast amounts of money and energy being spent on the revitalization of NY Harbor. If this does not particularly interest you, walk two blocks west at any point and continue north on Water St.

Here, at the base of Fulton St., at no. 19, a mock-lighthouse information booth marks the entrance to the **South St. Seaport**, where the port of NY began. At the booth one can obtain information and recommendations. Arrive at the Seaport directly via Subway 2, 3, 4 or 5 to Fulton St., and walk east to the end of Fulton St.

The Seaport area is open daily until late evening. Sunday hours: retail shops noon-8pm, food stores 10am-6pm; ships are open 10am-5pm. Admission charge (gallery and ships together). An hour long cruise leaves the port at noon, 1:30pm and 3pm. The South St. Venture, at 210 Front St., puts on a multi-screen show every half an hour, usually from 11am-8pm, Tel. 669-9400, in the *Trans-Lux Theater*; admission charge, Tel. 732-7678 for reservations.

The Seaport is actually a small neighborhood. Note the cobblestone streets, closed to cars. The Seaport's major feature, **Fulton Market**, is a three-story complex of specialty food shops, cafés and restaurants. Next is Seaport Plaza, a new 34-

story office building with ground-level shops. Museum Row Block houses the **South St. Seaport Museum**, the *Trans-Lux Seaport Theater* and small specialty shops. One can visit the museum; open in summer 10am-6pm and in the winter 10am-5pm, admission charge. Schermerhorn Row Block, built between 1810-1812, is one of the oldest complexes still standing. Its 12 buildings house restaurants and antique, craft, clothing and gift shops. Across the way is **Pier 16** on the East River, where several preserved ships now serve as museums. The three-story glass-and-steel **Pier 17 Pavilion** juts into the river, its grand arcade opening onto 120 restaurants, cafés and shops. The outdoor terraces provide a spectacular view of the river.

There is an archeological museum **New York Unearthed** at 17 State St. Battery Park. Open Mon.-Sat., noon-6pm. (The entrance is on Pearl St.). There is no entrance fee and the museum is worth a visit especially to those interested in "modern archeology".

Here, at South St., was the harbor of mercantile NYC in 1800. The first transatlantic freight and passenger lines debarked from here, as did voyages upstream to the Erie Canal, which greatly expanded inland trade routes when opened in 1825. The Seaport boomed in the 1840s and 1850s, the streets lined with merchants, counting houses, sail makers and other maritime businesses. By the 1860s, large-volume Hudson River docks began to dominate the harbor. Notwithstanding its new life as a tourist attraction, the old Seaport still remains an active fish market. Be present at around 4am, Mon.-Fri. and watch as the daily catch is brought ashore, scaled, cleaned and fileted. Trucks crowd the narrow cobblestone streets, loading up with seafood. It's all over by late morning, when the museums, shops and visitors take over.

Seaport Liberty Cruise operates a 90-minute tour by boat several times a day, Tel. 630-8888, and special night cruises with music, dances and beautiful views of the seaport and Ellis Island.

Exit the Seaport area and head north on Front St. To your right, at 146 Beekman St., the *Meyer & Thompson Fish Co.* begins smoking cod at 3am, as it has for over 70 years. By 11am, the floor has

The Fish Market at South St. Seaport

been swept and hosed down. Come by an hour later, Tuesday through Saturday, and you'll find, in the same place, an art gallery devoted solely to Naima Rauam and largely to fish market scenes (open till 6pm). The name of this establishment is "Art in the Afternoon" (fish in the morning).

Return to Front St. and continue north. One block ahead, at the far right hand corner of Front St. and Peck Slip, is one of the largest and most detailed examples of *trompe l'œil* artwork anywhere. Richard Haas' perspective of the Brooklyn Bridge.

Follow Front St. to its end at Dover St. To your right is the famous *Jeremy's Ale House*. Appearances aside, Jeremy's is a lunchtime and "happy-hour" favorite of both construction workers and Wall Streeters. Turn west on Dover St.

If you are short on time or energy by now, save the remaining daylight sites (City Hall, the Woolworth Building, the Courthouses) for another day.

We resume by continuing along Dover St. noticing the top of the **Municipal Building**, peaked by the gilded statue of *Civic Fame*, in the distance to the right. Crossing Pearl St., we find Dover St. renamed Frankfort St. On your right is the base of the Brooklyn Bridge. Continue along Frankfort St., crossing Gold and Rose Sts. On you left is **Pace University** (est. 1906). As Frankfort curves to the left to become Park Row, we arrive at the southern boundary of the **Civic Center**. To get here directly, take the 4, 5, or 6 Subway to the Brooklyn Bridge and exit near Pace University.

Stop at the corner of Spruce St., observing the spire of St. Paul's Chapel against the gleaming WTC tower. The statue of Ben Franklin was presented by Alexander de Groot to the press and printers of NYC in 1872, when this was the newspaper publishing district (the publishing industry catalyzed NYC's rise to intellectual supremacy by migrating here from Boston in the 1850s).

Cross Park Row to City Hall Park. On 23rd Park Row you will find *Jandr Music World*, a very good store for electronics and records. From there follow the park's border south to Broadway. Across the street, at 233 Broadway, is the **Woolworth Building**, the Gothic masterpiece designed by Cass Gilbert (also architect of the beaux-arts Custom House). The lavish lobby – marble walls, carved and gilded moldings, arched, mosaic ceilings – is not to be missed.

Head north on Broadway. Crossing Broadway at Park Pl. and following the park northward, we come to a statue of Revolutionary War hero Nathan Hale, unveiled in 1893. Sculptor Frederick MacMonnies intended the work to depict the hero at the moment he uttered his famous words: "I only regret that I have but one life to lose for my country!" before he was executed.

Facing the sculpture at the corner of Broadway and Steven Flanders Square, turn right and cross the square toward City Hall on your left (note the first arch of the Brooklyn Bridge in the distance).

The Woolworth Building, with the Twin Towers in the background

NYC's third **City Hall** was at the city's northern extremity when built from 1802-11. Its rear facade was surfaced not in marble but in cheaper brownstone in expectation that no one would ever see it. Everything, excluding the original marble under the porch ceiling, has been resurfaced since then. Open Mon.-Fri. 9am-5pm, admission free.

The elegant lobby's centerpiece is a beautiful double-circular marble stairway beneath a central rotunda. Visit the upstairs Governor's Room, now a portrait gallery facing the park, and the City Council Chamber, very much in use today. Enter the Chamber if it is open, and behold the enormous ceiling mural – *The City of New York as the Eastern Gateway of the American Continent* – a mammoth tribute to the city by Taber Sears, installed in 1903. The city's Art Commission subsequently withdrew its approval of the mural, though to no avail as it had already been mounted.

Exit City Hall and turn left toward the **Brooklyn Bridge**. Turn left at the first street you encounter, Centre St. Unless you wish to walk or jog across the Brooklyn Bridge, via a central pedestrian walkway, to the lovely community of Brooklyn Heights (see "Brooklyn"), continue north on Centre St. to Chambers St.

There, directly behind City Hall, is the infamous **Tweed Courthouse**. Though the Italian *palazzo*, completed during William "Boss" Tweed's administration (known for political graft) is architecturally exquisite, the building is better known for its cost: fourteen million dollars! Embarrassed by the building's shady political past, the city allowed it to fall into disrepair and thought of tearing it down, but it has recently been designated as a landmark.

The World Financial Center

Cross Centre St. at Chambers St. and before you, you will see the stately columns of the **NYC Municipal Building**, designed by McKim, Mead & White, one of the most popular architectural firms at the turn of the century. Behind the columns is a maze of city offices. Continue north on Centre St. At the brick courtyard of St. Andrew's Plaza you will find the Catholic **Church of St. Andrew**, dating back to 1842. This is a modest, somber church both inside and out. The huge structure further inside the plaza is the **NYC Police Headquarters**.

Continue on Centre St. The next building on your

right is the **US Federal Courthouse** (1922-36), the last work of Cass Gilbert, architect of the US Custom House, the Woolworth Building and the Supreme Court in Washington DC. Though the courthouse was one of NY's tallest skyscrapers in the 1930s, its imposition on the street below was minimized by Gilbert's use of a portico and cornice on the facade.

NYPD – New York Police Department

The neo-classical **NY County Courthouse**, constructed 1926, just beyond, was designed by Guy Lowell. The first major structure on Foley Square, its Corinthian portico exudes authority and commands respect for the American legal system. Looking at the facade, you cannot discern the building's rather unusual hexagon shape. Here stand the Archives of the County Clerk of New York County, one of America's most important legal repositories (housing the records of almost every major NY State Court in the County of NY since colonial times). Enter the Courthouse, cross the vestibule and walk down a long corridor into the central rotunda. Though in need of restoration, the rotunda is a beautiful architectural landmark. Softly illuminated by natural light, it features a set of murals depicting the *Story of Law in Western Civilization*, as well as historical exhibits at ground level to encourage historians to make further use of the collection.

Before heading for Chinatown (only a few steps away) walk slightly farther north on Centre St. and stop at No. 100, between Leonard and White Sts. You have come to the **Criminal Courts Building and Prison**, better known as **The Tombs**. Its 835 cells had been unused for a few years, but they're back in action now. The nickname derives not from the fate of its inmates – NY does not have the death penalty – but from the Egyptian Revival architecture of the previous prison which stood just across the street. Head back to Worth St. and turn east. To get to

Outside NY County Courthouse

Chinatown, bear left on Park St., cross Mulberry St. and keep going until Mott St. You're now in the heart of Chinatown, a great place to rest your feet and delight your palate

The City's skyscrapers line South St. Seaport

Chinatown – Like Being in Another Country

Chinatown, a few paces from the WTC and City Hall (see "Lower Manhattan"), may also be reached by the R or Subway 6 to Canal St. Head east on Canal St. to Mott St. and south from there. The major attraction here is the marvellously authentic and inexpensive Chinese cuisine. Come for dinner; don't worry about walking around at night. The streets are generally bustling and quite safe.

The streets of Chinatown are dotted with pagoda phone booths. Festive celebrations spill into the open during the Chinese New Year in February. Chinatown, perhaps more than any other NYC ethnic neighborhood, truly gives one the feeling of being in a foreign country.

The immigrants who thronged in the 1880s to what is today's Chinatown were largely a group of bachelors, a consequence of the 1882 Chinese Exclusion Act which kept wives and children in the old country. Confined to two business options – restaurants or laundries – the newcomers lined the streets with the restaurants we see today. Fifty years ago, however, hand laundries (approx. 5,000 in metropolitan NYC at the time) served as the main source of income for Chinese-Americans, as well as extended families back in China. Chinatown remains one of NYC's most cohesive ghettos. The visitor is shielded from the severe poverty lurking behind the storefronts, and you will marvel at the bustling activity, the street markets with their exotic produce and, of course, the restaurants.

Stroll down Mott St., the heart of Chinatown, and choose a restaurant that appeals to you (one patronized by Chinese people is most likely to be good and non-Westernized) for lunch or dinner. Most menus are printed in both English and

Frying Chinese delicacies

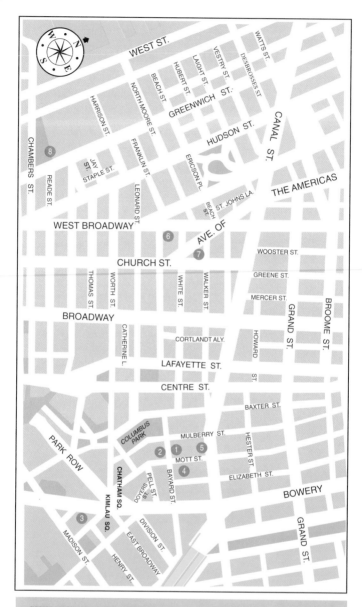

CHINATOWN AND TRIBECA

1. Hong Fat
2. Lung Fong
3. Shearith Israel Cemetery
4. Chinatown Ice Cream Factory
5. Kam Man Food Products
6. Franklin Furnace
7. Alternative Center for International Arts
8. The Triplex

Chinese. Try *Hong Fat*, 63 Mott St., Tel. 962-9588, 732-5899, for a satisfying chinese meal. One of the best Chinese bakeries is *Lung Fong*, 41 Mott St., open 9am-10pm daily. If you want to eat cheap, try the *Wanton Garden*, at 52 Mott St. which has a special atmosphere.

Follow Mott St. south to Chatham Square, where it intersects the Bowery. Across the square on St. James Place (between Oliver and James Sts.) is a remnant of pre-Chinatown days: the **Shearith Israel Cemetery**, the first burial ground of the congregation, established in 1654, by Spanish and Portuguese Jews.

A pagoda-shaped telephone booth in Chinatown

Return to the Bowery, head north and turn west on Bayard St. for the *Chinatown Ice Cream Factory* at No. 65 near Elizabeth St. and its exotic Oriental flavors such as ginger, papaya and mango. Open daily from noon to midnight. Continue on Bayard St., turn right at Mott St. and walk until you reach Canal St. At this street you will find many small stores for electronics and textile, and also stores for fish and shellfish sold fresh from aquariums. *Kam Man Food Products*, 200 Canal St., is not to be missed. Browse around, venture downstairs, check out the many exotic foods, fresh and preserved.

Tribeca – Art on the Loading Dock

Tribeca, acronym for the "Triangle Below Canal", encompasses the blocks between Broadway and the Hudson River, north of Barclay St. and south of Canal St. Worth a short visit for its art galleries, restaurants and clubs. Tribeca is a short walk west of Chinatown on Canal St., north of the WTC on West Broadway or west from City Hall on Chambers St. (alternately, take the Subway 1, 2 or 3 to Chambers St., exiting at the intersection with W Broadway).

Tribeca, a neighborhood of 19th century mercantile buildings, is one of the latest Manhattan districts to undergo "gentrification", when affluent people invest in the improvement of a neighborhood, sending property and rent values up... and the poorer residents out. A frequent first step is the discovery and "colonization" of a neighborhood by artists. Galleries, performance spaces and some excellent dance clubs still remain.

A sure sign of a neighborhood's revival is the appearance of fine restaurants, and we are at the doorstep of several. *One Hudson Café* at Hudson and Chambers Sts., near the subway exit, specializes in seafood, a wide variety of wines by the glass and jazz every night but Sunday. Open Mon.-Fri. noon-3pm (lunch), Tues.-Fri. 3-6pm (light entrées) and Tues.-Sat. 6-11pm (dinner). Music: Tues.-Fri. 5-11pm, Sat. 6-11pm, Tel. 608-5835.

From Chambers St., walking north on W Broadway, we come upon an alternating series of recommended restaurants/clubs and galleries. *The Odeon*, a converted cafeteria at 145 W Broadway, is the hub of NYC's downtown café society, where

Inside one of Tribeca's many supreme galleries

artists, actors and musicians meet. The cuisine is nouvelle, prices high. Open seven days a week for lunch and dinner, Tel. 233-0507. *Franklin Furnace*, east on Franklin St. at No. 112, is a free-admission experimental art space with a large collection of published art work (books, postcards and magazines) and exhibits of performance artists as well. Just north of 38 Franklin St. is *Artists Space*, at 223 W Broadway, which exhibits visual and

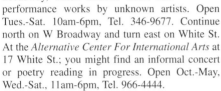

performance works by unknown artists. Open Tues.-Sat. 10am-6pm, Tel. 346-9677. Continue north on W Broadway and turn east on White St. At the *Alternative Center For International Arts* at 17 White St.; you might find an informal concert or poetry reading in progress. Open Oct.-May, Wed.-Sat., 11am-6pm, Tel. 966-4444.

As you stroll east on White St., notice the beautiful cast-iron buildings with their curved, arched windows. Dating from the early to mid-1800s, these originally mercantile edifices now serve as warehouses and textile showrooms.

North of White St., at 6th Ave., you will notice the **brown brick building**, against the small Tribeca Park. The building belongs to the *AT&T Telephone Company*, and it is noteworthy for the angels which adorn it.

Return to W Broadway, head north (note the Empire State Building in the distance) and turn west onto N Moore St. Pass the warehouses and

loading docks. Ignore the grime: you're en route to Hudson St., Tribeca's premier row of art galleries. Most are open Tues.-Sat. 11am-6pm.

A terrific, inexpensive meal is yours at *Hamburger Harry's*, 157 Chambers St., south on Hudson St., then west on Chambers St. The walls are painted an unusual cobalt-blue; the burgers are grilled over mesquite.

Continue past Greenwich St. to the Borough of Manhattan Community College. The reason for coming here is the school's theater, *The Triplex*, at

199 Chambers St. Inquire in advance about performances, Tel. 346-8000; the visiting artists are usually world-known groups from abroad. Closed Jun.-Sept.

There are two good reasons for winding up an evening in Tribeca, regardless of where you've spent the day. They are actually north of Canal St., on Varick St.: *Heartbreak*, 179 Varick St., and *Sounds of Brazil*, 204 Varick St. *Heartbreak*, an inexpensive cafeteria-style restaurant by day (10am-4pm), turns into a dance club at night, featuring 50s style rock & roll for a "hip" crowd. Cover charge, packed on weekends, Tel. 966-3935. *Sounds of Brazil*, also known as *S.O.B.*, offers Latin-influenced live jazz. Tel. 924-5221.

For a late night snack or early-morning breakfast, walk up Hudson St. and turn left onto Laight St. At the end of Laight St., at West St., is one of Manhattan's three *Market Diners*, all open 24 hours a day, seven days a week.

To truly understand NYC's vitality, remember that as you burn the night away in Tribeca, you are only a few steps away from the most historic section of the city, now the financial center of the world.

The Lower East Side and Little Italy – Blintzes and Bargains

More than any other neighborhood, the Lower East Side – south of E Houston St., and east of the Bowery – is symbolic as the immigrants' first home. Do not expect to go sightseeing here, but come instead for the ethnic foods and bargains on clothing and housewares.

The greatest waves of immigration arrived on American shores between 1880 and 1920, mostly from Italy and Russia – the former fleeing a stifling agri-cultural economy, and most of the latter Jews in search of freedom. Both groups settled mainly in the underfed, overpopulated Lower East Side, after earlier Irish and German immigrant groups had moved up the socio-economic ladder and away from that area.

In 1880, approximately half of all New York City dwellers lived above the rented storefront restaurants of the Lower East Side and, though educated in other fields, often worked in those restaurants as well. Restaurant labor was frequently the only option available: ownership required only a minimal capital investment and a familiarity with one's native cuisine. These eateries provided their owners with economic opportunities and their patrons a taste of the life they had left behind – companionship, familiarity and an easier adjustment to a new country.

Each successive wave of newcomers brought new culinary tastes. The post-World War II exodus of European ethnic groups cleared the way for a steady stream of newcomers, including Puerto Ricans, Dominicans, East Indians, Central and South Americans. Although most Jewish families have since moved elsewhere, they still own many businesses here and the area has retained a distinct Jewish flavor. We therefore recommend that you do not

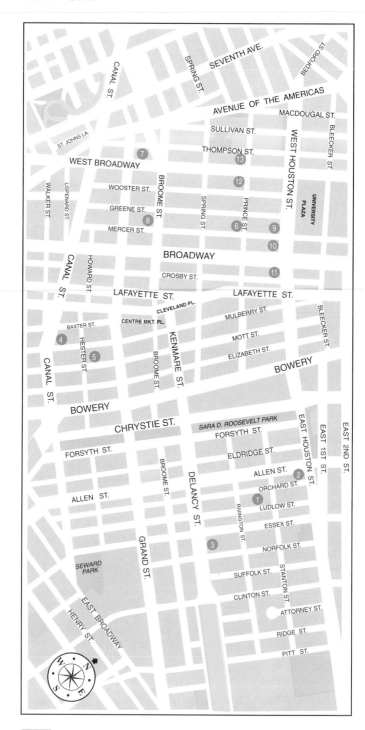

visit on Saturday, the Jewish Sabbath, but on Sunday. Everything's open then, and the area is packed with people.

Take Subway 4, 5, 6 or R to Canal St., walk east along Canal St. until you reach Orchard St. The Lower East Side's busiest shopping street, the section north of Delancey St. as far as E Houston St. turns into a **pedestrian mall** on Sundays from 8am till 6pm.

With all the stores and restaurants open and the streets packed, you will find plenty of excitement as well as well-camouflaged petty thieves; guard your wallets and purses. Far from the fancy boutiques of Madison Ave., bargaining is common practice here; use your own judgement and discretion. Since the worst you will do is to find a store owner who won't budge, it will never hurt to try for a better deal than the marked price. If you do not mind the crowds and the seeming chaos of sidewalk commerce, this is the place for incredible bargains on designer clothing, suits, hosiery, undergarments, linens and more. Spend a few hours just wandering around.

Some of the shops to visit include *Leslie Bootery* for discount men's and women's shoes with stores at 36 and 37 Orchard St., *Forman's* for designer women's clothing at 82 Orchard St., *Fine and Klein* for high-quality discount handbags and leather goods at 119 Orchard St. and *Ezra Cohen* for bedding and linens at 307 Grand St. near Orchard St. As you make your way north on Orchard St. you will be part of

---

LOWER EAST SIDE, LITTLE ITALY AND SOHO

1. Orchard St. Pedestrian Mall
2. Russ and Daughters
3. Ratner's
4. Il Cortile
5. Puglia's
6. Annina Nosei Gallery
7. Manhattan Brewing Co.
8. Global Village
9. Sperone Westwater Gallery
10. New Museum of Contemporary Art
11. John Gibson Gallery
12. Mary Boone Gallery
13. Leo Castelli Gallery

a merchandising history that has not changed much in 100 years.

Turning west on East Houston, you will discover some of the most wonderful vendors of smoked fish, salads and cheeses on the very first block. Get your bagels at *Moishe's*, at 181 East Houston St., and then head for *Ben's Cheese Store* for a chunk of his unbaked blueberry, raisin-walnut or vegetable farmer cheese. The result is as sweet and tasty as cheesecake but without as many calories. Next door at No. 179, is *Russ and Daughters*, the archetype of all delicatessens, bursting with sliced smoked fish, caviar, salads, halvah and chocolates,

all served by the very helpful countermen. Don't leave without some lox, New York's version of smoked salmon. Norwegian lox, herring in cream sauce and whitefish are all top notch. Slightly further west, in a very unglamorous storefront at the corner of Forsythe and E. Houston Sts., is the *Yonah Schimmel Knishery* with its menu of potato, kasha, spinach and fruit knishes. Both *Russ and Daughters* and *Yonah Schimmel* proudly serve the third- and fourth-generation offspring of many of their customers.

Heading east again, we pass Orchard St. and come upon *Katz's Delicatessen* at 205 E. Houston St., Tel. 254-2246, a non-kosher restaurant that is quite famous and becomes extremely crowded, especially during lunch. Continue south to Delancey St. To the east you will see the entrance to the *Williamsburg Bridge*, constructed in 1903 to connect Manhattan and Brooklyn.

Ratner's, at 138 Delancey St., Tel. 677-5588, began as a bakery and is arguably the city's most famous dairy restaurant. Though its history is more impressive than its food, here is where you can try veal cutlet without a stitch of meat on it!

A block westward is **The Bowery**, lined with stores stocked with the kind of heavy-duty, professional kitchen equipment with which many home-owners like to outfit their kitchens. Chinese cooking utensils, woks, strainers, etc., are available in several shops on Chrystie St. between Hester and Grand Sts. North of Spring St., however, the Bowery becomes a depressing place, full of bums and derelicts.

Culinary alternatives to the Jewish-style restaurants are at hand in nearby Chinatown and Little Italy.

A lively street in Little Italy

Little Italy

To reach **Little Italy** from the Lower East Side, walk west on Grand St. across the Bowery or take Subway 6 or R to Canal St., walking east from there to Mulberry St.

Little Italy occupies just a few streets north of Canal St., of which Mulberry St. is the most important. Little Italy seems to shrink as Chinatown expands north of Canal St. The term "Little Italy" originally referred to a section of Harlem; the Lower East Side neighborhood, the poorer of the two, was known then as "New Italy." While many Italian families have since prospered and moved on, some still remain.

Dining out in Little Italy

Stroll through Little Italy on a warm evening; dine at one of the many good restaurants and enjoy cappuccino and pastry. An especially lively time to visit is during September's week-long Festival of San Gennaro, the Neapolitan feast honoring the saint martyred by the Romans in 306 AD. The street fair is a crowded, joyous celebration with rides, games and lots of food.

Begin at Canal St. and head north on Mulberry St. The wood-paneled *Il*

Cortile, at 125 Mulberry St., is one of the fancier restaurants in the area – good if somewhat pricey. Open Mon.-Thurs. noon-midnight, Fri. and Sat. noon-1am, Sun. 1pm-midnight, Tel. 226-6060. Steps away is *Umberto's Clam Bar*, 129 Mulberry St. at Hester St., famous as the site of a gangland slaying several years ago. The food is decent; open daily 11:30am-6am, Tel. 431-7545. East on Hester St. is *Puglia's*, an informal and convivial establishment founded in 1919. It is located at 189 Hester St., Tel. 966-6033, 966-6006, and is reasonably priced; occasional song and music add to the friendly atmosphere. Open Tues.-Sun., noon-midnight, closed on Mon. Back on Mulberry St. at no. 133, Tel. 925-3120, is *SPQR*, a combination restaurant and nightclub that is quite fancy and expensive. The food is not remarkable, though the atmosphere is opulent. Open Mon.-Thurs. noon-11:30pm; Fri.-Sat. noon-12:30am; Sun. noon-11pm.

Save dessert for one of two places. One is *Ferrara's* (est. 1892), located at 195 Grand St., Tel. 226-6150, quite famous for its pastries and espresso which you can enjoy at an outdoor table. Open 7:30am-11:30pm daily. The pastries are perhaps even better at *Café Roma*, slightly north at 385 Broome St. near Mott St. Open Mon.-Sat. 8am-midnight, Tel. 226-8413.

Artistic graffiti at the Lower East Side

Be aware that most restaurants in the Lower East Side and Little Italy **do not** accept credit cards.

Soho –
The Novice Galleries Grow Up

"Soho" is an acronym for the area **SO**uth of **HO**uston St. – or, more precisely, the area bordered by West Houston and Canal Sts. on the north and south,
and Broadway and Sixth Avenue on the east and west.

One visits Soho for its art galleries, fashion shops and some delightful restaurants. The busiest browsing and shopping streets are Spring, Prince and
especially West Broadway. Though our tour takes you through some of the
quieter streets as well, stick to the main ones if your time is limited. The best
time for "people-watching" is a nice Saturday or Sunday afternoon.

Most boutiques are open Tuesday through Sunday, and closed Monday; most
galleries are open Tuesday through Saturday, noon-6pm. We shall incorporate
several of the better known galleries into the walking tour; check newspapers
and magazines for current exhibitions and leave enough time for random
viewing.

You can reach Soho by subway as follows: the R
to Prince St., walking west from there; the 6 to
Spring St., walking west; or the E to Spring St.,
walking east. Some street parking is available.
There is also a small parking lot on Wooster St.,
between W Houston and Prince Sts.

Today's Soho was Indian territory through the 17th
century. Of the many cast-iron row-houses which
date from the early 19th century, the
oldest still standing is at 107 Spring
St. Though an exclusive residential
district in the mid-1800s (the elegant
Lord & Taylor haberdashery was
located on Grand St.), Soho later
shifted to light industry, so much so
that it was zoned exclusively for
manufacturing in the late 1950s. The
first artists to move in then did so
illegally.

Since Manhattan as a whole began to
enjoy a renaissance of sorts in the
mid-1970s, rising out of near-bank-
ruptcy, to become a fashionable
place in which to live and work,
Soho's complexion changed dramatically. In the 1960s and 70s more
buildings were converted for
combined studio and residential use,
and more artists moved in. The prefabricated cast-iron loft buildings

*Looking for bargains
at Soho*

provided large living-working spaces, prized by artists willing to ignore the bustle of trucks and loading docks in the low-rent neighborhood.

Galleries came at the artists' heels; restaurants and boutiques were not far behind. Rising rents ultimately chased the artists out, leaving the galleries and boutiques behind to prosper. Today's Soho is trendy rather than funky and safe rather than "fringe." Despite vast differences in the art displayed, most galleries in Soho are similar in design: roomy halls, high ceilings and a clean, spartan look. Certain details – cast-iron columns and pressed-tin ceilings – have survived from warehouse days, offsetting the newly-bleached wood floors and white walls which provide an unobtrusive showcase for paintings and sculpture.

Begin the tour at Prince St. and Broadway, walking west on Prince St. to the *Annina Nosei Gallery* at No. 100 and its neo-expressionist exhibitions, Tel. 531-9253.

Nearby at No. 116 is *Agnes B.*, part of an international boutique chain featuring French ready-to-wear clothing for men, women and children. French film posters decorate the walls. Prices are relatively reasonable.

On the same St., at No. 160, the *Vesuvio Bakery* sells wonderful Italian bread and biscuits. An excellent choice for casual lunch or dinner is *Elephant and Castle*, at 183 Prince St., Tel. 925-8248, which specializes in omelets, burgers and an extensive burgundy-by-the-glass wine list. Prices are reasonable.

Turn south on Sullivan St., then east on Spring St. and south on Thompson St. Note the Twin Towers of the World Trade Center in the distance.

Across Broome St. at 40 Thompson St. is the **Manhattan Brewing Co.** and its in-house taproom. While it is not America's first commercial brewery (the first one was established in 1632 by the Dutch East India Co.), it is the only one still operating after so many years. Venture upstairs to the taproom. Note the monstrous brass brewing kettles. Pub-style lunch and dinner is served with a variety of *Manhattan Brewing Co.* beers. Open Tues.-Sun. 11:30-1am.

Return to Broome St. and continue east, passing or entering several galleries, en route to Global Village, located on 454 Broome St., Tel. 966-7526. A video establishment devoted largely to documentary films, its 75-seat viewing hall is used for scheduled screenings and discussions. Call in advance; admission charge.

A left turn from Broome St. will take you to Greene St. Continue north to discover the heart of historic 19th-century cast-iron Soho, officially designated as such in 1973. Prefabricated cast iron, though cheaper than masonry due to mass-production, lent building facades the appearance of masonry. As you stroll along Greene St., look up at the line of fire escapes. After a day in the art galleries, one cannot help but notice that the sunlight filtering through the fire escapes imparts them a look of an asymmetrical outdoor sculpture. The cobblestone street adds to the ambiance.

The *Soho kitchen* is on 101 Greene St., Tel. 925-1866, decorated with large abstract paintings. The attractive bar allows you to sample 125 different wines and champagnes by the glass. The inventive, light fare is reasonably priced. Open for dinner Mon.-Fri. 4pm-midnight, Sat. from 5pm. The bar is open till 2am on Fri. Brunch is served on Sat. Closed Sundays.

See huge at "Think Big!"

Greene St. is home to several more galleries, including *Sperone Westwater* at No. 142, and its display of contemporary European and American art. Walk two blocks east on West Houston St. and turn south on Broadway for some more modern-art exhibits. The **New Museum of Contemporary Art**, 583 Broadway, Tel. 219-1355, is devoted exclusively to "art of our time," mostly art which has been neglected by the large and more famous museums. Open Wed.-Sun. noon-6pm, Admission charge. Free Sat. 6-8pm, and for children under 12. Closed in the summer. Across the street at 568 and 578 Broadway, is a block of new or newly-located galleries well worth visiting. Among them you will find the *John Gibson Gallery*, Tel. 925-1192, and the *Twining Gallery*, Tel. 431-1830. These exhibit a variety of contemporary paintings, sculptures and photography. Most of the galleries are open Tues.-Sat. noon-6pm.

In a way, we have saved the best street for last. Continue west on Spring St. to W Broadway. Turning north on W Broadway you will find a boutique, gallery or restaurant at every storefront. Cover the east side first, then the west side so as not to miss anything. Be sure to visit the "heavyweight" galleries: *Mary Boone* at No. 417, and *Leo Castelli* nearby. Mary Boone became quite famous some years ago, epitomizing the young, aggressive dealer with an eye for budding talent. Castelli is one of Soho's most established galleries.

On 386 W Broadway is *Think Big!* where the mundane turns into mammoth giants, such as man-sized paper clips or six-foot crayons.

Our tour has not covered every street in Soho, focusing rather on those of major interest. Of these, an exploration of West Broadway, Prince and Spring Sts. will give you a feeling of the area. Be sure to try at least one of the area's restaurants, most of which serve brunch on Saturdays and Sundays.

If you find yourself here in the evening and want

to have dinner, walk south on Broadway and re-enter the heart of Soho and its abundance of good restaurants by turning west on Spring St. The *New Deal* at 152 Spring St. Tel. 431-3663, serves reasonably-priced pre-theater dinner specials in a tranquil atmosphere, with background jazz offered later in the evening. *Tennessee Mountain* at 143 Spring St., Tel. 431-3993, offers perhaps the best barbecued ribs in town, also at reasonable prices. The *Spring St. Natural*, at 66 Spring St., serves excellent all-natural fare.

For an expensive, elegant dinner, walk south on W Broadway as far as Grand St.; the best choice is *Chanterelle* at 89 Grand St., Tel. 966-6960, whose nouvelle cuisine menu changes every two weeks. For a less expensive quick bite, continue west on Grand St. to the *Moondance Diner* at the corner of 6th Ave. This smallish 1950's-style diner will satisfy your appetite in a fun setting.

After dinner, enjoy a wonderful production of a new play or musical at the informal *Ark Theater* at 131 Spring St., Tel. 431-6285. For more experimental theater, check the billings at the *Performing Garage*, 33 Wooster St., Tel. 966-9796.

One source of avant-garde entertainment is nearby. The *Film Forum* at 57 Watts St., Tel. 627-2033, screens foreign and non-establishment films.

Greenwich Village –
Anything Goes

Greenwich Village is known as a hothouse for new ideas, be they socio-cultural, political, fashion or, more accurately, anti-fashion. Compared with calm, conservative Uptown, the Village lives on the "fringe": American Communism, the 1950s "beat" generation, the 1960s anti-war movement, the gay-rights movement and the punk rockers all sounded their first rumblings here.

Performing by the arch at Washington Square Park, erected in 1889 for the centennial of George Washington's inauguration as President

Once an Indian village, 18th-century Greenwich Village was dotted with wealthy country estates. Late in the 19th century it became home to artists and writers such as Winslow Homer, Mark Twain and Henry James, who even wrote of a wealthy family living next to the village park in his 1881 novel *Washington Square*.

Indeed, **Washington Square Park** is rich in history. An English elm known as the "Hangman's Tree" because of the function it fulfiled in the late 1700s, still stands in the park. Emma Goldman, the noted anarchist, who lived around the corner and advocated her belief in unrestrained freedom for everyone, was accused, without proof, of complicity in the assassination of President McKinley in 1901. Other famous residents of the Village include Edna St. Vincent Millay, O. Henry, Diego Rivera and Eugene O'Neill, who formed one of the earliest off-Broadway theater companies, the Provincetown Players.

Contributing to the atmosphere in the Village are the institutions of higher education and the concentration of students. The Village alone is home to NYU, the New School, the Parsons School of Design, and the New School for Social Research.

An inherently intellectual atmosphere? An ambience of rebellion for its own sake? Either way, the Village's bizarre fashions, informal bars and convivial coffee-houses attest to an open exchange of ideas.

Enjoy the West Village by day and far into the night – strolling, shopping, dining, club-hopping. We've provided two separate day tours and an evening tour as well. As you will see, the neighborhood abounds with activity. The best time to visit is from mid-afternoon into the late evening. There is no need to rush; shops are usually open late, there are not many sites, and strolling the streets is the most fun.

Day Tour No. 1

Take Subway R, 4, 5 or 6 to Union Square 14th St. and walk a couple of blocks west to 5th Ave., from there walk south. The Village begins at 14th St.

The 5th Ave. limestone buildings tend to be larger, taller and more ornate than those lining the nearby side streets. For example, note the solid edifice at 62 5th Ave. (at the corner of 12th St.), which houses the **offices of Forbes Magazine and Gallery** exhibiting the private collection of founder Malcolm Forbes. Open Tues.-Sat. 10am-4pm. Thurs., group tours only, entrance free. Tel. 206-5548.

The **Graduate Faculty of Political and Social Sciences**, located at 65 5th Ave., an arm of the New School for Social Research, was founded in 1933 as a graduate school to be staffed by European scholars who escaped the Nazi regime.

Turn west onto W 12th St. The houses, **No. 34 to 44**, built in 1860 in late Italianesque style recalling India House on Lower Manhattan's Hanover Square, were considered among New York's most elegant when constructed.

Speed and noise at the Subway

Returning to 5th Ave., we find the **First Presbyterian Church** between 11th and 12th Sts., entrance at 12 W 12th St. New York's Presbyterian community dates back to 1716, when it was coldly received by the English colonists, officially members of Wall street's Trinity Church. During the Revolution, the Presbyterians sided with the rebels while Trinity sided with the British. After the necessary postwar reassessment, Trinity

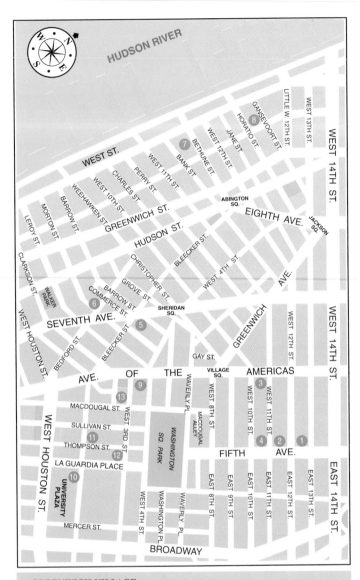

GREENWICH VILLAGE

1. Forbes Magazine and Gallery
2. First Presbyterian Church
3. Second Cemetery of Shearith Israel
4. Church of the Ascension
5. Second Childhood
6. Cherry Lane Theater
7. Westbeth
8. Gansevoort Wholesale Meat Market
9. The Blue Note
10. "Time Landscape"
11. Circle in the Square Theater
12. The Chess Shop
13. Minetta Lane Theater

temporarily offered its premises to the Presbyterians, whose own church was being rebuilt. Completed in 1845 in 15th-century Gothic style, the church was modelled after the Church of St. Savior in Bath, England, while its tower resembles that of Magdalen College, Oxford. President Theodore Roosevelt, born in NYC, was baptized here. When you visit the church, have a look at the stained glass windows, three of which were designed by Louis Tiffany, the American glazier famous for his multi-colored iridescent glass.

Continue south on 5th Ave. and turn west on W 11th, a pretty street of well-maintained town houses. **No. 60**, built in 1842, is a characteristic product of Andrew Lockwood, "master builder" of W 11th St., in its combination of Federal and Greek Revival styles. Further west, toward the corner of W 11th and 6th Ave. is the second cemetery of the Spanish and Portuguese Synagogue, **Shearith Israel** (the first cemetery of this congregation, founded in 1654, is in Chinatown). Used between 1805 and 1829, the second cemetery has been crowded into a tiny triangle by the surrounding houses.

If it's lunchtime, cross 6th Ave. for a pizza at *Ray's*, the famous Village establishment. Return to 5th Ave. and continue south. At the corner of W 10th St. is the **Church of the Ascension**, an English Gothic structure designed by Richard Upjohn, built in 1840 and redecorated around 1888 from plans drawn up by architect Stanford White. White's firm, the popular McKim, Mead & White, was responsible for much of the city's turn-of-the-century architecture, including the huge General Post Office on 8th Ave.

The interior of the Church is graced by a mural, *The Ascension* by American-born painter John La Farge, whose work also hangs in the **Church of the Incarnation** at 35th St. and 209 Madison Ave. La Farge was a friend of Henry James and greatly influenced James' works – most of which feature an artist as a main character. The church is open daily, noon-2pm and 5-7pm. Tel. 689-6350.

Turn west onto W 10th, another lovely residential block. Samuel Clemens – better known as Mark Twain – lived at No. 14.

Looking south on 5th Ave. you will see the arch which opens onto **Washington Square Park**, erected by NYC in 1889 for the centennial of George Washington's inauguration as President.

The park, its fountains and its street jazz musicians will cool your spirits in summer. On weekends, from April until snowfall, *La Boule New Yorkaise* meets at the south end for *petanque*, a French version of Italian *bocce* in which one throws or rolls hollow steel balls so that they stop as close as possible to a little target ball. Spectators are welcome.

The attractive park is safe during the day. At night, unless entertainment is being offered, stay out; the park becomes a market for drugs and is very dangerous.

An eastward stroll on Waverly Place from the north end of the park leads you to several restaurants. An inexpensive cup of coffee or light meal is available at the *Waverly Coffee Shop* at the corner of Mercer St. Popular with NYU students, the

Waverly offers what must be New York's largest daily selection of muffins – to eat there or to take out.

From the southern end of the park, walk west along W 4th St. to 6th Ave. Basketball courts between 3rd and 4th Sts. feature games which attract large crowds. Across 6th Ave. at 3rd St., the *Waverly Twin Theater* screens first-run movies during the day and evening, Tel. 929-8037. The Waverly, like several other Village cinemas, offers a special midnight show, often a cult film or an "oldie." When films such as the *Rocky Horror Picture Show* are shown, movie-going becomes a participatory event with audiences dressing as characters and speaking the dialogue with the actors.

West of 6th Ave., down W 4th St. at No. 161, is the *Pink Pussycat Boutique* with an inventory of every erotic novelty imaginable.

At the Washington Square

If you want to continue walking, you will find some of the more interesting shops on Greenwich Ave. and 8th St. From Sheridan Square, head east on Christopher St. along Sheridan Square Park. This short stretch of Christopher St. has several nice clothing and toy shops, etc. Turn west at Greenwich Ave. between 6th and 7th Ave., this is a great street for clothes shopping.

Return east to 6th Ave. and walk several blocks north to *Balducci's*, between 9th and 10th Sts. *Balducci's* is the Village's gourmet food shop, a feast for the eyes as well as the stomach. If it hasn't got what you want, forget you ever wanted it.

Retrace your steps southward on 6th Ave. and turn east on W 8th St., another fun shopping street and habitat of some truly bizarre fashions in clothing, hairstyle and jewelry. Stores and clientele tend to look wild. This stretch abounds with shoe stores, some carrying bargain merchandise. You may want to stop into the *Be Bop Café*, very 1950s in decor and music. Further east, at 52 W 8th, is the *8th St. Playhouse*, another cinema with midnight shows.

For evening and late-night ideas, see the section "By Night", further on.

Day Tour No. 2

Now we shall explore some of the Village's prettiest streets, best restaurants and some more theaters, starting from Sheridan Square. Either walk there from W 8th St., where tour No. 1 ended, or take Subway 1 to Christopher St.

From Sheridan Square, walk south along 7th Ave. and turn east onto Bleecker St. This stretch of Bleecker is home to several good shops and restaurants.

Second Childhood, 283 Bleecker, Tel. 989-6140, is a wonderful little antique toy store with trains, wind-ups, tin soldiers and farm animals. *Golden Disc,* at no. 239, buys and sells collector LPs.

Now return west on Bleecker for more fun shops and terrific restaurants.

Upon reaching Bank St., skirt the playground to the north and then turn south onto Hudson St. Do not miss *Second Hand Rose*, situated at 573 Hudson, with its stock of 1920s-1950s furniture and large selection of vintage wallpaper, all extremely well-preserved.

Continue to Christopher St. and turn east. Behold a little Village enclave consisting of some of the quaintest blocks in the entire city – trees, window boxes and extremely well-maintained row houses. Don't be dissuaded by the seemingly confused street layout. Follow our directions and you will be treated to a unique reminder of what the city was like a century ago.

On 61 Christopher is the *Duplex Jazz Club*, Tel. 255-5438. Downstairs in the piano bar, patrons and staff sing along. Upstairs is a nightly cabaret show. Turn right onto Bleecker and stroll to Grove St. Walk west on Grove, then turn south on Bedford St. *Chumley's*, one of New York's famous bars, stands at No. 86; entrance is through the alleyway just around the corner on Barrow St.

After a stroll in this enclave, turn south to Barrow St. Head east until it becomes Commerce, the prettiest street of all. As you cross Bedford, look to the left and notice the house at **75 1/2 Bedford**. This is New York's narrowest building, only 9.5 ft. (less than 3 m) wide. Further along Commerce, at No. 38, Tel. 989-2020, you will find the *Cherry Lane Theater*, an intimate playhouse. A few steps away is the *Blue Mill Tavern*, an unpretentious little bar-restaurant established in 1926, a perfect place for a break.

Now retrace your steps west. Turn north on Hudson, and west onto W 11th St. At the corner of 11th and Washington Sts. is the *Black Sheep*, Tel. 242-1010 , a charming country French restaurant with a fixed-price menu. Continue on W 11th to West St., the Village's western border parallel to the Hudson River. South of here are several gay clubs and cinemas. Turn north on West St. for **Westbeth**, the artists' complex at West and Bethune Sts. The original tenant of this site was the *Bell Telephone Laboratory* (*Western Electric*) which, in 1896, invested $119,000 in buying this land for its manufacturing shop. Here the first talking movies were made, the transistor was discovered, and television was demonstrated to the public for the first time.

The solid concrete and steel buildings were dedicated in 1970 and renamed Westbeth. Conceived as an answer to artists' need for large, affordable working space, and evidence of New York's commitment to its artist residents, the Westbeth project required tax abatements, liberalization of zoning regulations and FHA sponsorship. It received all three. The inexpensive housing here is available only for serious artists.

Enter the complex through the courtyard entrance on Bethune St. You will find a theater for film and drama, ground-floor galleries for permanent public display of residents' work and a shared studio for

sculptors. Dance studio space is rented by choreographer Merce Cunningham for public performances.

Near Westbeth, dinner can be had at the previously-mentioned *Black Sheep* or at the *Yellow Rose*, a Mexican restaurant at 521 West St.

A stroll north of Westbeth along West St. will take you through the **Gansevoort Wholesale Meat Market**, namesake of the Gansevoort Docks of yesteryear. The author Herman Melville once worked here as a customs inspector because he could not support his family from writings such as *Moby Dick* and *Billy Budd*. The market is an interesting, though not a pretty, sight.

By Night

The West Village, especially the few streets just south of Washington Square Park, is just the place to spend the evening and the late night hours. Reach the square either from the day tours we outlined or directly by taking Subway A or E to W 4th St. On a nice evening, you can simply walk around or call up a jazz club, make a reservation, and arrive early enough to walk around a little.

Begin at W 4th St. and 6th Ave., walk south on 6th Ave. and turn east onto W 3rd St. The *Blue Note*, 131 W 3rd, Tel. 475-8592, is an intimate jazz club that attracts the most famous and talented performers. Crowded tables surrounding a small stage generate camaraderie between performer and audience. A jazz performance here will be one of the highlights of your visit to NYC. The cover charge and minimum can be satisfied with drinks or dinner.

Continue along W 3rd to *Bleecker Bob's Golden Oldies Record Shop*, 118 W 3rd. St., one of several Village record shops specializing in hard-to-find oldies. Most such shops are open late into the evening.

Turn south at La Guardia Place and cross Bleecker. There you will find the *"Time Landscape"*, a recreation of Manhattan's pre-colonial mixed oak forest and rolling topography. To resume the search for urban night-life, turn west onto Bleecker. This stretch of Bleecker, between La Guardia and 6th Ave., is the liveliest of late-night venues. Every corner seems to sprout a sidewalk café, perfect – weather permitting – for nursing a drink or an espresso and watching the young, arty street scene. Beside these are several superior clubs, some more legendary than the musicians performing inside.

Jazz players and their audiences haunt the Blue Note jazz club

Preachers, 145 Bleecker, Tel. 533-4625, offers late-evening pop and rock music. *The Bitter End*, 147 Bleecker, Tel. 673-7030, is a music club and neighborhood landmark which launched the careers of many artists, including Woody Allen and Robert Klein, but most of today's performers are unknown. *The Village Gate*, across the street at 160 Bleecker, Tel. 475-5120, serves food, drink and music in its large downstairs room, reserving the smaller *Top of the Gate* for cabaret-style musicals. *Circle in the Square Theater*, 159 Bleecker, Tel. 254-6330, is a wonderful, intimate theater with 300 seats arranged on three sides of the stage.

At 315 Bowary and Bleecker St. is *CBGB'S*, a dim black cave, which was the place for punk in the 1970's. Today it functions as a showcase for talents of all kinds. Tel. 982-4052.

An excellent Spanish restaurant, *El Rincon de España* on Thompson St. north of Bleecker at No. 226, Tel. 260-4950, offers reasonable prices and noteworthy *paella*. For dessert, try one of the many nearby cafés. A 24-hour newsstand will provide you with a *Sunday Times* after your late-Saturday night on the town.

The *Chess Shop*, 230 Thompson, is open noon-midnight every day for players and on-lookers alike. Backgammon, Go and cribbage as well as

At the Chess Shop

chess are played. Lessons are available too. There is a charge per game for playing. Tel. 475-9580.

The *Sullivan Street Playhouse* is on 181 Sullivan St., south of Bleecker, Tel. 674-3838. Turn north on MacDougal St., one block west of Sullivan. Just off MacDougal is the *Minetta Lane Theater*. Further north on MacDougal is the oldest off-Broadway theater company, the *Provincetown Playhouse*, founded by Eugene O'Neill, 133 MacDougal St., Tel. 477-5048.

Head west of 4th St. and turn left on Cornelia St. for *Sabor*, 20 Cornelia St., Tel. 243-9579, and its delicious Cuban food. Open only at dinner time.

At No. 29, is the *Cornelia Street Café*, featuring pop, rock and folk music, Tel. 989-9318.

Continue west along W 4th St. and browse through the shops. At the corner of Jones St. you will find the *Peculier Pub*, 120 W 4th, a small bar that somehow manages to offer 200 types of domestic and imported beer, Tel. 353-1327. A left turn onto Barrow St. will take you to *One If By Land, Two If By Sea*. Situated at No. 17, it is an expensive Continental restaurant with a cozy atmosphere in what was in Revolutionary days Aaron Burr's coach house, Tel. 255-8649.

Return to W 4th and continue west until you reach Sheridan Square, the intersection of W 4th, Christopher St. and 7th Ave. This junction offers everal options for your evening. The *Circle Rep.*, theater company at 99 7th Ave. South, Tel. 24-7100, offers consistently well-staged shows with tickets, often available on the day of perfor-mance. At 100 7th Ave. South is the *Actors' Playhouse*, Tel. 691-6226. In addition to its regular erformance schedule, the *Playhouse* offers free tudent presentations on Mondays at 8pm. Next oor at 88 7th Ave. South is *Sweet Basil's*, one of New York's finest jazz clubs, Tel. 242-1785. lightly further north, at 178 7th Ave. South at 1th St., is the world-famous *Village Vanguard*, a asement jazz club now celebrating its 55th irthday, Tel. 255-4037.

hop in the afternoon and dine in the evening at ny one of the fine restaurants and cafés. Take in a how or an early jazz set, then a late jazz set in a ifferent club. Most clubs have two sets on veekend evenings. Round off the night with some ecord-buying, and pick up the *Sunday Times* efore the cab ride back to your hotel.

The East Village – Astounding Creativity

The East Village only recently evolved into an "in" place to visit; it alway had a lot to offer – theaters, galleries, dance clubs, a variety of inexpensiv restaurants, and the most exciting avant-garde art in 20 years. Dress any wa you like for your visit to this very modest neighborhood. The best time to vis is late afternoon or evening, especially on Fridays or Saturdays. **Galleries ar closed on Mondays**.

The East Village, like the West, runs from Houston St. to 14th St. East an West are demarcated by 5th Ave. from 14th St. south to 8th St., and b Broadway from 8th St. south to Houston. Though you will see no differenc between East and West from Broadway itself, the socio-economic difference become more pronounced the further East or West you go.

The West Village looks the wealthier of the two, with its boutiques and fanc expensive restaurants; the East is a community of artists, actors and imm grants. East Village galleries show more experimental work, and dining i less expensive. The East is evolving; the West is more stable. The Wes although far from conservative, has been an established artists' neighborhoo for many years, a place where the Uptown crowd has long flocked for lat night jazz or a glimpse of the bizarre street life.

If you visit the East Village by day, take Subway I to E 8th St., head for the corner of Broadway an E 8th and walk north on Broadway. Big showcas windows at the corner of Broadway and E 10th *Broadway Windows*, add to the street scene wit their changing exhibits of large artwork. Th windows are the gallery. Directly across the stree is **Grace Church**, a beautiful Protestant Episcopa

In front of the exquisite Gothic Grace Church

Church of Gothic design, completed in 1846. Designed by James Renwick, Jr., the church is famous for its stained glass windows, high arches and carved pulpit, Tel. 254-2000. On Broadway, across from the church, are several antique shops, most notably *Fifty-Fifty*, 793 Broadway, Tel. 777-3208, with its stock of vintage mid-20th century furniture and furnishings. This part of the East Village – Broadway north

Grace Church

to 13th St., and 11th and 12th Sts. one block west – abounds in such shops. Many sell only to other tradesmen but some are open to the public.

Two shops which are a "must" are situated at Broadway and 12th. On the northwest corner at 821 Broadway, is *Forbidden Planet*, Tel. 473-1576, the ultimate science fiction store with its stock of toys, masks, games, books and over 15,000 different comic books. Employees eagerly demonstrate mechanized robots, and you are perfectly welcome to browse. Crossing to the northeast corner, will feel equally welcome at the *Strand Bookstore,* 828 Broadway, Tel. 473-1452, which claims to be New York's largest used bookstore.

Strand Bookstore, a huge outlet for used books

Located in a former clothing outlet, the *Strand* stocks over two million current, rare and out-of-print books, often at amazing bargain prices. Pick up reviewer's copies of recent books for 50% off the publisher's price list. If there's anything you can't find, ask the employees. *Strand* also has a number of smaller branches scattered throughout the city.

Continuing north on Broadway, look up at 13th St. for a glimpse of the Empire State Building in the distance. Turn west on 13th, then south on University Place (the nearby NYU owns much of the property in this area). University Place is home to several clubs worthy of return visits in the evening: two jazz clubs, *Bradley's* at No. 70, Tel. 228-6440, and the *Knickerbocker Saloon* at No. 33, Tel. 228-8490. The *Knickerbocker* is a restaurant decorated with memorabilia from the early 1900s. There is no cover or minimum charge.

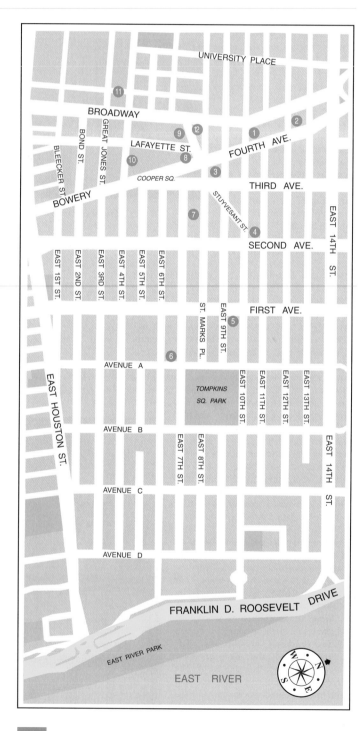

Music until 2:30am. The popular *BBQ*, 21 University Pl., serves excellent roast chicken.

Head south on University and turn east on E 10th. The *Margo Feiden Galleries* at 75 University Pl., Tel. 228-8490, house more than 1,000 original drawings by noted caricaturist Al Hirschfeld. Now an octogenarian and an artist for the *New York Times*, Mr. Hirschfeld has been drawing theater people for more than sixty years. His trademark, aside from his distinct style, is the cleverly hidden inclusion of his daughter's name in most of his caricatures. Search for "Nina" and enjoy the collection free of charge, Mon.-Fri. 10am-6pm, Sat.-Sun. 1-5 pm. Some items are for sale, and posters are available.

The statue of Peter Cooper, founder of the School for the Advancement of Science and Art

Turn south onto Broadway and then east onto E 8th St. Cross Lafayette. On your right, where Lafayette meets 4th Ave., is **Cooper Union Foundation Building**, named for Peter Cooper, the noted inventor and philanthropist. The School for the Advancement of Science and Art, founded by Cooper in 1859, has never charged tuition fees. The entrance is on E 7th St. Stop inside and check the schedule of upcoming free exhibits and concerts, or Tel. 353-4100.

E 8th St. turns into St. Marks Place when you cross 4th and 3rd Aves. Here you will find vintage clothing shops such as *Trash and Vaudeville* at No. 4, Tel. 982-3590. Turn north onto 2nd Ave. On your left, at 133 2nd Ave., is the *St. Marks Cinema* which screens feature films and midnight showings of cult films or classic oldies. Next door at No. 135, is the **Ottendorfer Library**, a century-old facility which, as such, is the oldest public library branch still in its original home. Estab-

The Cooper Union Foundation Building at Astor Place

lished as a haven for German immigrants by Oswald Ottendorfer, owner of a German-American newspaper, the library has adapted to changing times by adding Polish, Ukrainian, Chinese, French and Spanish books to its shelves.

Here, from 2nd Ave. eastward, is the immigrants' and artists' village. The area between 4th and 11th Sts., and Aves. A and C abounds with galleries, experimental theaters and inexpensive ethnic restaurants whose gastronomical delights you should definitely sample. Cuisines reflect three major cultures, with the restaurants themselves as different in nature as in menu. The Polish-Ukrainian restaurants are decorated in the "1950's Functional" style of formica, glass and tiles in bright earth tones, in accordance to their role as their immigrant clientele's political and cultural centers. You can eat quickly and inexpensively; the service is very friendly. The Hispanic restaurants, though amiable to outsiders as well, exist primarily to serve "their own." The decor, usually in bright colors, often includes flags and maps of the country of origin. The ubiquitous Indian restaurants exude "exoticism". Dim lights, colorful fabrics and native sitar music give the sense of being transported to a foreign land.

At the northwest corner of 2nd Ave. and 10th St., is the **St. Marks-in-the-Bouwerie Church**. The late-Georgian edifice, constructed in 1799, replaced the chapel which the last Governor of Nieuw Amsterdam, Peter Stuyvesant, built in 1660 on his *bouwerie* (cattle) farm. Stuyvesant and seven generations of his descendants are buried here; his stone marker is embedded in the church's foundation. With Alexander Hamilton's legal assistance, St. Marks opened as the first Manhattan parish independent of Trinity Church, setting up prayer chapels throughout the city to serve the needs of immigrants without invoking the then-discriminatory practice of pew rental. Today, St. Marks often serves as an artists' forum. The Poetry Project has presented weekly readings there for some 25 years. Isadora Duncan and Martha Graham danced here. *Theater Genesis*, founded in 1965, was one of the first off-off Broadway theaters to produce the early works of Pulitzer-Prize winner Sam Shepard. Tel. 674-6377 for performance information (no performances June.-Sept.)

At 162 2nd Ave. you will find the *Theater for the New City* (Tel. 254-1109), one of the many experimental theater companies that operate in the East Village.

For camping equipment or sporting goods the place to go is *Hudson's*, one block west, occupying a full block of 3rd Ave. between 12th and 13th Sts. Search for Broadway show albums and out-of-stock records at *Footlight Records*, 113 E 12th St.

Astor Place Haircutters – not the place for conformists

A stroll east on 11th, beyond 1st Ave., takes you into an increasingly seedy neighborhood with an abundance of drug trafficking. This lower-rent district, however, is home to several hot new East Village art galleries with exhibits of work hailed as "the most energetic and provocative in the country." Although this art defies categorization, several common characteristics seem to prevail: the works are small in size, humorous, political, intentionally unpolished and infused with energy, seemingly ripped from the easel. Of the more than 60 galleries and clubs inhabiting today's East Village, several leading ones are on 10th and 11th Sts.

The **Tenth Street Turkish Baths**, 268 E 10th, is considered NYC's only surviving traditional Turkish bathhouse. Called *"the schvitz"* (Yiddish

At the Flea Market in East Village

slang for steam bath), the interior can become unbearably hot. Bathhouses were commonplace in New York when many apartments did not have their own facilities for bathing. While many such establishments have become locales for sexual intimacy among the male clientele in recent years, the Tenth Street Baths retains much of its 19th-century atmosphere of a place where people can come just to relax. Gangsters used to come here to discuss business, checking their weapons with an attendant whose main qualification for the job was his deafness. Admission charge to the bathhouse and *platzka*, a vigorous scrubbing with soap and a hand broom made of oak leaves, Tel. 473-8806.

By heading west to 1st Ave. and turning south, you approach several different choices for evening entertainment. **P.S. 122**, at 150 1st Ave. near 9th St., is a former school transformed into an important experimental arts center, with the *P.S.* no longer standing for "Public School" but for "Performance Space". Though not fancy, it exhibits work as good as that of the nearby galleries and is a perfect place to view the latest in dance, music and theater. Tel. 228-4249 for further information.

The *Pyramid Club*, further west at 101 Ave. between 6th and 7th Sts., tends toward the wild and bizarre in dance. The crowd, wildly uninhibited, displays every imaginable style of clothing and dance. There is an admission charge. After sampling the Village's other entertainment possibilities, you might want to return late at night.

Walk west to 1st Ave., which now seems like the height of civilization compared to "Alphabetland" (Aves. A, B, C). Turn north and you will come to *Polonia Polish Restaurant*, 126 1st Ave., between 7th and St. Marks Place. Like the Ukrainian restaurants we mentioned earlier, *Polonia* is a tiny, friendly and inexpensive spot, perfect for a fast lunch. Try the homemade soup and potato *peiroge* or dumplings. You might also try *Teresa* at 103 1st Ave.

All of 6th St. in East Village, between 2nd Ave. and A Ave. is full of Indian restaurants and food stores.

As you turn the corner onto St. Marks Place, you will see *Theater 80 St. Marks*, another cinema which offers midnight showings of screen classics, Tel. 254-7400. Now turn south and west onto 7th St. Here, at 15 E 7th., is *McSorley's Old Ale House* (1854), a neighborhood landmark and a favorite watering hole. Open only to men until 1970, *McSorley's* was finally forced to admit women after a court battle, Tel. 473-9148. Try *Surma*, two doors away at 11 E 7th, for Ukrainian books and beautiful, intricately decorated Easter eggs, Tel. 477-0729.

Continue west on 7th St., crossing 3rd and 4th Aves. Pass the front of Cooper Union and turn south onto Lafayette St. Before heading south, notice *Astor Wines and Spirits* at 12 Astor Place on the far side of Lafayette, perhaps New York's largest liquor store, Tel. 674-7500.

Turning south onto Lafayette, you will find the *Public Theater* at No. 425, originally home of the Astor Library. The renovated Public Theater, actually houses several theaters in addition to the headquarters of the NY Shakespeare Festival (free summer performances at the *Delacorte Theater* in Central Park). *Hair* and *Chorus Line*, the longest-running Broadway shows ever, were first staged here. While full-price tickets are available at the box office, the *Public Theater* also offers a discount system, *Quiktix*

sold for half-price tickets on the day of performance.

The *Astor Place Theater,* across the street at 434 Lafayette, also stages high-quality shows. The theater itself is an historical landmark, one of the four survivors of Colonnade Row or LaGrange Terrace, an ensemble formed by nine columned edifices built in the 1830s. The 28 elegant Corinthian columns bracketed the residential enclave majestically. John Jacob Astor, whose library stood across the street, and Washington Irving, author of *Rip van Winkle* and *Legend of Sleepy Hollow*, lived here.

Also on Colonnade Row is *Indochine*, 430 Lafayette, a restaurant specializing in Vietnamese cooking and owned by one of the founders of Tribeca's *Odeon*. You will share *Indochine's* airy, colorful dining room with New York's art and fashion mavericks, models and photographers. Prices are quite reasonable but portions are small. Open 6pm-12:30am daily, Tel. 505-5111.

Continue south on Lafayette and turn east on E 4th St. No. 29 is the **Old Merchants House of New York**. Built in 1831-32, it is Manhattan's only 19th-century house to survive with its original furnishings and family memorabilia intact. Open Sundays 1-4pm, and at other times by special appointment, Tel. 777-1089.

The Bouwerie Lane Theater, 330 Bowery and 2nd St., Tel. 677-0060, houses the *Cocteau Repertory*, which specializes in resurrecting neglected classics. *La Mama (E.T.C.),* 74A E 4th, Tel. 254-6468, stages excellent productions of new and avant-

garde plays and performance pieces. Early works by Sam Shepard were presented here.

Walk north on the Bowery and turn west onto Great Jones St. for the Great Jones St. Café, No. 54, Tel. 674-9304, a good place to end the evening. It's a tiny place; you will probably have to wait for a table. The food is good, reasonably priced and is served until 4am.

Tower Records, New York's largest music store

Now head west to Broadway. This stretch of Broadway is always alive and active. At the corner of Broadway and E 4th St. is **Tower Records**, New York's largest music store, with another branch on the Upper West Side. Its jazz collection is especially extensive. Open 9am to midnight, 365 days a year. *Tower's* classical music bargain annex, located around the corner and entered from E 4th and Lafayette, is open 9am-11pm daily, Tel. 505-1500. Don't miss it.

Several blocks west, at 15 W 4th St., is the *Bottom Line*, a pop and rock music club that often features big-name performers live. Advance tickets are often required, Tel. 228-7880.

Some of New York's best vintage and one-of-a-kind clothing shops are located north on Broadway. One of these, the *Antique Boutique*, at 712-714 Broadway and Washington Pl., Tel. 460-8830, should not be missed. It carries a wide array of vintage clothes from yellow tuxedos to bowling shirts and costume jewelry.

There's a highly recommended pastry shop – *Veniero's*, on 342 East 11th St. Tel. 674-7264. This shop was established around 100 years ago and is said to be the best in East Village. It is so popular that one must take a number and stand in line!

Our East Village tour ends at *Astor Place Haircutters* on the corner of Broadway and Astor Place. This is an establishment of a different sort, one which offers you a more personalized souvenir of your trip to the Village. Everything new and radical in hair design is happening here. Give your name and take your place in a line that often snakes around outside. Peer through the large showcase window at the stylists as they hack away with artistry and precision; that's part of the fun. When you hear your name called over a loud-speaker, it is your turn. This is inexpensive entertainment – choose from a variety of styles and colors to match or clash with the vintage outfit you may have just purchased, Tel. 475-9854.

Gramercy Park – A Serene Enclave

Gramercy Park neighborhood is considered the area bounded by 14th St. to the south and 27th St. to the north, 5th Ave. to the west and the residential complexes of Stuyvesant Town and Peter Cooper Village to the east – with the park itself in the center.

This attractive residential enclave, though not particularly exciting for the tourist, does offer high-quality discount men's clothing, several bookstores, good restaurants and small, specialized museums.

Like Greenwich Village, Gramercy Park was once the home of many important literary figures (Washington Irving and O. Henry, for example) and, together with the Village, was decreed by the NY Municipal Art Society, in 1957, as a historic district worthy of preservation. The Society claimed that the buildings forged an historic link with the original Gramercy Park of 150 years ago.

Take Subway R, 4, 5, or 6 to **Union Square**, the junction of 14th St. and Broadway. One hundred years ago, 14th St. was considered a noble thoroughfare; Union Square was one of the prettiest of NYC's small parks, with *Tiffany's* and *Lord & Taylor's* close by. Since those days, the area has undergone many changes. At the north end of the **Union Square Park**, farmers and other suppliers gather on Wednesdays, Fridays and Saturdays at the outdoor **Union Square Greenmarket** with inexpensive fresh fruits, vegetables, eggs and other produce.

Union Square

From Union Square walk east on 14th St. to Irving Place; then head north. The headquarters of *Consolidated Edison*, NYC's supplier of electricity is on your right at No. 4 Irving Place. Inside is the **Con Edison Energy Museum**, chronicling the age of electricity. It is open free of charge, Tues.-Sat. 10am-4pm. Enter just around the corner at 145 E 14th St., Tel. 460-4600.

Continue north on Irving

Place. Washington Irving (1783-1859), the first professionally successful native-born American author (*Rip van Winkle, The Legend of Sleepy Hollow*) lived at No. 49, at the corner of 17th St. More contemporary entertainment – jazz, salsa and blues

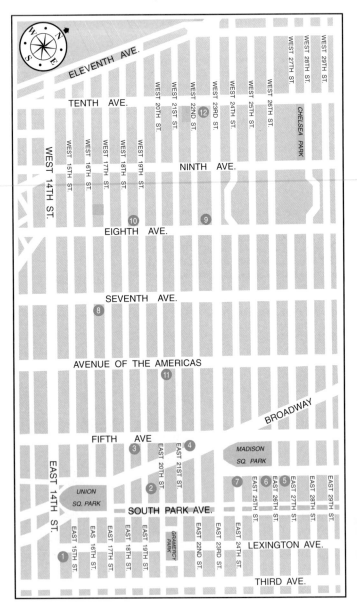

– is at hand at *Irving Plaza*, located at 17 Irving Place near 15th Street, Tel. 777-6800. There are two good Italian restaurants nearby, between 17th and 18th Sts. on Irving Place – *Paul and Jimmy's*, Tel. 475-9540 and *Sal Anthony's*, Tel. 982-9030.

A good but slightly expensive Chinese restaurant is *The Cottage* at 35 Irving Place between 15th and 16th streets, Tel. 505-8600.

Pete's Tavern is across the way at 66 Irving Place, Tel. 473-7676. It is said that the notable short-story author, O. Henry, frequented the latter establishment around the turn of the century, while writing his famous *The Gifts of the Magi*.

Just a block north on Irving Place is **Gramercy Park**. NYC's only remaining private park, the owners of the surrounding plots share its ownership. The south and west sides of the park are still fronted by the truly lovely original town houses. You almost expect to see horse-drawn carriages rather than automobiles at the curb side.

Take particular note of Nos. 15 and 16 Gramercy Park South. No. 15 was designed by Vaux & Radford in 1867 for Samuel J. Tilden, NY State Governor (1874) and Democratic Presidential nominee (1876) in the most controversial election in U.S. history. Though Tilden appeared to have won, the Republicans refused to concede, bargained with undecided Southern Democrats and wooed those states' electoral votes by promising to remove Federal troops from the post-Civil War South. Republican candidate Rutherford B. Hayes indeed gained the votes he needed, a full four months after the November election! Tilden died

GRAMERCY PARK AND CHELSEA

1. *Con Edison Energy Museum*
2. *Roosevelt's Childhood Home*
3. *Barnes & Noble Bookstore*
4. *Flatiron Building*
5. *NY Life Insurance Building*
6. *Madison Square Courthouse*
7. *Metropolitan Life Building*
8. *Barney's*
9. *Chelsea Hotel*
10. *Joyce Theater*
11. *Limelight*
12. *Empire Diner*

in 1886 leaving a five million dollar estate, of which three million dollars helped found the NY Public Library. The public is now welcome to visit the **Grand Gallery**, open Tues.-Sun. 1-6pm (closed July-Aug.).

Next door at No. 16 is **The Players**, established in 1888 as a home-hotel for actors, and redesigned by architect Stanford White in 1906. Note the flagpole, lanterns and the masks of *Comedy and Tragedy* over the doorway.

Lexington Ave. begins at the north end of the park. Look north on Lexington Ave. for a perfect view of the **Chrysler Building**, the Art Deco masterpiece further uptown.

Walk along Park Ave. and turn west on 20th St. A recreation of the 1858 birthplace of Theodore Roosevelt, the only native New Yorker elected to the Presidency, is located at 28 E 20th St. The museum, **a replica of Roosevelt's Childhood Home**, features five Victorian-period rooms. Open Wed.-Sun. 9am-5pm; last tour leaves at 3:30pm; concerts are offered on Sat. at 2pm. Admission charge; children under 16 free. Tel. 260-1616 to confirm concert schedules.

Continue south on Park Ave. to 17th St. for the highly-recommended *Roundabout Theater*, in its home in a renovated neo-Federal building at 100 E 17th St. The *Roundabout* stages revivals of renowned plays starring famous performers, Tel. 719-9393. Walk west on 17th St., and turn north onto Broadway. At 867 Broadway and 18th St., is *Paragon Sporting Goods*, a large store with a wide selection of ski outfits, camping gear, etc., Tel. 255-8036.

Gramercy Park is NYC's only remaining private park

Turn to 5th Ave. for several major bookstores and fine men's clothing outlets. The **Barnes & Noble Bookstore Sales Annex,** on the corner of 18th St., is an enormous store where everything is discounted. Window-shop elsewhere but buy here, Tel. 807-0099. The *French and Spanish Bookstore*, at the corner of 19th and 5th Aves.,

has an extensive selection of French, Spanish and other foreign language books and dictionaries, Tel. 581-8810. *China Books and Periodicals* 125 5th Ave. between 19th and 20th Sts., focuses exclusively on China – books, magazines, notices concerning China-related events throughout the city, Tel. 966-1599.

Continue north on 5th Ave. The **Flatiron Building**, designed by D. M. Burnham and built in 1902, occupies the entire triangle between 22nd and 23rd Sts. on the east side of 5th Ave. An immediate symbol of New York's architectural supremacy, it was the subject of famous photographs by Alfred Steiglitz and Edward Steichen. Following a period of decline, the building has been rediscovered as an architectural gem.

Across 23rd St. on the east side of 5th Ave. is **Madison Square**, one of the lovelier of the city's smaller parks. Among its statues, the most famous is the **Admiral Farragut Monument** at the northwest corner, designed by Stanford White and sculpted in 1881 by Augustus Saint-Gaudens, the American neo-Classicist who traveled in the same circle as White and painter John La Farge. Stand at the west side of the park and face east, looking at the wonderful buildings facing you from the park's Madison Ave. side. From north to south you see the NY Life Insurance Building, the low-rise courthouse of the Appellate Division of the State Supreme Court, the Metropolitan Life Building and the Metropolitan Tower. Behold the spectacular variety of architectural styles this row presents.

The **NY Life Insurance Building,** the modern sky-scraper at 41 Madison Ave., was completed in 1928 from plans by Cass Gilbert, who also designed the Woolworth Building, the US Customs House, and the US Courthouse in Lower Manhattan. Here was the original Madison Square Garden, the sports and entertainment arena built in 1890. It's here that its designer, Stanford White, was shot to death by Harry K. Thaw while watching a performance featuring showgirl Evelyn Nesbit, White's former girlfriend and Thaw's wife (The new Madison Square Garden is located in the Pennsylvania Station complex between 31st and 33rd Sts. and 7th and 8th Aves.).

The **Madison Square Courthouse**, at the northeast corner of Madison Ave. and 25th St., is home to the Appellate Division of the State Supreme Court in Manhattan. Designed in 1896, it is a beautiful white marble structure with columns and statuary. Exhibitions of a legal historical type are presented in the lobby entrance on 25th St.

The **Metropolitan Life Building**, with its huge gates, is connected by a span to the tower just south, on Madison Ave. Designed by Le Brun & Sons in Italian Renaissance eclectic style, and built in 1908-1909, its tower has four clock faces, one on each side, each 26.5 ft. (over 8 m) in diameter, with minute hands weighing half a ton (approx. 500 kg) each. The largest of the four chimes, which play a tune by Handel every quarter hour, weighs 7,000 lbs. (over 3,000 kg).

Walk east on 23rd St. The *Madison Hardware Company*, 105 E 23rd St., is in fact a center for model-train hobbyists. Its inventory includes toy trains up to forty-five years old – still in their original boxes – and its repair shop can fix almost any train manufactured within the last eighty years. Visit Mon.-Fri. 8am-6pm, Sat. 8am-4pm, Tel. 427-5679, 996-6274.

On Third Ave., on the corner of 22nd St., is *Rolf's*, The popular German-American restaurant (in an area once known as "Little

Germany" for its immigrant population who relocated from the Lower East Side) offers inexpensive fare and a bar which is always crowded, Tel. 477-4750.

The Gramercy Park neighborhood offers several excellent options for after-dinner, late-evening entertainment. Further south on 190 3rd Ave., near 17th St. is famous *Fat Tuesday's* top jazz performers, cover charge and minimum purchase, Tel. 533-7900. *Tramps*, 125 E 15th St., offers jazz and blues. Again: cover charge and minimum, Tel. 777-5077.

If your tastes run more to the legitimate theater, try either the *Roundabout* at 100 E 17th St., Tel. 719-9393; *Repertorio Español* at 138 E 27th between Lexington and 3rd Aves, Tel. 889-2850; the *Vineyard Theater* at 108 E 15, Tel. 353-3366, or the *Jewish Repertory Theater*, 344 E 14th near 1st Ave., Tel. 996-1100. They are all closed during summer.

The Metropolitan Life Building

Chelsea – Dining and Dancing to a Young Beat

Chelsea curiously offers the visitor only a couple of hours of daytime sights and diversions, despite its dimensions, extending from 14th St. north to 30th St. from 5th Ave. west to the Hudson River. Brimming with new restaurants, experimental theaters and exciting dance clubs, Chelsea comes to life by nightfall.

Take Subway 1, 2, or 3 to 14th St. and head north on 7th Ave., between 15th to 18th Sts., for some impressive shopping. The climax, and reason enough for a visit to Chelsea, is *Barney's*, along the entire east side of 7th between 16th and 17th Sts. Once exclusively a men's store, *Barney's* now displays designer fashions e.g., Perry Ellis, Issey Miyake, Missoni, Ralph Lauren and Giorgio Armani for men, women and boys. Enjoy a refined shopping experience; make it even better by reserving a salesperson and tailor through the shopping-by-appointment service, Tel. 929-9000. *Barney's* also offers a small but tasteful house-wares department named *Chelsea Passage*, and an antique jewelry section and café upstairs.

Continue north on 7th Ave. Walk east on 19th St. for a glimpse at the Empire State Building tower.

At 23rd St. (a two-way boulevard) turn west. Orig-inally one of NYC's most exclusive residential promenades, the Broadway-8th Ave. section of 23rd St. was overtaken in the 1880s by hotels, pubs, theaters and... stables. This metamorphosis came about in a large part by the construction of the Elevated Railroad (the "El"). 23rd St., the midpoint of the line, became a natural spot for commerce and entertainment. As you head west, notice the **Chelsea Hotel** . Opened in 1884 as one

of NYC's first cooperative apart-ment houses, the *Chelsea* was converted into a hotel in 1905 and has since been a favorite for artists and writers such as O. Henry, Dylan Thomas, Thomas Wolfe, Sarah Bernhardt, Jackson Pollack and Arthur Miller. Notice the beautifully ornate flower pattern of the bal-conies and visit the lobby's art gallery. Check in for the night if you wish, though the quarters are far from fancy.

A southward turn on 8th Ave. from 23rd St. brings us to **Historic Chelsea**: 22nd St. to 20th St. between 8th and 10th Aves. 20th and 21st Sts. are particularly lovely, lined with turn-of-the-century town houses and apartment buildings.

Return to 6th Ave. and head north for the **Master Eagle Gallery**, 40 W 25th St., the showroom of the *Master Eagle Reproductions Company*. Illustrations by students and professionals are often on display on the sixth floor. The gallery is open Mon.-Fri. 9:30am-4:30pm, admission free, Tel. 924-8277. Another daytime attraction in Chelsea is NYC's **Flower District** (27th to 30th Sts. on 6th Ave.). Most, though not all, of its shops limit themselves to wholesale trade.

As for Chelsea night life, choose from a wide selection of restaurants, off-Broadway theaters and late-night music and dance clubs. Begin with dinner in central Chelsea, (8th Ave. between 16th and 19th Sts.), where an array of worthwhile, reasonably-priced Mexican, Creole, American regional and cafeteria-style restaurants await you. *Claire's*, is nearby at 156 7th Ave. Finally, *Meriken* at 162 W 21st St. serves new-wave Japanese food to a very trendy young crowd, Tel. 620-9684.

Now we turn to entertainment. New York theater and dance goes deeper than Broadway, with a proliferation of intriguingly-named offbeat companies whose work, experimental at times, rarely compromises on quality. Chelsea specializes in precisely this type of entertainment.

It is always advisable to verify performance times in advance. Beginning with dance, Chelsea offers two marvellous venues. The *Joyce Theater*, 175 8th Ave. and 19th St., just north of the 8th Ave. restaurant cluster, has foregone its cinema function for dance performances of in-town and visiting companies alike, Tel. 242-0800. The *Dance Theater Workshop*, devoted to the promotion of new dance, performs in the *Bessie Schonberg Theater* at 219 W 19th St., Tel. 691-6500. The *Schonberg Theater* also hosts poetry readings and pantomime.

Roller-skating at Chelsea

Other respected theater companies in the area include *The Production Company*, 15 W 28th St., located just east of Broadway, Tel. 689-1997, and the *Actors' Outlet*, at 120 W 28th St., Tel. 255-7293. Still other less well-known Chelsea companies, venture deeper into the avant-garde. Reservations are recommended, though you can usually pay for your tickets when you arrive. This is inexpensive entertainment at its best, served up in small theaters where any seat is generally a good one.

Nightclub fans will certainly not be disappointed in Chelsea. *Caroline's*, 332 8th Ave. at 28th St., hosts comedy performers who have paid their dues at some of the smaller clubs. You may recognize some from appearances on television programs. Show time is 9pm Tues.-Sun., with an additional 11:30pm performance Fri.-Sat. Cover charge; you must have at least two drinks, Tel. 924-3499.

Chelsea abounds in late-night dance clubs. This entertainment is costly. Besides expensive admission costs, a tip for the coat keeper and drinks are expensive too. When leaving the premises invitations to other clubs are handed out, these usually entitle you to a discount on the entrance fee. Some discos, usually the newest and hottest ones, let the doorman decide – as you wait in line – whether or not you will contribute to the type of ambience the club is trying to promote.

The *Peppermint Lounge*, 100 5th Ave. at 15th St., has three separate levels and plays dance music ranging from the 50s to today's new-wave, Tel. 262-6029. The *Roxy Roller Disco*, 515 W 18th between 10th and 11th Aves., acts as a roller rink during the week, and as an extremely popular disco during weekends. You will meet all kinds of people here, Tel. 675-8300. One of NY's hottest dance clubs is *Limelight,* situated in a converted church at 6th Ave. and 20th St. and 47 W. 14th St. Though "hot" in NYC changes from week to week, Limelight, equipped with a good sound system and acoustics, maintains its popularity, Tel. 807-7850. *Private Eyes*, behind the chrome façade at 12 W 21st St., is more a bar and video club than a dance club. One of the neighborhood's newer

A view of the city from Chelsea, with the Empire State Building to the right

establishments, it is riding the crest of music-video popularity, Tel. 206-7770.

Tunnel, 220 12th Ave (27th St.), is open from 10pm. It is a huge complex, each floor suited to a different type of young audience, Tel. 695-8238.

The *Palladium*, 126 E. 14th St. (near 4th Ave and Union Square) is a relic of the original type of disco. A huge place with unsurpassed sound and lighting.

Jacki 60, Washington St. 432 W. 14th St., is open on Tues. and Wed. from 10pm. This is a medium-sized place with a good crowd. There are two floors of dancing and shows.

The *Webster Hall* at 125 E. 11th St. is a huge complex suited to a variety of patrons; blacks up a flight, homosexuals down a flight, etc. dancing and billiards too. Opens at 10pm. Tel. 353-1600.

The *Squeeze Box* in Pon Hills, Spring St., 511 Greenwich St. on the border of the Village and Soho, is compact in size but huge in quality.

Don't quit Chelsea without a last stop at the *Empire Diner*, 210 10th Ave. at 22nd St. This archetype of diners – stainless steel and chrome – fills up with all the beautiful people from the neighborhood clubs after they close. Open 24 hours a day, every day, except Mon. 5-8am, nothing really "cooks" here until 2am. Tel. 243-2736.

Chelsea's panorama

Herald Square – Macy's and More

We shall begin at 34th St. and 5th Ave. Take Subway R or N to 34th St. and walk one block east, or take Subway 6 to 33rd St. and walk west. This section of Midtown, south of 42nd St., has some of the most famous department stores in the world. Let us begin, however, with the first item on every visitor's "must see" list: the Empire State Building.

Rising out of the corner of 5th Ave. and 34th St., the **Empire State Building** is without question the most renowned symbol of NYC, and possibly the most famous building in the world. Designed by *Shreve, Lamb & Harmon Associates* and completed in 1931, it thrusts 1,472 ft. (nearly 450 m) skyward. The **86th floor** features an **indoor observatory** with a concession and souvenir stand and an outdoor promenade equipped with high-range binoculars. At the very top is the **102nd floor observatory**, indoors at 1,250 ft. (approx. 381 m) above street level. The view from here is spectacular. Visibility on a clear day approaches 80 miles (nearly 130 km); By night there is a stunning view of the city lights. The observatories are open daily from 9:30am-midnight. Purchase tickets on the Concourse Level below the main lobby. Admission charge, reduced entry for senior citizens and children under 12.

The Empire State Building

The building's granite and limestone surface, trimmed with stainless steel mullions, seems to sparkle. Since 1977, the upper 30 floors have been illuminated from 9-11pm by high-power floodlights positioned on the building's retreats or "setbacks." Lighting designer Douglas Leigh has recently added 32 high-pressure bulbs around the mooring mast (designed for the docking of zeppelins), creating the halo effect envisioned in the original 1930 design. The marble in the lobby was imported from Italy, France, Belgium and Germany. 73 elevators ply seven miles (approx. 11.20 km) of shaftway; 1,860 stairs climb from street level to the 102nd floor.

The **Guinness World Records Exhibit Hall** (concourse level) displays 250 record-breaking events through video, photographs, holograms, etc. Open daily, 9am-10pm. Admission charge (under 5 years old, free), Tel. 947-2335.

Department stores? Among others in the area, try *Altman B. & Co.*, *Lord & Taylor* and the king of them all, *Macy's*. Each has its own style and image, carefully cultivated by the management. Many offer a personal shopping service: tell your "personal shopper" what you would like, and he/she will select several items fitting the description. That way you save time and never overlook anything.

For *Lord & Taylor*: Walk north on 5th Ave. At the corner of 38th St. The store, exudes a calm, relaxed atmosphere with attentive salespeople at your service. Three indoor restaurants refresh you after heavy shopping. *Lord & Taylor's* Christmas windows are a major holiday-season attraction, not to be missed, Tel. 391-3344.

Perched atop the Empire State Building

From *Lord & Taylor*, return south to 5th Ave. and 31st St., and head west to Broadway. At 31st St. and Broadway is *Olden Camera and Lens Co. Inc.*, Tel. 226-3727, with its well-priced selection of antiquated photo equipment, if you can be bothered rummaging around for something that works. Before shopping for anything at *Olden* or any NY camera store, by the way, it is best to consult the *Sunday Times* "Arts and Leisure" section or a major photo magazine as to the right prices.

Continue north to 33rd St. and Broadway. This is the site of the new ***Herald Center***, formerly *E.J. Korvettes'* department store. Each of the seven floors uses a different NYC neighborhood as its motif. The Central Park floor even has a carrousel – a great place to take children.

At 33rd St. and 6th Ave. is a shopping center, which has a 9-storey interior open space design, well worthy of a glance. It also houses a visitor's information desk. ***A&S Plaza*** is open Mon., Thurs. and Fri. 9:45am-8:30pm; Tues. and Wed. 9:45am-6:45pm; weekends 11am-6pm.

The entire block of 34th St. from Broadway west

HERALD SQUARE AND EAST SIDE 26TH-42ND STS.

1. *Empire State Building*
2. *Altman B. & Co.*
3. *Lord & Taylor*
4. *Herald Center*
5. *Macy's*
6. *Madison Square Garden*
7. *General Post Office*
8. *Port Authority Bus Terminal*
9. *Marble Collegiate Church*
10. *Church of the Transfiguration*
11. *Church of the Incarnation*
12. *Pierpont Morgan Library*
13. *NY Public Library*
14. *American Standard Building*
15. *W.R. Grace & Co. Building*
16. *Lincoln Building*
17. *Grand Central Terminal*
18. *Philip Morris Building*
19. *Sniffen Court*
20. *69th Regiment Armory*

to 7th Ave. is *Macy's*, one of the world's largest department stores and, due to its sheer abundance and variety of goods, is a "must" even for a non-shopper. For direct subway access, take Subway 2 or 3 to 34th St. The main floor is a beautiful art deco hall bursting with jewelry, leather goods, cosmetics and fragrances. The balcony above serves the *Metropolitan Museum of Art Gift Shop* and the *Café l'Étoile*, open from 3-5pm, where you can get a great health shake. Between the main floor and men's clothing is the arcade, with its trendy boutiques and NYC souvenirs. *Macy's* has it all, but perhaps the most surprising department to try is *The Cellar* for imported caviar, fresh pasta, delicious baked goods, a variety of deli items and cheeses, and every invention for the well-equipped modern kitchen. Then venture upstairs on one of the old-fashioned wooden escalators. Tel. 695-4400.

Macy's is an especially joyous, if crowded, experience at holiday time, beginning with the annual Thanksgiving Day Parade. This nationally televised event, which takes a full year of planning, sends bands and floats down 5th Ave. under huge helium balloons of Bullwinkle Moose, Kermit the Frog, Superman and others. Thanksgiving marks the start of the Christmas shopping season. *Macy's* entered American Christmas folklore forever with

*A view from the
Empire State Building*

Inside Macy's, the famous department store

the wonderful 1947 film, *Miracle on 34th Street*, in which young Natalie Wood comes to believe in Santa Claus. If you visit in December, be sure to see Santa in **Santaland**, a Macy's tradition. If the thought of holiday crowds overwhelms you, use the "Macy's By Appointment" personal shopping service, Tel. 736-515.

Exit *Macy's* on the 7th Ave. side. This is **Fashion Avenue**, the heart of the Garment Center since the turn of the century when the apparel industry, looking for better working conditions and proximity to the large department stores, relocated here from the Lower East Side. High Midtown rents now threaten to push the garment manufacturers to less expensive locations, leaving only the showrooms. As for rental of prime Midtown real estate, Manhattan has surpassed London as the world's most expensive commercial location. The garment industry, however, will not vacate overnight; you will still have to dodge the wheeled racks of clothing that clog 7th Ave.

The blocks south of 34th St. are considered the **Fur District**. Walk north on 7th Ave. and look to your right on 35th St. As far as Broadway, the street resembles a canyon, with tall buildings allowing no penetration of direct sunlight. The towers at 7th Ave. and 37th St. are known as the "Bridal Buildings" because, until recently, they were occupied almost exclusively by wedding fashion showrooms. One block south is the *Fashion Atrium*, formerly a run down hotel renovated for $15 million into a quality women's sportswear showroom. Though many showrooms here are open only to the trade, an informative tour of the neighborhood, including access to its inside operations, is offered by the **International Ladies' Garment Workers Union**, Tel. 265-7000 – the famous ILGWU (est. 1900), instrumental in the labor movement's early efforts for higher wages and safer working conditions.

The importance of Jewish labor and leadership in the garment industry is silently but strongly depicted on the neighborhood's streets. Take note of *The Garment Worker*, a statue by Judith Weller in the court-yard of 555 7th Ave. at 39th St. Seated in a folding chair at his pedal-operated sewing-machine with his sleeves rolled up, the statue of a skullcapped garment worker is a tribute to the genera-tions of Jewish men and women who plied this trade. One block east, the northwest corner of 39th and Broadway has been named **Golda Meir Square** for the late Prime Minister of Israel; a bust of Mrs. Meir by Beatrice Goldfine stands in the courtyard, facing north. At 34th St., just west of 7th Ave. is the **Garment Center Con-gregation** for Jewish worshippers in the area.

We shall return to the vicinity of *Macy's* for other important sites, neither involving the garment trade and each occupying two square blocks. The first is the new **Madison Square Garden**, designed by *Charles Luckman Associates* as successor to the hall which actually fronted Madison Square. The building, built above Penn Station, between 31st and 33rd Sts. and 7th and 8th Aves., is probably America's most-used entertain-ment complex, with over 600 events including the Ringling Brothers Barnum and Bailey Circus, the annual Westminster Kennel Club Dog Show and the annual Singles Expo devoted to the needs and special concerns of NYC's single adults. Admis-sion charge. Garden information, Tel. 877-4300.

The original Penn Station building (McKim, Mead & White, designers) was razed in 1962, but the subterranean rail complex still serves as NYC's train, linking it with Connecticut (*Metro-North*), Long Island (the *Long Island Railroad – LIRR*) and the rest of the country (*Amtrak*). *LIRR*, as a commuter railroad, is particularly frantic at rush hour, as lines for the information and the ticket booths seem to intersect. It's nevertheless an excellent way of reaching Long Island and its sites (i.e., Jones Beach).

At Madison Square Garden

The noble grandeur of the old Penn Station survives in the majestic **General Post Office**, which was also designed by McKim, Mead & White, located on 8th Ave. between 31st and 33rd Sts. Note its magnificent staircase and the immortal inscription above: "Neither Snow nor Rain nor Heat nor Gloom still detain these Couriers from the Swift Completion of their Appointed Rounds." The Post Office, one-and-a-half million sq. ft. in area, was opened to the public in 1914, replacing the old post office at City Hall Park. Aside from regular postal services, you will find several historic exhibits highlighting the construction of the building and bygone methods of postal delivery.

The Post Office is also notable as Santa Claus's mailing address. Thousands of letters addressed to St. Nick arrive here every year. Operation Santa Claus, inaugurated by mail clerks 50 years ago, makes these adorable letters from children available to the public in December (Room 3016). Read them; send a reply if you choose.

The General Post Office has an area of one-and-a-half million sq. ft.

Further west, between 11th and 12th Aves. and 34th and 38th Sts., is the **Jacob K. Javits Convention Center of NY**, designed by I. M. Pei who also designed the Louvre's transparent Pyramid, in Paris. The center bears the name of NY's three term U.S. Senator and civil rights and public welfare activist. At 22 acres, it is said to be the largest building of its kind. Its initial $375 million budget ballooned to $462 million, yet the show goes on. The center will provide exposition space, conference rooms, shops, restaurants, a movie theater and the most advanced, continent-spanning conferencing technology available.

One of NYC's last middle-class neighborhoods, **Clinton**, is yours to explore beginning on 9th Ave. between 37th and 40th Sts. This is also known as "Hell's Kitchen" because of a period of gang warfare at the turn of the century. It stretches from 34th to 59th Sts., from 8th Ave. to the Hudson River. That three-block stretch of 9th Ave. has some wonderful food markets which supply some of the finest chefs in town. Interesting rather than exciting, the walk takes under an hour to complete.

At 488 9th Ave., is a very special place, *Manganaro Grosseria Italiana*: a small, homey restaurant with deli-style sandwiches and salads, and a grocery up front with fresh breads, smoked meats and cheeses, sun-dried tomatoes, etc. Apart from its mouth-watering aroma, *Manganaro's* is also home of the six-foot hero sandwich. See for yourself. The restaurant is very crowded at lunchtime; Tel. 563-5331. Further down at 592 9th Ave. is *Empire Coffee and Tea*, with over 200 blends of coffee, tea and spices. The owner will even grind your own blend of beans in a vintage 1926 machine, Tel. 586-1717 for home delivery. Across 9th Ave., between 38th and 40th Sts., is the **Central Fish Market**, worth a visit even if you are not buying.

In the days of Nieuw Amsterdam, the neighborhood of Clinton was known as Blooming Dale. Its main road, today's Broadway, was Bloomingdale Road: 42nd St. was a creek, and green meadows bordered the Hudson River. By 1803 the area was considered suitable for farm-land, and was bought up, in part, by John Jacob Astor (formerly a poor immigrant who made a fortune in fur trading and real estate). At the time, 14th St. was NYC's northern boundary.

A City Commission completed the mapping of Manhattan's streets in 1811. As construction

A contrast of colors at the Central Fish Market

moved northward, Astor's neighbors sold their lots at high profits. Astor, however, retained his land renting out the building lots which he and his heirs were forbidden to sell. This strategy resulted in the amassing of a huge family fortune. On the other hand, unfortunately, it also resulted in a pattern of cheap construction, since developers could not hope to retain the land once their leases expired.

Clinton went commercial in the 1850s after railroad tracks were laid down the middle of 11th Ave. to a terminal at 30th St. The neighborhood was subsequently taken over by immigrants; this was the "Hell's Kitchen" period.

From the 1850s until just before World War II, 9th Ave. was known as **Paddy's Market** where push-carts bursting with fresh produce competed with grocery stores. When the 9th Ave. "El" was razed, the thoroughfare was widened and the pushcarts relocated to an open lot on 39th St., an unsuccessful and short-lived arrangement. The **Port Authority Bus Terminal**, constructed in 1950,

The Port Authority Bus Terminal links NYC to the rest of the country and Canada

was vastly renovated and expanded in 1982. Bringing all independent bus companies under one roof, the terminal links NYC to the rest of the country and Canada.

Today, Clinton is a neighborhood in transition. As its working-class residents try to renovate the buildings and maintain affordable housing, sky-rocketing Manhattan real estate prices and a major "clean-up" of Times Square and its environs threaten Clinton with "gentrification."

East Side, 26th-42nd Sts. – Books, Books and More Books

The streets from 26th to 42nd east of 5th Ave. favor architecture buffs more than shoppers. Here you will find several beautiful churches, some of NYC's most famous buildings, such as the NY Public Library, many hotels and quite a few decent restaurants. Well worth a couple of hours, the area combines with your tour of the East Side from 42nd to 51st Sts.

Take Subway R to 28th St. and walk east to 5th Ave.; alternately, take Subway 6 to 28th St. and walk west to 5th Ave.

The **Marble Collegiate Church** (1854) on 29th St. and 5th Ave. is a parish of the Reformed Protestant Dutch Church of New York, established in 1628 under Peter Minuit (the first Governor of Dutch Nieuw Amsterdam). The church houses the **Holy Land Museum and Library** and exhibits authentic historic artifacts from the Holy Land, including symbols of Christianity, Judaism and Islam. Open Tues. 10am-4pm; guided tours on Sun. at 12:15pm, Tel. 686-2770.

One-half block east on 29th St. is the **Church of the Transfiguration**, a Gothic structure, constructed in 1856, affectionately known as The Little Church Around the Corner, open daily 8am-6pm. Its notable features include a pretty garden in front, and windows named in memory of various actors.

Continue east and turn north on Madison Ave. At the corner of 30th St. and Madison Ave. is the **American Academy of Dramatic Arts**, designed by architects McKim, Mead & White for the Colony Club.

The **Old Grolier Club** is one-half block east of Madison Ave. at 29 W 32nd St. Designed in 1890 in Romanesque style, its arched columns are curious neighbors to the loft buildings on either side.

The **Church of the Incarnation** is at the northeast corner of 35th and Madison. Designed in 1864 by E. T. Litell in Gothic style, its interior is graced with stained glass windows by Tiffany, woodwork by Daniel Chester French (sculptor of the Seated Lincoln at the Lincoln Memorial in Washington) and a sanctuary mural by the noted painter of the period, John La Farge.

A noble lion statue stands outside the New York Public Library

Aside the steps to the New York Public Library

The **Pierpont Morgan Library**, is at the northeast corner of 36th St. and Madison in one of New York's great edifices, an Italian Renaissance palazzo designed by McKim, Mead & White in 1905. John Pierpont Morgan Sr. (1837-1913), was perhaps the most influential man of his time – railroad baron, financier of the merger that created *US Steel* (the country's first billion-dollar company) and collector of art and literature in his later years. The ornate interior of his library, now a museum, offers permanent and visiting exhibits of artwork and manuscripts. Open Tues.-Fri. 10:30am-5pm, Sat. 10:30am-6pm; Sun. noon-6pm. Closed Mon. and holidays. Admission charge. Tel. 685-0610.

Proceed north and then west to 40th St. At the southeast corner of 5th Ave. (and 42nd St.) is the Mid-Manhattan branch of the **NY Public Library**, the city's largest circulation library guarded by the famous lions (which wear wreaths on Christmas). The library building, erected in 1915, was originally a large department store. The *Metropolitan Museum of Art* Gift Shop is situated on the ground floor. For more information call Tel. 869-8089.

The adjacent **Central Research Library**, designed by *Carrere & Hastings*, built for nine million dollars in 1911, is considered America's finest example of the Beaux-Arts style and one of the world's five largest research libraries. It occupies 5th Ave. between 40th and 42nd Sts., a site which was once a graveyard for the poor and then a reservoir which doubled as a major tourist attraction with its walls 25 ft. (7.62 m) thick, topped by a promenade. Inside the main lobby – the beautiful white-marble Astor Hall, named after John Jacob Astor, you will find an information desk, bookshop and museum exhibits. Free tours are held. Enquire at the information desk. If it's sunny, join the locals for lunch on the steps, where you might enjoy a free outdoor concert by street musicians.

Walk west on 40th St. At No. 20, is the **Wendell L. Willkie Building of Freedom House**, named after the 1940 Republican Presidential nominee who, after having lost to FDR, went on to write *One World* – a call for understanding between all nations. Now headquarters of the organization concerned with world-wide human freedom, the structure was originally designed by Henry J. Hardenbergh (designer of the Dakota apartment house and the *Plaza Hotel*) as home of the New York Club.

Continue west and you will come to the splendid **American Standard Building**, completed in 1924 and still unique in its color scheme. Designed and built by Raymond Hood, also architect of much of Rockefeller Center, for the *American Radiator Co.*, its black brick and gold stone exterior has been described as the most daring experiment in color in modern building.

Between 40th and 42nd Sts. is **Bryant Park**, the Central Research Library's backyard. Named for noted poet and editor William Cullen Bryant, this much-needed break in the skyline is a soothing spot with flagstone paths, trees, ivy and a central lawn where, on summer weekdays at noon, you will enjoy free outdoor jazz and band concerts. Here, at America's first World's Fair (1853-54), the Crystal Palace was introduced. After the supposedly "fire-proof" Palace burnt to the ground in 1858, the site became a Union training ground during the Civil War. Today it hosts a flower market, a book stall and two outdoor cafés.

The Bryant Park Music and Dance Tickets Booth, 42nd St. between 5th and 6th Aves., is the place for half-price same-day tickets, or full-price advance sale tickets for concerts and dance performances. Open Tues.-Sun. noon-7pm, Wed. and Sat. 11am-7pm, Tel. 382-2323.

Across the street is the unusually-shaped **W.R. Grace & Co. Building**, its upward sweep covered in white travertine marble and glass. At its end, on 43rd St., is **Grace Plaza** with its occasional free outdoor concerts.

Face the rear of the library from 6th Ave. and take in the view: the American Standard Building on your right, the

Grace Building on your left and the Chrysler Building tower at the far left.

Walk east on 42nd St., crossing 5th and Madison Aves. Enter the **Lincoln Building** at No. 60 and note the vestibule walls, covered with Abraham Lincoln's quotations. A miniature bronze copy of the original "**Seated Lincoln**" (at the Lincoln Memorial in Washington) sits in the lobby.

At 42nd St. and Lexington Ave. is the magnificent beaux arts-style **Grand Central Terminal**. The original terminal, built in 1871 by shipping and railroad magnate Commodore Cornelius Vanderbilt, yielded to the present structure, an urban gem which became the object of a bitter preservation battle during the 1970s. A trio of Jules Coutan statues – *Mercury*, *Hercules* and *Minerva* – adorn its 42nd St. facade; just beneath them and directly above a statue of Vanderbilt is a 13ft. (approx. 4 m) clock. The terminal incorporates 33.7 miles (nearly 54 km) of track, a main concourse 375 ft. (approx. 114 m) long by 120 ft. (over 36 m) wide, a vaulted ceiling 125ft. (38 m) high, decorated with constellations of the zodiac, and windows 75 ft. (nearly 23 m) high. When sunlight streams through, you can understand why this room is loved by photographers and a favorite location for film-makers. For information on free tours set out from under the Concourse clock, call Tel. 582-6875.

The grand architecture of the Grand Central Terminal

As you exit the terminal at 42nd St., notice how Park Ave. was rerouted through a viaduct that rises above 42nd St., circumvents Grand Central and the MetLife Building (previously called Pan Am Building) directly behind, and exits northward through the Helmsley Building. Right here on Park Avenue at Grand Central is the deluxe **Grand Hyatt Hotel**.

The Romanesque **Bowery Savings Bank** resides across from Grand Central on 42nd St. On the southwest corner of 42nd St. and Park Ave. is the **Philip Morris Building**, a 26-story gray granite structure which boasts two completely different kinds of façades – vertical stripes on the Park Ave. side and horizontal stripes on 41st and 42nd Sts. *NY Times* architecture critic Paul Goldberger, has attacked this experiment for the way the two façades clash, a very real problem since the building is most often viewed from the corner.

When it comes to sponsorship of the arts, however, the *Philip Morris Corporation* is beyond reproach: witness its gift to the city, the Midtown branch of the **Whitney Museum of American Art**, inside the Philip Morris Building. Its ground-floor room with its windows and 45 ft. (13.7 m) high ceiling, is a serene hideaway bedecked with sculptures and a gallery of changing exhibits. No admission charge. Tel. 878-2550. Lectures on art are given on Mon., Wed., Fri. at 12:30pm. Tel. 570-3676. Museum open: Fri.-Sun., Wed., 11am-6pm; Thurs. 1-8pm.

Park Ave., a wide, two-way thoroughfare, is so called because its divider was once wide enough to include benches and pedestrian pathways. Express buses depart every 20 minutes for Newark Airport from the southeast corner of Park and 41st St.

Continue east on 42nd and turn south on 3rd Ave. This is **Murray Hill**, named for Robert Murray, whose country home stood here in the late 1700s. An elegant quarter in the late 1800s, its side-streets are lined with lovely brownstones and town houses. An unusual architectural arrangement exists at 150-152 E 38th St.: an unattached brick house set far back from the street, with a gate leading from the street into a slate courtyard backed by a wall for privacy's sake. Atop the wall, guarding the entrance, sit two copper dolphins.

Walking west on 36th St., be sure to notice **Sniffen Court**, at No. 156. Its charming Civil War buildings, once used as stables, surround a lovely slate courtyard adorned with plants and lanterns. The buildings themselves are only two stories high, unusual for modern Manhattan.

26th St. offers you the **69th Regiment Armory**

with its convex side walls. Here the famous 1913 Armory Show, the International Exposition of Modern Art, gave America its first taste of cubism and fauvism (Picasso, Braque, Matisse, etc.) and ended her isolationism in the art world. The public and critics were particularly outraged by Marcel Duchamp's masterpiece *Nude Descending a Staircase*.

HELICOPTER EXCURSIONS

One last address in this neighborhood: the **Heliport** on the edge of East 34th St. Tours lift off at 9am-9pm daily (Jan.-March 9am-6pm), except Christmas and New Year's. Minimum of two passengers per flight, Tel. 248-7240.

At the Grand Central Terminal

The Theater District – Curtain Up!

While theaters exist in every NY neighborhood, there is a definite Theater District, bounded roughly by 42nd to 57th Sts. west of 6th Ave. Because of the extensiveness of the area, we have organized our attractions, restaurants, etc., around the respective theaters. Ventures far from the heart of the district are called "excursions."

No visit to NYC is complete without a night at the theater, and that usually means in the Theater District. All the commercial Broadway, theaters and many "Off-Broadway", are found here. These terms refer more to a type of theatrical experience than to an address. "Broadway" houses are the large commercial theaters just east and west of Broadway, which generally "showcase" the big hit musicals and dramas. "Off-Broadway" houses are further away from Broadway, in spirit and in location. Here the plays are somewhat more experimental, the tickets slightly less expensive. As the cost and risk of mounting original new Broadway shows have escalated, producers have been taking successful Off-Broadway shows and moving them to Broadway houses. As Off-Broadway becomes a testing-ground for Broadway, the line between the two becomes blurred.

Remember that there are rarely performances on Sunday evenings.

Theatre tickets (see "Tickets" below) may be purchased at the *TKTS* in Times Square (Tel. 768-1818), or *Ticket Central* at 406 W 42nd St. (Tel. 279-4200). Note the theater's address and plan your day (museums, shopping, dinner, etc.) accordingly. Remember that evening performances usually begin at 8pm. If you are running late inform your waiter, as the "natives" do, that you have to "make a curtain." Theater District restaurants are accustomed to this kind of pressure.

Shows, shows and more shows – all spell Broadway

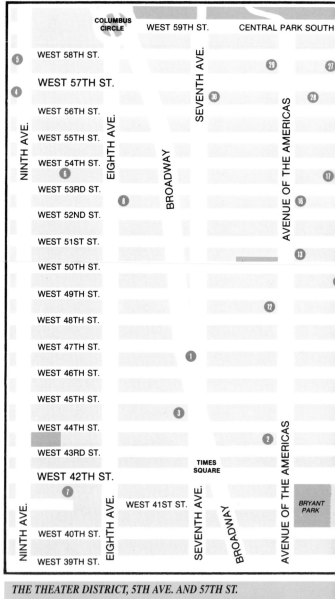

THE THEATER DISTRICT, 5TH AVE. AND 57TH ST.

1. *TKTS*
2. *Town Hall*
3. *Theater Museum*
4. *Hearst Magazine Building*
5. *Caribbean Cultural Center*
6. *Children's Museum of Manhattan*
7. *Original McGraw-Hill Building*

8. *Roseland Ballroom*
9. *NY Public Library*
10. *Diamond Row*
11. *RCA Building*
12. *McGraw-Hill Building*
13. *Radio City Music Hall*
14. *St. Patrick's Cathedral*

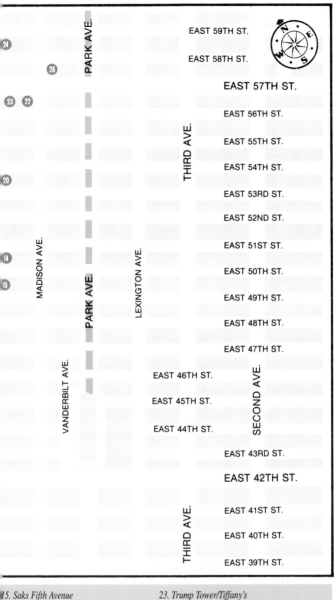

Liberty for sale at a shop in Times Square

Times Square is the heart of Broadway. The area – 42nd St. between 6th and 9th Aves. and the adjacent stretch of Broadway – is certainly not Manhattan's prettiest. But its flashing lights scores of pornography shops movie houses and strip joints make it colorful, especially at night. A few reminders: don't stroll alone down a street that seems too deserted, try to stay with others, keep a tight grip on your bag, remain alert and try not to look lost. With this in mind, you have little to worry about.

Though not a place for meandering, Times Square is a "must." The Square is a symbol of NYC's rush and vitality, dazzling in neon light. This is also America's most famous spot for greeting the New Year. Since 1906, every December 31st at 11:59pm, a mammoth aluminum ball begins a one-minute pulley-guided descent from the top of the building at One Times Square. The ball – which has taken the shape of an apple in recent years, symbolic of NYC's nickname, "The Big Apple" – measures 6 ft. (close to 2 m) in diameter and bristles with red lights. Jan. 1st simply does not begin until the ball reaches the bottom and splits in half.

There are two notable buildings in the area: the **Knickerbocker Building** at the southeast corner of 42nd St. and Broadway, and the **New Amsterdam**, 214 W 42nd near Broadway. The Knickerbocker, commissioned by John Jacob Astor – great-grandson of the German immigrant who started the family financial empire – was built as a hotel in 1902. Today it's an office building with a modern interior but its ornate facade and mansard roof remain unchanged. The *New Amsterdam,* the first theater on the block to receive landmark status, introduced Fanny Brice, Eddie Cantor and Will Rogers to NYC audiences.

Local attractions take us in three different directions:

DIRECTION 1: TO THE HEART OF THE THEATER DISTRICT

Town Hall, constructed in 1921, 123 W 43rd St. is the only concert hall in the immediate vicinity.

Billings in this McKim, Mead & White landmark include the *Select Debut Young Artists'* series and an operetta-in-concert program, Tel. 840-2824.

The **Theater Museum**, just west of Times Sq. in the *Minskoff Theater* arcade between 44th and 45th Sts., displays theater history in an entertaining and informative way. Open Wed.-Sat. noon-8pm, Sun. 1-5pm. Tel. 869-0550. Truly fervent theater *aficionados* will wish to visit the *Drama Bookshop*, a hidden treasure on the 2nd floor at 723 7th Ave., just north of 48th St. Mingle with young actors who browse between auditions amidst the most extensive stock of plays, scripts and theater and cinema books. Open Mon.-Fri. 9:30am-6pm, Wed. till 8pm and Sat. 10:30am-5pm, Tel. 944-0595.

DIRECTION 2: OUT OF THE THEATER DISTRICT

Close by is the *Mysterious Bookshop*, at 129 W 56th St. favorite for its unusual collection of new, used and rare suspense fiction, Tel. 765-0900. Walk northwest to 57th St. and Broadway, where *Coliseum Books* carries a large selection of current titles, Tel. 757-8381.

Note the odd design of the **Hearst Magazine Building**, 9th Ave., between 56th and 57th Sts. Its design called for seven stories more than were ultimately built and the ornamentation – pillars,

A theater, one of hundreds on Broadway

statuary and urns – seems to overpower its truncated form.

Cultural attractions in the area include the Caribbean Cultural Center, the Horticultural Society and the Manhattan Laboratory Museum. The **Caribbean Cultural Center**, 408 W 58th St. near 9th Ave., maintains large exhibits celebrating Caribbean culture. Open Tues.-Fri. 11am-6pm. Sat. 1-5pm. Admission charge, Tel. 307-7420. The **Horticultural Society**, 128 W 58th St. between 6th and 7th Aves., offers lectures, courses and tours on plant life. Open Mon.-Fri. 10am-6pm, Wed. till 7pm, Tel. 757-0915. Finally, the **Children's Museum of Manhattan**, 212 W 84th St. between 8th and 9th Aves., is a combination museum, classroom and art center which often presents participatory exhibits that are fun for both children and adults. Open Mon.-Thurs. 1:30-5pm; Fri.-Sun. 10am-5pm. Closed Tues., July-Aug. Admission charge, Tel. 721-1234.

An excellent lunch or dinner possibility is *Juliana's*, a small café at 53rd St. and 8th Ave., serves light Italian fare, Tel. 598-9884.

DIRECTION 3: TOWARD OFF-BROADWAY THEATER ROW, FOR A "NIGHT TOUR"

The south side of 42nd St. between 9th and 10th Aves., is split by Dyer Ave. Head west on 42nd St. from Times Sq. The original **McGraw-Hill Building**, designed by Raymond Hood (architect of Rockefeller Center and the NY Daily News Building) and built in 1931, is at 330 W 42nd St. Its unique art deco design has earned it designation in

the National Historic Register. The metallic blue, silver and gold bands at street level are ornamentation of a type usually associated with earlier Art Deco design.

The first thing to know about **Theater Row** is that you need tickets! For information on the numerous possibilities of purchasing tickets see "Tickets." A partial list of theaters can be found in the entertainment section at the back of the book. Though some stages may be "dark" (i.e., not playing a show) there is always something worthwhile playing on the block.Theaters aside, notice Richard Haas' *trompe-l'oeil* deco murals on either side of Dyer Ave. Visit the *Theater Arts Bookshop*, 405 W 42nd St., a lovely little store with a good selection of theater and performance books. You may find some famous performers browsing.

Alternative entertainment is just around the corner: the *Westside Theater a*t 407 W 43rd St., Tel. 315-2244, or if your tastes run more toward stand-up comedy than legitimate theater, try the *Improvisation*, 358 W 44th St. just east of 9th Ave. Here you'll enjoy food, drink, comedy and song in a small, cabaret atmosphere. Cover charge and minimum. Tel. 279-3446.

Dining in this area is best done on **Restaurant Row**, 46th St. between 8th and 9th Aves. Of its line up, we recommend three: *Orso*, *Barbetta* and *Joe Allen*. *Orso*, no. 322, is fairly new; prices on the Italian menu are reasonable. You may spot a rising star dining at a nearby table, Tel. 489-7212.

Barbetta at no. 321, also Italian, is a pretty restaurant with a garden open in warmer weather. Though expensive, the food is authentic and is usually well-prepared, Tel. 246-9171. Pub-style, inexpensive *Joe Allen*, no. 326, is an actors' favorite, Tel. 581-6464.

Theater Row restaurants include *La Rousse* at 414 W 42nd St., a performers' favorite, Tel. 736-4913, *China*, at 411 W 42nd St., Tel. 947-1933, the *West Bank Café* at 407 W 42nd St., an attractive little restaurant with a light menu, Tel. 695-6909, and *Lois Lane's*, the health food restaurant and store at 42nd St. and 9th Ave., Tel. 695-5055.

Times Square's flashy lights

Nightclub entertainment is yours at *Don't Tell Mama*, 343 W 46th St., a quality cabaret piano bar which offers, among other things, a children's "nightclub" – Sat. at 3pm. Cover charge, minimum purchase, Tel. 357-0788. Two blocks south at 234 W 44th St. is *Sardi's*, famous scene of opening-night cast parties where producers and actors await the reviews. The food is neither great nor cheap but people go there to see and be seen, Tel. 221-8440.

Several possibilities for celebrity-spotting are slightly further north. *Wally's & Joseph's*, 249 W 49th St., serves well-prepared steaks and lobsters, Tel. 582-0460. *Rosa's Place*, 303 W 48th St., has reasonably-priced, well-prepared Mexican food, Tel. 586-4853. *Mama Leone's*, 239 W 48th St., is a touristy, festive and fun place, but the food is noted more for quantity than for quality, Tel. 586-5151.

Another four recommended restaurants lie closer to Times Sq. *Hisae's*, 318 W 45th St., serves reasonably-priced Oriental-style seafood, Tel. 489-6100. The *Barking Fish Café*, 676 8th Ave., just south of 45th St., has a home-style, affordable Cajun menu (from the swamp regions of Louisiana, namely French & Carribean cuisine), Tel. 947-9322. *Café Un, Deux, Trois*, 123 W 44th St. between 6th Ave., and Broadway, is a spacious, pastel-colored establishment which caters to a young and trendy crowd, Tel. 354-4148. Just around the corner is *Cabana Carioca*, 123 W 45th St., delicious Brazilian food, Tel. 581-8088.

Artistic peddling on Times Square

Mike's American Bar and Grill, a western outpost of the Theater District at 650 10th Ave., at 46th St., serves highly affordable home-style cooking. Do not let the unimpressive exterior deter you, Tel. 246-4115.

On 277 Park Ave. and 47th St., a three-storey greenhouse atrium awaits you. It has 50 varieties of flora, trees and terraced pools. Open 7 days a week, 24 hours a day.

Closer to Carnegie Hall, City Center and the northernmost Theater District houses are two of the city's best delicatessens – the *Stage Deli* at 834 7th Ave., north of 53rd St., Tel. 245-7850, and the *Carnegie Deli*, 854 7th Ave., north of 54th St., Tel. 757-2245. Both serve delicious sandwiches, the *Carnegie* having a slight advantage in quality. The size of the portions will astound you. Also nearby is *Seeda Thai*, 204 W 50th St., a handsome, authentic and reasonable Thai restaurant, Tel. 586-4513.

Entertainment in the Theater District does not end when the curtain comes down. The *Carnegie Tavern*, just behind Carnegie Hall at 165 W 56th St., will top off your night with some talented jazz piano. The bars in several of the hotels in the area are also worth a visit. The *Sheraton Center*, 7th Ave., between 52nd and 53rd Sts., is equipped with no fewer than three restaurants and two bars. Catch a glimpse of local politicians who enjoy dropping

Inside the Hard Rock Café

in. For a more breathtaking view of the urban scenery, visit the *Wine Bistro* on the 7th floor of the new *Novotel Hotel* Broadway and 52nd St. Sip wine to the sound of piano music and the sight of the twinkling neon landscape to the south, Tel. 315-0100.

Fox-trot at the world-famous discotheque – the **Roseland Ballroom**, 239 W 52nd St. where music ranges from big-band to salsa depending upon the time and day. Open Thurs.-Sun. 2:30pm onwards, Tel. 247-0200. The discos that are hot at the moment are closer to the Hudson River on 56th and 57th Sts. Cap things off at the *Hard Rock Café*, 221 W 57th St. Conceived in London, the waiting line for this bar/restaurant seems endless. The decor is rock-and-roll memorabilia. Open till 4am, Tel. 459-9320.

Excursions

Two river excursions debark from this part of Manhattan. One is the *Circle Line*, a three-hour, 31-mile (approx. 52 km) narrated cruise around Manhattan (late March through mid-Nov.), which docks at the foot of West 42nd St., at Pier 84 on the Hudson River, Tel. 563-3200. The other is *World Yacht*. Tel. 563-3200, which anchors at Pier 81, west of 41st St. Tel. 630-8100.

Docked at Pier 86, West 46th St. at the Hudson River, is the **Intrepid**, once an aircraft carrier and now a sea/air/space museum which holds, among other things, a rocket-carrier submarine. View the informative, dramatic exhibits and films; walk through the control bridge and command center. Children shouldn't miss it. Open Wed.-Sun. 10am-5pm; summertime daily. Admission charge, free for children under the age of 6. Tel. 245-0072.

The Intrepid Museum – once an aircraft carrier

For something totally different try 51st St. on the corner of Broadway. What was once a theater is now a church-theater called *Times Square Church*.

Open Sun., Tues., Thurs. and Fri. As for the goings on here, there are strange musical prayers for all types of Christians. They take place in a theater hall whose owners went bankrupt and leased it out to this church. The prayers take place on a stage with a red velvet curtain, ushers and sometimes even an orchestra. Full house, free entrance and well worth a visit.

Pigeons galore at Times Square

Fifth Avenue – "The" Avenue

5th Avenue from 42nd to 59th Sts. is New York's premier shopping boulevard, with most of the exclusive shops concentrated between Rockefeller Center and 57th St. Here you will find the world-famous *Saks Fifth Avenue* and *Bergdorf Goodman*, the sparkling jewels of *Tiffany's*, and the marble grandeur of St. Patrick's Cathedral, the city's most beautiful church. The famous promenade, lined with limestone skyscrapers, is also a famous parade route.

A New Yorker of the 1800s, returning to 5th Ave. today, would recognize St. Patrick's and nothing else. The avenue, once lined with mansions designed after the great homes of Europe and populated by the likes of the Vanderbilts and the Astors, was considered the world's most prestigious residential avenue. The turning point came in the 1920s; when *Saks* relocated here from Herald Square, the *Times* declared upper 5th Ave. a new shopping street, and Rockefeller Center was built during the following decade. Today it is hard to imagine 5th Ave. without that lovely Art Deco amalgam of culture, business and entertainment. More recent additions to the avenue include the glass skyscrapers of Olympic Tower and Trump Tower. One mansion remains: the Morton F. Plant House, today's Cartier Building.

Take Subway 4, 5, or 6 to 42nd St./Grand Central; walk west on 42nd St. to 5th Ave. and head north. Give it a full afternoon, though not on a Sunday, when most shops are closed. Here we shall describe all the exclusive shops, restaurants, clubs and architecturally significant buildings within one block east and west of 5th Ave.

The **New York Public Library**, that wonderful Carrere & Hastings beaux arts gem guarded by Edward C. Potter's lions, is just south on 42nd St. (see "East Side 26-42 Sts.") Turn west on 43rd St.

The Rockefeller Plaza

The **Century Club** at No. 7 – note its flag of a white Aladdin's lamp on a blue background – occupies a vintage 1889 building designed by McKim, Mead & White, the most sought-after architects of their day. Speaking of clubs in the area, don't forget the **Harvard Club**, 217 W 44th St., another McKim, Mead & White design built in 1894 for graduates of Harvard College. Further west at No. 37 is the **NY Yacht Club**, designed by Whitney Warren of Warren & Wetmore (1899). The America's Cup, the foremost prize of international yacht racing, has been kept here since 1857. Won by "America" in Britain's "Hundred Guinea Cup" race of 1851, the trophy became an international prize when deeded to the Yacht Club in 1857. American yachts reigned supreme for about 130 years, until an Australian crew using a novel racing hull won it in 1985. Since then it has become highly controversial what kind of boats are allowed to race for the Cup and now it is fought over mainly in the courts. A New York court awarded it to New Zealand and then the US Supreme Court took it back.

Walking down 5th Avenue

No. 42 is the classical-style home of the **Bar Association of the City of NY**, designed by Cyrus Eidlitz and built of Indiana limestone and marble in 1896. One of the country's largest law libraries is maintained here. Next door is the *Royalton Hotel*, designed by Stanford White of McKim, Mead & White in 1899.

Across the street at 59 W 44th St., is the famed *Algonquin Hotel*, once home of the literary Round Table, that witty, sarcastic group that included urbane humorists Robert Benchley and Dorothy Parker. Still a favorite among writers and theater people, the *Algonquin Hotel* offers several restaurants, the most famous being *The Oak Room*, Tel. 759-3000.

East of 5th Ave., at the corner of 44th St. and Madison Ave., is *Brooks Brothers*, est. 1818, the clothing shop for men and women where "preppy" – khaki slacks, button-down Oxford shirt and a navy blue blazer – have been "in" for years, Tel. 682-8800.

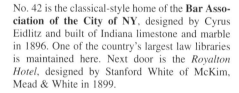

At the corner of 45th St. is the **Fred F. French Building**, an art deco tower built in 1927. Note the gilded, arched doorway on 5th Ave. and the winged horses over the ground-level windows.

At 45th to 46th St. one can find the **world's largest atrium**. It's only half the size of the Empire State Building and hosts New York's only revolving rooftop restaurant with a panoramic view, Tel. 398-1900.

Turn west onto 47th St. from 5th Ave., and you will find yourself in **Diamond Row**. Wall-to-wall jewelry stores await you between 5th and 6th Aves.; 80 % of all US trade in diamonds is conducted here. Among the larger establishments are the *National Jewelers Exchange*, the *NY Jewelry Center* and the *Diamond Center of America*. Business on this street is conducted in a highly unusual manner. Since no two diamonds are alike, each is sold individually, with the seller opening negotiations. The buyer, if interested, writes his offer on a small envelope which he seals after enclosing the diamond within. The seller may neither open the envelope nor show the diamond to anyone else until he accepts or rejects the offer. If he accepts, buyer and seller shake hands and say "*mazel and brocha*" – Yiddish for blessing the buyer and wishing the seller luck.

In the middle of all this is the *Gotham Bookmart and Gallery*, 41 W 47th St. (second floor) and its changing art exhibits. This establishment has been a gathering place for writers and book lovers for 65 years. Here you'll find a huge inventory of excellent books both in and out of print. Every December it displays a Christmas tree decorated with hundreds of rare ornaments. No admission charge, Tel. 719-4448.

On 575 5th Ave. is *Rusty Staub's*, a diner owned by baseball star Rusty Staub, which specializes in barbecued ribs. Recommended. Tel. 682-1000.

Return to 5th Ave. and continue north. Stop in at *Scribner's Bookstore* at 597 5th Ave., Tel. 486-4070, with its unmistakable, lovely iron-and-glass facade. Designed by Ernest Flagg and built in 1913, *Scribner's*, though recently purchased by

Rizzoli International Bookstores, retains its independent name and reputation.

On 5th Ave., we approach **Rockefeller Center** – a city within a city and one of New York's unsurpassed highlights. It stretches from 48th St. north to 52nd St., and from 5th Ave. west to midway between 6th and 7th Aves. Its heart is the RCA Building at 30 Rockefeller Plaza, a 70-story limestone shaft dramatically illuminated at night by white floodlights. Direct access by subway: B.D.F. and K.

Located on a site originally owned by Dr. David Hosack (who cared for the Revolutionary leader Alexander Hamilton following his fatal duel with Aaron Burr), and later by Columbia University, the center traces the history of the Metropolitan Opera's search for a new home in 1926. The "Met" enlisted the support of John D. Rockefeller, Jr., who signed a lease with Columbia University. Lacking funds for development, however, the "Met" backed out, leaving Rockefeller without a commercial tenant on the eve of the 1929 Stock Market crash. Rockefeller had to develop the site himself because the rent he owed Columbia far exceeded the revenue he earned from the residential tenants.

The Rockefeller Plaza at Christmas time

A series of disastrous architectural designs subjected Rockefeller's project to contempt (one group, the *Fine Arts Federation of NY*, actually proposed construction of a new avenue between 5th and 6th from 42nd St. to Central Park, right through the center of the complex) until a team of architects headed by Raymond Hood (designer of the American Standard Building) drew up the final plan. The rental office invented some unconventional methods for wooing tenants – awarding construction contractors preference for the actual construction if they would agree to lease office space, and granting exclusive renting privileges to service businesses while keeping competitors out. President Hoover chipped in with tax deferrals for foreign retailers.

The result is a beautiful art deco gift to the city. The **RCA Building**, now recognized as one of the world's greatest skyscrapers, is flanked on 5th Ave. by the *Maison Française* and the *British Building*, with the downward slope of the *Channel Gardens*, adorned by sea-creature fountain-heads by Chambellan, in between. At Christmas the gardens are graced with sculpted angels outlined in tiny white lights, ushering the visitor to the colorful illumination of the towering Christmas tree in front of the RCA Building.

Among the shops lining Channel Gardens, are *La Librairie de France* (Tel. 581-8810), over 50 years in this location, with its vast selection of French books.

At the end of the Promenade is **Rockefeller Plaza**, a sunken square surrounded by flags of foreign nations. In winter, either watch ice skaters glide past the gilded statue of *Prometheus*, mythical founder of civilization, or rent some skates yourself (after paying admission charge and rental fee). In summer, the restaurants at the Plaza's lower level spill out into the open air.

As you explore the Plaza, note the powerful carvings which bracket the doorways and border the eaves. Lee Lawrie's *Wisdom* graces the Plaza entrance of the RCA Building; other Lawrie carvings usher you into the Maison Française and

NBC – New York's Broadcasting Center

"Prometheus" at the Rockefeller Plaza

the British Building from the Channel Gardens. A theme common to all the Center's artwork is *New Frontiers and the March of Civilization* – with special reverence for man, the builder. The murals inside the RCA Building illustrate this theme admirably. The first artists approached to carry out the murals were Picasso and Matisse, because of the prestige and value their fame would lend the Center, but they were unavailable and uninterested. Accordingly, Rockefeller settled for Sert and Brangwyn for the side murals and Diego Rivera for the central fresco. The communist Rivera, though, proved too controversial, and when he refused to remove the unmistakable image of Lenin which he'd painted into his design, the mural was destroyed. It was replaced by a marvellous work by Sert in which you can identify Abraham Lincoln as *Man of Action* and Ralph Waldo Emerson, poet and advocate of self-reliance, as the *Man of Thought*. The embittered Rivera repainted the mural in Mexico City, adding a portrait of John D. Rockefeller to a section depicting *Debauchery*.

Once inside the RCA Building, go downstairs first to the Shopping Concourse which includes restaurants, gift shops, boutiques, and a gallery devoted to the Center's history. Open Mon.-Fri. 9am-5pm.

Return to ground level for tickets to the **NBC Network's Radio and Television Studios**, about $10, entitling you to 20% off at the NBC Gift Shop. You will be guided through a control studio, the famed Studio 8-H, the network's two radio stations and the sets used on *Saturday Night Live* and *The Today Show*. Tours depart Mon.-Sat. every 15 mins. from 9:30am-4:30pm, Tel. 664-4444, no entrance to children under 6. Several NBC programs – *Saturday Night Live*, *The Phil Donahue Show* and the *Jay Leno Tonight show*, are either broadcasted live or filmed in front of a studio audience. Write to *NBC* at *Rockefeller Plaza* for tickets; free-ticket winners are chosen at random from all such requests, but unfortunately, out-of-towners are unlikely to win tickets on dates which coincide with their visits. In any case, you can also enjoy a guided tour of the center and Observation Roof, 850 ft. (approx. 260m) high. Tours meet at the front desk of the RCA Building, Mon.-Sat. 9:30am-4:30pm. Admission price depends on the tour you take, Tel. 489-2947. The *Rainbow Room Restaurant*, Tel. 632-5000, offers a spectacular view of the city skyline, but you may be denied entry if you're too casually dressed.

The McGraw-Hill Building with its plaza

Exit the RCA Building at 6th Ave. Ranked by height from south to north, are three skyscrapers of similar design – the **Celanese Building**, the **McGraw-Hill Building** and the **Exxon Building** – each fronting an entire block from 47th to 50th Sts. Mini-parks behind the Exxon and McGraw-Hill Buildings, the latter with a walk-through waterfall, are open only in warm weather. Admission charge, Tel. 869-0345. The **Time and Life Building** comes next, between 50th and 51st Sts.

At the northeast corner of 50th St. and 6th Ave. is

Radio City Music Hall, the art deco triumph, famous for its combined stage and movie presentations of the all-female dance group, the *Rockettes*. In recent years, Radio City has diversified into rock and pop concerts. Box office: Tel. 247-4777.

You can also tour Radio City for an admission charge, to view the fabulous murals and lounges, Tel. 632-4041.

Turn east on 50th St. and pass the Associated Press and International Buildings on your left. The **Italia Building**, at the northwest corner of 50th and 5th Ave., is most notable for the artwork that is no longer above the doorway. Today's grapevine-and-wheat design replaced a fascist decoration that came down in 1940, just before the United States entered World War II.

In the court of the International Buildings, on 5th Ave. between 50th and 51st Sts., stands the arresting sculpture of Atlas clutching a globe of zodiac symbols.

Directly across 5th Ave. is the marble splendor of **St. Patrick's Cathedral**. New York's most beautiful church was designed by James Renwick, Jr. and built in 1879, a reflection of the rising prominence of Roman Catholics in NYC. Christmas Eve Midnight Mass at St. Patrick's Cathedral is one of the most sought-after events in town; request tickets in Sept. or Oct. There is direct access to the Cathedral by Subway N or R to 49th St. then walk east from 7th Ave., or the B, D, or F to 47th-50th Sts.

Two vast breaks in the 5th Ave. skyline – one at St. Patrick's and the other at 56th St. – allow the avenue and its highly reflective limestone buildings to bask in natural light at midday.

An ornament at the St. Patrick's Cathedral

Just south of St. Patrick's, directly opposite Channel Gardens, is *Saks Fifth Avenue*. Known worldwide for its designer clothing, *Saks* is the only department store thus far to be designated a landmark. Its 10-story classical-style home was modelled in the 1920s after an Italian palazzo. Inside, too, *Saks* looks rich with its deep-hued mahogany walls and separate rooms for individual designer's lines. *Saks' Fifth Avenue Club* includes a Personal Shopping Service, an International Shopping Service and the Executive Club. The

St. Patrick's Cathedral – New York's most beautiful cathedral

latter, for a fee, guarantees the same consultant each visit as well as same-day delivery, priority alterations, and reminders before birthdays and anniversaries. *Saks Fifth Avenue* is open Mon.-Fri. 10am-8pm; Sat. 10am-6pm; Sun. noon-5pm, Tel. 753-4000.

Walk north on 5th Ave., passing St. Patrick's and the Olympic Tower. North of 51st St. you will find *H. Stern* for jewelry and *Mark Cross* for luggage. At the southeast corner of 52nd St. and 5th Ave., in the former Morton F. Plant Mansion, is *Cartier*. Though the exquisite rings and necklaces you'll see are very, very expensive, *Les Musts de Cartier* offers a more affordable gift selection, Tel. 838-5454.

West of 5th Ave. at 21 W 52nd St., is the famous **21 Club** – clublike indeed, as you will sense when the doorman greets you and escorts you past rows of lantern-bearers into the bar, with its model cars and planes suspended from the ceiling. Tradition-laden *21 Club* began as a speakeasy during the Prohibition of the 1920s. Regulars, predictably, get preferential treatment. Tel. 582-7200.

Continue west to the tower of **CBS Studios** at the northeast corner of 52nd St. and 6th Ave., designed by famed architect Eero Saarinen and built in 1965. *CBS* offers free public screenings of its new programs Mondays through Fridays, year round. Inquire about tickets at the main desk inside the 52nd St. entrance.

Walk north on 6th Ave. and then east on 53rd St. until you reach the **American Craft Museum,** at 40 W 53rd St., open Tues. 10am-8pm; Wed.-Sun. 10am-5pm. Entrance for children under 12 is free of charge. Tel. 956-3535. The museum exhibits a wonderful collection of pottery, weaving and other handicrafts.

The outstanding **Museum of Modern Art (MOMA)** is further east at 11 W 53rd St. Founded in 1929 with considerable support from Abby Aldrich Rockefeller (wife of John D., Jr.) and her son Nelson, MOMA has introduced the public to post-Impressionist and to contemporary art; it exhibited Picasso and Jackson Pollack, for example, when other museums wouldn't. One of its first offerings – a small exhibit entitled *International Exhibit of Modern Architecture* – helped change NYC's urban landscape. The *International Show*, as it came to be called, displayed the stark steel and glass slabs of Le Corbusier, Gropius, and Mies van der Rohe. Though quite daring at the time, these glass and steel buildings, cheaper and easier to build than buildings of stone, are familiar to us today as the standard design of American corporate headquarters. MOMA is still a pioneer of art frontier, and has broadened its concept of art to include film and furniture design. The museum is open Sat.-Tues. 11am-6pm; Thurs., Fri. noon-8:30pm. Closed Wed. Admission charge, free for children under 16 accompanied by an adult. After 5:30pm admission is 'pay what you wish', Tel. 708-9750, 908-4110.

Don't miss MOMA. Obtain that day's schedule of films at the information desk (film tickets are included in the price of museum admission) and plan your tour around it. If it's warm, visit the ground floor outdoor sculpture garden and its works by Rodin and others. The painting and sculpture collections are on the second and third floors; photography is on the second, prints and drawings on the third, architecture and design on the fourth. The **Titus Film Theaters** share the lower level with temporary exhibition galleries. The addition of Cesar Pelli's condominium tower and the sale of its flats enriched MOMA's coffers and doubled the exhibition space. Among the great masterpieces in the permanent collection are Vincent van Gogh's *Starry Night* and Andrew Wyeth's *Christina's World*. Have lunch at the ground-floor garden café. Open Fri.- Tues. 11am-4:30pm and Thurs. 11am-8pm. Gallery lectures weekdays, 12:30pm and 3pm, and Thurs. 5:30pm and 7pm. Photography is permitted only in the permanent

collection. Tel. 708-9696. Direct access by Subway 6 to 51st St., then walk west, or take the E or F to 5th Ave.

Continue east on 53rd St. The southwest corner at 53rd St. and 5th Ave. is occupied by the **Tishman Building** at 666 5th Ave., crowned by *Top of the Sixes*, a roof restaurant with a spectacular view, Tel. 757-6662; the northwest corner belongs to the Episcopal **St. Thomas Church**. St. Thomas seems to cry out for a second tower, if only for symmetry. Note the ornately-carved marble reredos and the deep-blue stained-glass windows behind them. Among the religious figures of the reredos is a depiction of George Washington at the extreme right, third from the bottom.

Continue west on 52nd St., crossing 5th Ave. to the **Museum of Radio and Television** at 25 W 52nd St. Though there are always one or two special TV

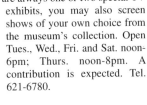

exhibits, you may also screen shows of your own choice from the museum's collection. Open Tues., Wed., Fri. and Sat. noon-6pm; Thurs. noon-8pm. A contribution is expected. Tel. 621-6780.

Just next door is a welcome little **outdoor plaza** – a refreshment stand, tables and chairs beside a waterfall – dedicated to Samuel Paley, father of CBS mastermind William S. Paley.

Across 53rd St. is the **Harper and Row Building**. The huge hanging globe next door identifies the *Rand McNally Shop* and its wide selection of foreign and domestic maps and travel books, Tel. 758-7488.

At 53rd St. between 3rd and Lexington Ave. visit the Citicorp Center with its 3 levels of shops and eateries. Discover the romantic cafés amidst trees and shrubs on the top floor.

Gucci, of the famed red-and-green stripe, occupies both the northeast and southeast corners of 54th St. and 5th Ave., with leather goods in the former and clothing in the latter. A sales annex is located at 2 E 54th, 7th floor, Tel. 826-2600. Cross 5th Ave. and take particular note of the **Aeolian Building**. This romantic gem, with its curved corners and ornamental urns below the roofline, was designed by Warren & Wetmore (designers of the NY Yacht Club) and built in 1925.

Not far from here, on 233 W 54th St. is an interesting attraction for pet lovers. The *Pet Department Store* offers you a Pet Deli, a dalmatian sofa for making portraits of your loved-ones, a treadmill for jogging, apart from a broad selection of collars, pet fashion, boots and treats to complete your visit. The place open daily. Tel. (800) 937-9571.

Walk half a block east on 54th St. to **Famolare, Inc.** The building, designed by McKim, Mead & White as a residence for industrialist William H. Moore, is noted for its windows. Diminishing in height as they ascend, they create an optical illusion of exaggerated height.

Across 5th Ave. from the Aeolian Building is the *University Club*, another McKim, Mead & White design erected in 1899. Be sure to visit *Godiva Chocolatier* at 701 5th Ave. for sinfully rich hand made Belgium chocolates and home-brand ice cream, Tel. 593-2845.

The southern corners of 55th St. and 5th Ave. are occupied by the near-twin *Gotham* and *St. Regis-Sheraton* hotels. *The Gotham*, 2 W 55th lies vacant and gutted because money ran out in mid-renovation. Notice the detail over the 55th St. entrance. The glamorous, beaux arts *St. Regis-Sheraton* (1904), by contrast, is alive and well.

The **Fifth Avenue Presbyterian Church**, on the northwest corner of 5th Ave. and 55th St., is unique among NYC's churches for its ashwood, rather than stone, interior and the circular, theater-like layout of its two levels. Duke Ellington gave two jazz concerts here.

At No. 712, adjacent to the

church, is the **1907 Building** and the **Coty Building**. Its neighbor at No. 714, is slated to give way to a skyscraper; preservationists and developers are fighting it out. Property value here is extremely high. The Coty Building attracted preservationists because of its windows, designed by the French craftsman René Lalique for the perfumery owner François Coty. Across the street you can see the **Coca-Cola Building**, a large and powerful structure that somehow fits quite well into the rest of the avenue.

A block east, at 55th and Madison, is the spectacular post-modern **Sony Building** (previously the AT&T Building; see "The East 50s"). **IBM Corporate Headquarters**, housed in a monolithic green granite triangle, is one block north at 56th St. Enter its atrium from the northwest corner of 56th and Madison and note the sculpture-fountain, a wonderful granite chunk of rough sides and smooth surface chiselled by Michael Helzer into right angles with a miniature river gushing out

from below. Have a seat amid the bamboo trees and enjoy coffee, tea and dessert on weekdays, when the kiosk is open. Free midday concerts are often performed here.

There is a *Warner Brothers* shop selling souvenirs and clothes from all the cartoons the company has created. It is located on 1 E 57th St. and 5th Ave. Tel. 754-0300. Another souvenir shop is the *Coca Cola* shop on 711 5th Ave. Tel. 418-9260.

On the east side of 5th Ave. between 56th and 57th Sts. stands **Trump Tower**, the most eagerly-awaited Midtown building of its time, designed by Der Scutt and Swank Hayden Connell, developed by Donald Trump. A dark-glass 68-story tower with many triangular retreats, its interior opens onto a shopping atrium 6-stories high, lined with unusual orange-hued marble trimmed with brass. The escalator seems to glisten beside an indoor waterfall. Inside you will find several boutiques, including *Charles Jourdan*, *Buccellati* and *Harry Winston Petit Salon*. The upper levels are residential condominiums with prices literally fit for a king: Prince Charles purchased one in the mid-1980s.

Next door at 57th St. and 5th Ave. is *Tiffany's*, with its fine jewelry and elegant gifts. Jewelry is downstairs, silver and glassware upstairs. The store itself, built in 1926, and immortalized in the movie *Breakfast at Tiffany's*, starring Audrey Hepburn and George Peppard, is a gem as well. The exterior is understated art deco; the interior is classically elegant. Ride the wood-paneled elevators, operated by helpful elderly women, Tel. 755-8000.

Time and quality are stable at Tiffany's

Continue north on 5th Ave.; cross 57th St., a wide two-way thoroughfare lined with exclusive shops and art galleries (which we'll cover in the next section) and head toward Central Park. At the northwest corner of 57th and 5th is *Bergdorf Goodman*. Beneficiary of a sparkling face-lift, *Bergdorf's* boasts the most elegant interior of the city's numerous department stores. Notice the gently-hued moldings and arched doorways of the jewelry department on the ground level. If not for the expensive merchandise, you might think you were in a French country estate. *Bergdorf's* also stocks designer clothing and accessories. The personal shopping service is called *Solutions*; its staff, which includes two people, works only by appointment, Tel. 753-7300. From *Bergdorf's* 57th St. corner, look south to the recently re-gilded **Crown Building**, another architectural beauty adding to the avenue's grandeur.

FAO Schwartz, 58th St. and 5th Ave. is one of the world's most famous toy stores. The huge stuffed animals are a particular attraction. It's a great place to take children, but only if you intend to buy them something, Tel. 644-9400.

Due north is the **General Motors Building** with *GM* cars on display at ground level, boutiques bordering its sunken outdoor plaza. To the west, at the foot of Central Park, is **Grand Army Plaza**. The **Plaza Hotel** is on the west side, its front doors facing the *Pulitzer Fountain*, designed by Thomas Hastings of Carrere & Hastings, and *Abundance*, a sculpture by Karl Bitter, both were completed in 1916. The statue of Civil War General William Tecumseh Sherman (who died in NYC) is by

Augustus Saint Gaudens. Here you will find the hansom cabs – horse and buggy – which will take you through the park or anywhere in town. Though romantic, it's expensive. Be sure to establish the price with the driver before you get in. Maximum of four people per carriage.

The skyscrapers of the Rockefeller Center, with the RCA Building in the middle

57th St. – Heavyweight Galleries

ike 5th Ave., 57th St. is high-class boutique turf, good for an entire weekday r Saturday afternoon of shopping and visits to several of the city's most stablished 20th-century art galleries. Note many boutiques and galleries are osed Sundays. Have lunch at the beloved *Russian Tea Room*, used as a set Woody Allen's *Manhattan* and Dustin Hoffman's *Tootsie*, and enjoy a oncert or film at the famous Carnegie Hall. In this chapter we shall point out ome highlights of the boulevard from 3rd to 7th Aves., a tour worth several ours.

ake Subway R, N, 4, 5 or 6 to 59th St. Devout hoppers may begin the excursion at ***Blooming-ale's*** (Lexington Ave. and 59th St.), a shopper's aradise which, if passed up now, should be eserved for another day (see "The East 50's"). In ither case, pick up 57th St. at 3rd Ave. and head vest.

our first stop is ***Hammacher & Schlemmer***, 147 E 57th St., synonymous with elite gadgetry – uriosities for people who have everything. ounded in 1848, it has been at this site since 926, Tel. 421-9000.

urther up the north side of the street are *Dunhill* *ailors*, 65 E 57th St., Tel. 355-0050; *Louis Vuit-on*, 51 E 57th St., Tel. 371-6111 and *Maud Frizon*, 9 E 57th St., Tel. 980-1460. *Dunhill* displays its British-style shirts and ties in a British-style shop, f course; *Vuitton* is famous for its *LV*-engraved uggage, and *Maud Frizon* is THE outlet for the rench designer's footwear collection.

Inside the enormous department store Bloomingdale's

Across the street at 48 E 57th St., Tel. 371-3943, is
Chaumet, the 200-year-old French jewelry firm
that once designed some "baubles" for Napoleon's
wife, Empress Marie Louise. Prices here reach six
figures. Next door, 46 E 57th St., Tel. 308-2900, is
Buccellati and its silver collection. *Guy Laroche*
nearby at 36 E 57th St., vends the ready-to-wear
wardrobe bearing this French designer's name,
Tel. 759-2301.

At 57th St. between Lexington and Park Ave. is a
unique atrium noted for its luxurious marble interior: An international and cultural center of art
and antiques. Open Mon.-Sat. 11am-6pm, Tel.
758-2900.

The **Fuller Building** graces the northeast corner of
57th St. and Madison Ave. Designed by Walker
and Gillette and built in 1928-29, this art deco
tower bears the name of a construction company
which relocated here from the Flatiron Building
near Madison Square. Notice the contrasting black
and white stone at the apex, and the strong figures
sculpted by Elie Nadelman over the 57th St.
entrance.

The *Wally Findlay Gallery*, 17 E 57th St., Tel.
421-5390, specializes in 20th-century paintings
and sculptures. Closed Sundays. *Hermes*, the
sumptuous leather shop, occupies the ground level
of Trump Tower, 11 E 57th St. Upstairs is the
Dyansen 57 gallery which exhibits the Erte sculpture collection, Tel. 754-3040. Next door is

Burberry's, home of the famous trench coat and signature plaid scarf, Tel. 371-5010.

Cross 5th Ave. for *Bergdorf Goodman*, the quietly elegant department store. Stroll through the ground-floor jewelry collection even if you do not shop, Tel. 753-7300. Nestled in Bergdorf's 57th St. corner is *Van Cleef & Arpels* jewelry boutique, Tel. 644-9500. The glimmering splendor of the Crown Building across 57th St., designed by Warren & Wetmore and built in 1922 (the gold-leaf gilding is new) adds significantly to the beauty of 5th Ave.

The *Festival Movie Theater* is at 6 W 57th St., Tel. 302-2434; next door is *Henri Bendel*, a very high-class flea market of sorts with elegant interior boutiques, Tel. 247-1100. Upstairs is the *Jean Louis David Salon*. An extravagance it is, but the beauticians are talented and do not always insist on an appointment.

Charivari 57 at 16-18 W 57th St., Tel. 333-4040, is the Midtown branch of the trend-setting *Chari-vari* clothing chain that has taken over the Upper West Side. The new home of the *Rizzoli Bookshop* is at 31 W 57th St. This Italian and Swiss-owned enterprise, new owner of *Scribner's Bookstore* on 5th Ave., specializes in beautiful fine art books, photo books and foreign editions, Tel. 486-4070.

The *Max Protech Gallery*, 37 W 57th St., Tel. 838-2340, often exhibits the work of 20th-century architects. Two well-known galleries, reliable for the quality of their offerings, reside across the way. The Marlborough Gallery, Tel. 541-4900, and the Kennedy Gallery, Tel. 541-9600, occupy the second and fifth floors, respectively, of 40 W 57th St. Marlborough displays the most famous of modern and contemporary artists; the Kennedy, which is over a century old, features American artists, reaching back to the 1700s and 1800s.

At the northwest corner of 6th Ave. and 57th St. is *Wolf's*, one of NY's finest delicatessen restaurants and an excellent choice for a reasonably-priced lunch, Tel. 422-4141.

Further west is the **Steinway Showroom**, 109 W 57th St., the geographic and artistic

neighbor of nearby Carnegie Hall and a pioneer in safety: its fully fire-proof building (1925) was equipped with a then-rare sprinkler system which is still in operation today. The ground-level array of grand pianos is surrounded by paintings on musical themes by famous American artists: Rockwell, Kent and N.C. Wyeth (father of Andrew), among others, Tel. 246-1100.

Across the street at 150 W 57th St. is the legendary *Russian Tea Room*. Its dark green walls, pink lamps, traditional Russian cuisine and Carnegie Hall celebrity clientele make it a superb choice for a festive weekday lunch or weekend brunch, Tel. 265-0947.

A pre-concert alternative to the *Russian Tea Room* is the opulent *Petrossian*, nearby at 182 W 58th St., Tel. 245-2215. This restaurant in the Alwyn Court Apartments furnishes an environment of polished pink-granite floors, Erte-designed mirrors, mink-trimmed banquette and window statuary as the setting for the jewel: caviar. Enjoy it with champagne or vodka; prepare to pay upward of $120 per order.

Next door is the New York branch of *Planet Hollywood*, a restaurant-club-bar belonging to the chain of the stars Sylvester Stalone, Bruce Willis and Arnold Shwartzneger. The stars themselves are not usually there but there are plenty of souvenirs from the pop and movie world of Hollywood.

The concert hall at 57th St. and 7th Ave. named for Andrew Carnegie, steel magnate and philanthropist, opened in 1891 with Tchaikovsky on the podium. An appearance in NYC, one of the world's music capitals, is a special thrill for a performer, and a solo concert at **Carnegie Hall** is considered among the highest honors. The acoustics of the Main Hall, host to the world's great orchestras and soloists, are among the finest anywhere. Tours of the Hall are available. A recital hall is situated upstairs; and a movie theater (entrance on 7th Ave.) is generally devoted to foreign or art films. Some Carnegie Hall concerts offer discounted, day-of-performance student and senior citizen "rush tickets," on sale from 1-1:30pm for matinees and 6-6:30pm for evening performances (ID required). The *Carnegie Café*, to the left of the auditorium, opens 30 minutes before performance time and stays open until the end of intermission. The Carnegie box office is open Mon.-Sat. 1am-6pm (until 8:30pm on performance evenings) and Sun. noon-6pm (only if there is a performance that day). Credit cards accepted until 1pm for matinees and 3pm for evening performances. For inquiries and ticket purchases, Tel. 903-9790.

East Side, 42nd-51st Sts. – Art Deco, Architecture and the UN

A walk through this neighborhood begins with some of the world's most representative Art Deco architecture, crosses the United Nations and penetrates the exclusive residential enclave of Beekman Place. Visit any day; set out in late morning.

Take Subway 4, 5, or 6 to 42nd St. Grand Central Station and walk east along 42nd St. (for a discussion of Grand Central and the vicinity see "East Side, 26th-42nd Sts.").

Let us first examine an outstanding and underrated Art Deco skyscraper, the **Chanin Building** at the southwest corner of Lexington Ave. and 42nd St. Much of its beauty is appreciable from just above eye level. Designed by Sloan & Robertson, it features exterior artwork on the 42nd St. and Lexington Ave. facades above the ground, and the fourth floors, in the form of a wide terra cotta band of paisley-swirled tropical leaves above and a bronze border of stylized sea monsters below. The buttresses above the Lexington Ave. entrance represent the skyscraper in miniature. Inside you will find a marble lobby adorned with bronze Art Deco patterns – brass radiator grills under allegorical, cubist bas-reliefs in the vestibules, executed by sculptor Rene Chambellan (designer of Rockefeller Center's Channel Garden fountains).

Across the way is the **Chrysler Building**, the

world's tallest building upon completion in 1929 – by virtue of a trick played by its architect, William Van Alen. With 40 Wall St. simultaneously under construction, Van Alen temporarily halted work to give the competing architects the impression that the Chrysler Building was complete at 925 ft. After the Wall St. builders added 2 ft. and claimed the "world's-tallest" title, Van Alen mounted a 123 ft. stainless-steel spire onto the roof. The last laugh, of course, belonged to the Empire State Building, completed a few months later.

With its tapering tower of diamond-shaped windows romantically outlined in neon at night (and best appreciated from afar), the Chrysler Building is the favorite of native New Yorkers. Of the different designs adorning each setback, the most revealing is at the fourth: winged radiator caps at the corners, with a band of brickwork reminiscent of capped wheels in the middle (this is, after all, the *Chrysler* Building). The lobby, once an automobile showroom, is lined with a rich Indian-red marble and intricate patterns of inlaid wood. The Edward Trumbull ceiling mural, 97 x 100 ft., (approx. 30 x 30.5 m) depicts varied forms of transportation in tones matching the marble.

The Chrysler Building with its tapering tower

Just north on Lexington Ave. and 44th St. is the home of the *Graybar Electric Co.*, whose chief business, communication devices, is illustrated in the artwork above the entrance; painted, gilded, god-like figures clutching items representing man's control of his environment through technology.

Return to 42nd St. on Lexington Ave. At 150 E 42nd St., is the **Mobil Building**, noted for its façade of punched-steel panels, a design innovation which prevents warping and allows the wind to keep the surface clean.

The **Daily News Building**, 220 E 42nd St., was designed by Howells & Hood (Hood of the

American Standard Building, near Bryant Park and Rockefeller Center) and built in 1929-30. The strength of the carved stone above the entrance is best appreciated from across the street. The

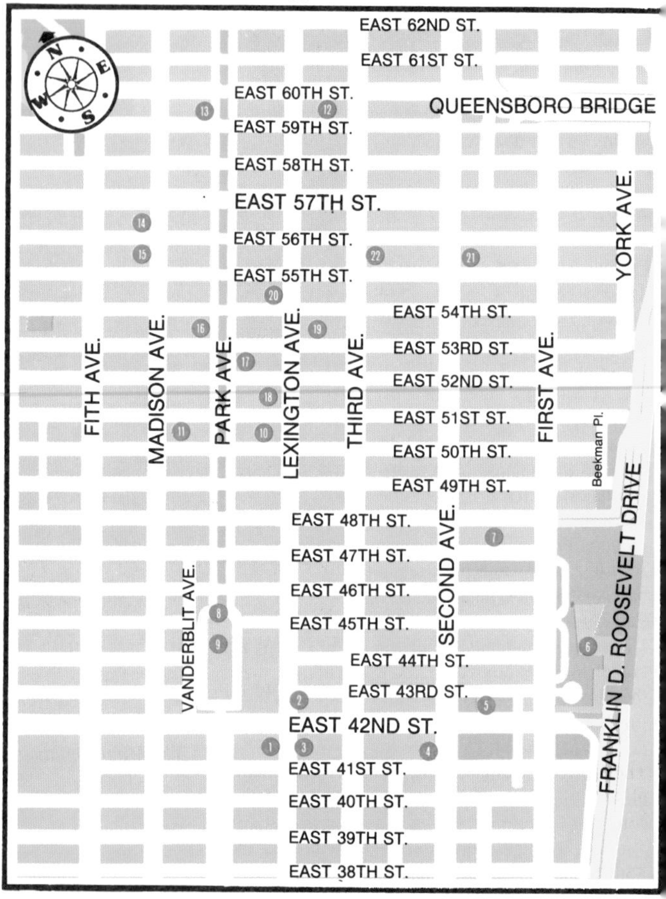

EAST SIDE, 42ND-60TH STS.

1. Chanin Building
2. Chrysler Building
3. Mobil Building
4. Daily News Building
5. Ford Foundation Building
6. United Nations Headquarters
7. Japan Society House
8. Helmsley Building
9. MetLife Building
10. St. Bartholomew's
    Episcopal Church
11. New York Palace Hotel
12. Bloomingdale's
13. Christie's
14. IBM Building
15. Sony Building
16. Lever House
17. Seagram Building
18. Four Seasons
19. Saint Peter's Church
20. Central Synagogue
21. Manhattan Art and
    Antiques Center
22. Michael's Pub

world's largest indoor globe – an excellent lesson in geography – sits in the lobby. Open Mon.- Sat. 9am-5pm. Tel. 210-2900.

Though the **Ford Foundation Building** entrance is at 320 E 43rd St., its beautiful garden is open to the public from 42nd St. The Foundation offices look onto the 12-story atrium with its trees, aquatic pool and shrubbery, which is changed periodically. Open to the public Mon.-Fri. 9am-5pm. Tel. 573-5000.

At 304 E 42nd St. is the *Tudor Hotel*, favored by UN delegates. Next door is the self-contained *Tudor City*, built in Tudor style by the Fred F. French Co. Entrance is via the stairways flanking 42nd St. east of the hotel. This once-seedy area was home to the unsavory Rag Gang from whom even the police flinched, and was filled with slaughterhouses and breweries. Most of Tudor City is now owned by Harry Helmsley, of hotel fame. Walk down the steps to the right of *La Bibliotheque*, and notice the verse from *Isaiah* carved into the wall. At the base of the stairs is Ralph J. Bunche Park, named in honor of the first black UN official and winner of the 1950 Nobel Peace Prize. *Peace Form One*, the aluminum sculpture, is by Daniel La Rue Johnson.

The Mobil Building

The **United Nations Headquarters** – international territory outside US jurisdiction, donated by John D. Rockefeller, Jr. – resides across 1st Ave., with the visitors' entrance up the stairs opposite 46th St. You may tour the buildings only in an escorted group. No children under age 5; children ages 5-12 must be accompanied by an adult. Photography is permitted. Tickets are available at the ticket booth past the information booth. Admission charge. Tours last 45-60 minutes and depart every 30 minutes daily from 9:15am-4:45pm. Tel. 963-1234.

Inquire about free first-come/first-served tickets to the **General Assembly** meetings at Tel. 963-7113. The Assembly convenes irregularly between Sept.-Dec. according to world events; the *NY Times* prints each day's agenda. The complex includes a duty-free gift shop, book shop and

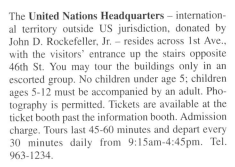

coffee shop, as well as the *Delegates' Dining Room*, where you too are welcome to lunch.

Outside, observe the world-famous configuration of the **UN Complex**. The 544 ft. (nearly 166 m), glass-steel slab, NYC's first such skyscraper, is the **Secretariat Building**. The low building with flared walls is the **Conference Building**, where the General Assembly meets. To the north is the lush **Public Garden**. To the east, beyond the Dag Hammarskjold Flagpole, is an unobstructed view across the East River to Long Island City in Queens. Walk through the sculpture garden toward the river. The promenade on which you stand runs above FDR Drive, which was built after World War II on rubble from bombed-out London and Bristol, England. The rubble had served as ballast for returning American cargo ships. Turn around, face west and behold the drama of the modern sky-scrapers rising above the park's trees. The mirrored UN Plaza Tower on the left (with the *UN Plaza Hotel* inside) and the slant-roofed Citicorp Building on the right, bracket the view.

The buildings of the United Nations Headquarters

Cross 1st Ave. The low building of horizontal terraces at 333 E 47th St. is **Japan Society House**, home of the Japan Society, devoted primarily to increasing understanding between Japan and America. Visit the gallery with its traditional and contemporary Japanese art or attend a film in the *Film Center* which has several screenings each week. The gallery is open Tues.-Sun. 11am-5pm. Art and documentary film – Fri. and Sat. at 6:30pm. Suggested contribution. Tel. 752-0824. For African art, there's the *African-American Institute Gallery* at 833 United Nations Plaza, 1st Ave. at 47th St., open Mon.-Fri. 9am-5pm, Sat. 11am-5pm. No admission charge. Tel. 350-2900.

Turn east on 49th St. and north onto Beekman Place, one of the most placid, removed and exclusive of the city's residential areas.

The lovely **Greenacre Park** is between 2nd and 3rd aves. Enjoy the granite-walled waterfall and fountains without having to pay a penny. Your tranquillity will be broken only by the rush of the water. The park is open and lit on summer evenings and there's also a snack bar.

The **General Electric Building**, built 1931, at the southwest corner of 51st St. and Lexington Ave. was designed as the RCA Building by Cross & Cross, who thoughtfully used the same materials that make up the low-lying St. Bartholomew's Church around the corner at 51st and Park. The quivering lines above the street-level windows and doors represent the vibrating *Victrola needles* of RCA Victor.

A statue with a message at the United Nations Headquarters

Walking south on Lexington Ave., pause for a moment at **Halloran House** on the corner of 49th St. Built as the *Shelton Hotel* in 1924, this Arthur Loomis Harmon creation is noted for its unconventional setback tower, a product of the zoning regulations enacted in 1916 after the Equitable Building (in lower Manhattan) sparked a "light-and-air" frenzy.

Three architectural curiosities await you on 3rd Ave. At the northwest corner of 48th St. is an office tower with windows arranged in a diamond pattern. Across the way at 767 3rd Ave. is a whimsy of artist Pamela Walters: huge metal footprints over the sidewalk gratings and a chessboard on the wall next to 767's Plaza. A block south at 47th St., 747 3rd Ave., are some brick hills embedded with benches, also Ms. Walters's handiwork.

Walk west to Park Ave. and face south. The view is of the **Helmsley Building**, built in 1929 after a Warren & Wetmore design, and re-gilded, with the MetLife Building (previously called the Pan Am Building) rising directly behind it. The car viaduct from Park Ave. South circles Grand Central at 42nd St. and exits through the Helmsley at 46th St. Walk through the pedestrian passages to 45th St. and the MetLife Building.

The **MetLife Building**, home office of the *Metropolitan Life Insurance Company*, was designed by Emery Roth & Sons, Walter Gropius and Pietro

The Helmsley Building with its gold-colored ornamentations

Belluschi, and was seve-rely criticized when built in 1963 for completely obstructing the view down Park Ave. At the same time, the dark curtain it drapes behind the Helmsley Building adds drama to the Helmsley's crown. The *Eastern Newsstand* on the east-concourse level of the MetLife Building, is arguably New York's largest, best-stocked business of its type, carrying three dozen foreign newspapers and some 3,000 different magazine titles.

Heading north on Park Ave., we come upon the famous twin-towered *Waldorf-Astoria Hotel*, established in 1931, at 50th St.

St. Bartholomew's Episcopal Church built in Byzantine style, with the General Electric Building towering over it

Across from the Waldorf is St. Bartholomew's Episcopal Church, built in 1919 in Byzantine style. Its front garden, the last breath of fresh air on Park Ave. became the focus of dispute in 1981 when church officials unveiled their plan to sell it to a developer, at a tremendous profit, for an office tower. The 1981 design envisioned a reflective-glass tower sure to clash with the church, unlike, for example, the new building at 560 Lexington Ave., or the General Electric Building at 51st St. and Lexington Ave., specifically built with materials similar to St. Bart's. Paul Goldberger, the NY Times' Pulitzer Prize-winning architecture critic, cited the GE Building as a textbook lesson in subtle juxta-position of a skyscraper to a low religious structure. A more recent design calls for masonry.

Walk west on 50th St. to Madison Ave. and pause at the wonderful Italianate brown-stone mansions at 451-455 Madison. These are the *Villard Houses*, designed by McKim, Mead & White for railroad tycoon Henry Villard and built in 1884. The urbane, elegant U-shaped group, one of NYC's greatest landmarks, now serves as the entrance to the *New York Palace Hotel*. The complex's south wing exhibits some of the most extravagant rooms of any NYC hotel: John La Farge murals, a St. Gaudens wall clock, Tiffany glass panels and a Maitland Armstrong mosaic ceiling. Most famous is the Gold Room, with its 30 ft. (approx. 9 m) ceiling. Enjoy afternoon tea 2:30-5:30pm daily, accompanied by a harpist. The sprouting *New York Palace Hotel* tower is an ugly addition to the exterior. Tel. 924-5221.

The United Nations Headquarters

The East 50s – Designer Skyscrapers

The East 50s are a showcase for modern architecture. Aside from the sheer abundance of commercial and residential skyscrapers, this neighborhood is the site of two pioneers in glass-and-steel construction: Lever House and the Seagram Building. Bracketing Park Ave., they remain two of the most original and visually striking buildings in the urban landscape. Only blocks away is an example of how far innovative architects have subsequently taken us: the remarkable Sony Building.

The façades of the buildings in this neighborhood conceal endless shopping territory, and of special importance is interior design: the **Decorator and Design Building**, 979 3rd Ave., has just about anything you might want for your home under one roof. Without leaving the neighborhood, you may visit any number of small showrooms, one of NY's largest art and antique auction houses, *Christie's* (*Sotheby's*, the other important auction house, is at 1334 York Ave.) and world-famous *Bloomingdale's*.

The world-famous Bloomingdale's

Bloomingdale's is where we begin: Take Subway 5, or 6 to 59th St., or R or N to Lexington Ave. Depending upon the effect *Bloomie's* has on you, the tour can last from several hours to the better part of a day. Allow yourself at least two hours.

Bloomingdale's claims, and correctly so, to be "like no other store in the world." It occupies the square block bordered by Lexington Ave. and 3rd Ave., 59th to 60th Sts. Enter on Lexington Ave., and notice the art deco façade, part of a 1930 addition to the store.

This is American retail marketing at its finest: floor after floor of newest-fashion clothing, glassware, furniture, artwork, appliances, electronics, kitchenware, bedding, gourmet foods, cosmetics and much, much more.

Bloomingdale's is open 10am-9pm Mon. and Thurs., 10am-6pm, Tues., Wed., Fri. and Sat. and Sun. noon to 6pm. Generally, the store is open until 9pm every night during the Christmas season, Tel. 705-2000.

Christie's, the world-famous auction house, maintains one of its NYC facilities at 502 Park Ave., on the northwest corner of Park and 59th St. Established in London in 1776, *Christie's* is the world's

*Bloomingdale's –
a shoppers' heaven*

oldest firm of fine art auctioneers. View furniture, decorative objects, etc., prior to auctions, free of charge, Mon.-Sat. 10am-5pm, Sun. 1pm-5pm, Tel. 546-1000. For future showings, sign up for *Christie's* mailing list by writing to Christie's Catalogue Dept., NYT, 21-24 44th Ave., LIC, NY, 11101.

Continue south on Park Ave. and pause at the **Ritz Tower** between 57th and 58th Sts., which was designed by Emery Roth. Though the name Emery Roth & Sons has come to signify glass-and-steel towers (the firm has designed more than 100 such buildings in Manhattan since World War II), Mr. Roth himself specialized in masonry buildings embellished with Renaissance detail.

The luxury *Drake Swissotel* stands at Park Ave. and 56th St., Tel. 421-0900, with the shop of shoe designers *Susan Bennis/Warren Edwards* on ground level: top-quality leather, avant-garde design, high prices. Across the way is the *Mercedes Benz Showroom*, designed by master architect Frank Lloyd Wright and built in 1955, Tel. 629-1666.

If you are considering an evening in this area, **Carnegie Hall** at 57th St. and 7th Ave., is one possibility: same-day tickets are sometimes available. Call Tel. 247-7800 for program and ticket information; (see "57th St." section). **City Center**, home to the *Alvin Ailey Dance Co.* also offers dance performances and occasional musical revues, Tel. 581-7907.

The **IBM Building**, a polished, green granite, triangular edifice, stands at 56th St. and Madison Ave. and, minus a ground-level corner at 57th St., appears to be pirouetting. Enter the **IBM Atrium** and notice the Michael Helzer sculpture, a dynamic, rough-sided granite chunk with right angles carved into its smooth surface and a rushing stream underneath. The atrium, a public space, is forested with bamboo, furnished with tables and chairs and equipped with a refreshment stand. Open Mon.-Fri. Free midday concerts are often performed here.

One block south is the magnificent **Sony Building** (previously the AT&T Building), perhaps the most controversial architectural design of its time, a dramatic step away from the unornamented glass-and-steel boxes of modernism, and the first post-modern corporate skyscraper. The base rises on tall rose-granite columns, forming an open colonnade. The center arch is 110 ft. (approx. 33m high). The crowning glory, and root of much of the controversy, is an unusual Chippendale roof. Inside the lobby stands the gleaming, re-gilded statue of *Golden Boy* (24 ft., 7.3 m tall with a 12 ft., 3.7 m wing-span) which crowned the old AT&T headquarters in lower Manhattan for many years. Take the elevator to the Sky Lobby, 77 ft. (23.5 m) above ground level. The entire building rises 648 ft. (197.5 m). This contribution to the skyline, designed by Philip Johnson and Guy Burgee, was completed in 1983. Don't miss the interesting exhibition inside (admission free). The building also houses the celebrated *Quilted Giraffe* restaurant; opulent interior, new-American cuisine – stressing fresh ingredients and simple preparation. Fixed-price menu, extremely expensive.

The IBM Building at 56th St. and Madison Avenue

Keep south and continue towards 53rd St. Follow 53rd St. east to Park Ave. for a look at two of the most important buildings in modern architecture: **Lever House**, built in 1952, was the second glass and steel skyscraper in NYC (the UN Secretariat was the first). It has been designated a city landmark, a crucial decision as to its survival, because today's zoning laws would allow a much larger building to stand here. Designed by Skidmore, Owings & Merrill, Lever House was the first such structure on Park Ave. and its revolutionary design was purposely kept small so as not to shock the neighborhood. Its ground-level columns are recessed, giving the illusion that the horizontal and vertical blocks are floating. Changing art exhibits are shown in the lobby. Admission free. The **Seagram Building** built in 1958, across the street at 375 Park Ave., was designed not to float but rather to meet the earth firmly and rise forcefully from its emphatically unembellished plaza. This Mies van der Rohe masterpiece was a great popular success – so successful, in fact, that zoning laws were changed in 1961 to encourage the genre. Unfortunately, few of the glass-and-steel slabs that consequently lined Midtown's streets truly equalled the quality and sleek beauty of the original.

The atrium at the IBM Building

Follow Park Ave. south to 52nd St. for the **Park Avenue Plaza** with its waterfall, cafés, shops and afternoon chess players practising their skills.

At 99 E 52nd St., between Park and Lexington

At the Park Avenue Plaza

Aves., is one of the city's favorite dining spots: the handsome, spacious *Four Seasons*. Here the New York elite enjoy cuisine, interior flora and accessories which change with the season. Tel. 754-9494. Choose between the *Grill Room* and the *Pool Room*.

Turn north on 3rd Ave. and proceed to 54th St. Note the slant-roofed **Citicorp Center** (1977) with the aluminium facade. Within is **The Market**, a three-story atrium lined with shops and restaurants. Don't miss *Conran's* simple, classic, moderately-priced housewares; equipped with tables and chairs surrounding a stage area. On the bill here are free concerts Mon.-Fri. 6pm, Sat. 8pm, Sun. noon, and children's entertainment, Sat. 11am. Tel. 677-3585.

Follow 54th St. west to Lexington Ave. **Saint Peter's Church**, on the corner, is a cultural as well as religious landmark, the chapel's walls graced with works by sculptor Louise Nevelson. Theatrical performances and concerts of first rate are held at the church. For information call Tel. 534-5366.

Head north on Lexington Ave. to 55th st. At the southwest corner is another religious edifice, the **Central Synagogue**, a Moorish Revival temple designed by Henry Fernbach and the oldest such building (1872) in continuous use in NYC.

Returning to Lexington Ave., you may want to note the 24-hour *Rialto Florist* at No. 707, Tel. 688-3234.

On the corner of 2nd Ave. is the **Manhattan Art and Antiques Center**, the largest of its type in town: 104 galleries and shops stocked with quality antiques, furniture and jewelry. Open Mon.-Sat. 10:30am-6:00pm, Sun. noon-6pm, Tel. 355-4400.

As for entertainment, the area of 58th St. and 3rd Ave. offers no fewer than seven movie theaters:

Cinema 1 and 2, Baronet, Coronet, D.W. Griffith, Manhattan 1 and 2, Sutton and Gotham. City Center and Carnegie Hall, too, are close at hand. *Michael's Pub*, 211 E 55th St., is a great little cabaret showcase for famous pop singers. Minimum, but no cover charge, Tel. 758-2272.

EXCURSIONS

The tram station to **Roosevelt Island** is located on 2nd Ave., at the top of the stairway between 59th and 60th Sts. The fare is a subway token, purchasable here or at any token booth. The ride, though short, provides a spectacular view. Take a free bus ride around the island or enjoy the Midtown Manhattan skyline from a park bench. The tram shuts down late at night so check the timetable.

Lapping up the sun on Park Avenue

UPPER EAST SIDE – INTRODUCTION

The Upper East Side stretches roughly from 60th-96th Sts. and from 5th Ave. to the East River. Almost entirely residential – though not homogeneous – its reputation conjures an image of conservative, respectable old-money wealth, a place where the gentry stroll on sunny days. This is true in part, harking back to the turn of the century when the 60s and 70s closest to Central Park were colonized by the city's wealthiest residents. With industry claiming more of the downtown around the time when the Park opened (1873), the NY upper class relocated to the serenity of the pasture land facing the park, to build mansions and elegant town houses. Most town houses between 5th and Park Aves. date from 1900-1920. Today, the area between 60th-79th Sts. and 5th and Lexington Aves. is an official historical district, not because each house is important or unusual in itself but because together they form a harmonious neighborhood. This is the area which confirms and consolidates the Upper East Side's reputation for wealthy serenity.

East of Lexington Ave., however – with the exception of East End Ave. and Gracie Square – the streets become less suggestive of wealth. The first village on the Upper East Side, Yorkville (1790) from 3rd Ave. to the East River and from 79th northward, was a farming and country estate village for a century before becoming an ethnic (mostly German immigrant) quarter. The Central European ambience survives to this day in the neighborhood's restaurants and shops.

South of 79th St., the same section sprouts luxury high-rise apartment buildings whose tenants tend to be younger and wealthier than those of Yorkville. Street commerce reflects the difference, with an abundance of singles bars, gourmet take-out food shops and fine restaurants. As more "Yuppies" (Young Urban Professionals) seek Manhattan housing, Yorkville has been losing its distinction as a neighborhood to the more fashionable "Upper East Side" designation.

Park Ave. remains a stretch of wealthy residences and hotels dotted with churches. Fifth Ave. is **Museum Mile**: the Metropolitan Museum of Art at 82nd St., the Museum of the City of NY at 104th St., and many others in between. Madison Ave. is axis of the historic district and the area's shopping boulevard, lined with designer boutiques and important art galleries. We begin our visit at the northern end of this promenade.

Upper East Side – a view from above

Madison Avenue – Old Money, New Fashions

It's "Never on Sunday" for Madison Ave., when most shops are closed. On a Saturday morning and/or afternoon, by contrast, you are likely to share a pleasurable day with shoppers of all ages, most of them well-dressed. You may want to detour west to 5th Ave. and visit a museum or two (see "Museum Mile").

Take Subway 4, 5 or 6 to 96th St.; head west, crossing Park Ave. to Madison Ave. and walk south from 96th St.; the first thing you will notice is a castle-like rampart on the east side of Madison from 96th to 94th: a remnant of the Squadron A Armory and now the rear wall of Hunter High School playground.

Let's begin shopping. West on 93rd St. at No. 29 is the Military Bookman, with a wide range of reading matter relative to the military, navy and aviation. It is open Tues.-Sat. 10:30am-5:30pm. South on Madison at 89th St. is The Glass Store, where beautiful blown glass objects are yours for the picking. Continuing south, notice the golden Minnesota limestone of the **Park Avenue Synagogue** extension, at Madison and 87th, designed by James Jarrett to blend in with the dignity of the neighborhood. The structure commemorates Jewish children who perished in the Holocaust.

Still further south we come to *The Soldier Shop* at 1222 Madison Ave., with its regiments of toy soldiers. Pause at the tiny *Butter Cake Square Bakeshop* for mouth-watering sweets, baked with 45 years of experience. *Gem Antiques*, 1088 Madison Ave., displays beautifully intricate glass paperweights.

Eeyore's, 25 83rd St., is a wonderful children's bookstore. The **NY Society Library**, NY's oldest (1745), resides at 53 E 79th St. off Madison, Tel. 288-6900.

Some interesting art Galleries are located at E 79th St. Among them *Lafayette Parke*, at No. 58, with its European and American paintings, Tel.

517-5500. The *Soufer Gallery* at 1015 Madison Ave., holds an interesting sculpture exhibition, Tel. 628-3225. *Aquavella*, 18 E 79th St., covers the Impressionist through the Contemporary periods. Open Mon.-Fri. 9:30am-5:30pm, Tel. 734-6300. Turn south at 5th Ave. for more art: the **French Embassy's Cultural Headquarters**, 972 5th Ave., occasionally offers art exhibits in the gallery just inside the iron doorway. The gallery is gorgeous in its own right: marble columns and floor, a round ceiling painted in lattice work entwined with vines and cherubs, Tel. 439-1400.

At the northeast corner of 5th Ave. and 78th St. is the James Duke House (1912), modelled by Architect H. Trumbauer after the Hotel la Bottiere in Bordeaux, France and now home of the **NYU Institute of Fine Arts**. Continue east on 78th St. for additional

Upper East Side

specimens of East Side architecture: the chrome-facade of the **Morris and Ida Newman Educational Center** at No. 60. Oddly out of place in this stretch of town houses, its irregular window shapes – curves, arches, slants, curls – add some whimsy to the street. The town house at No. 120, with its lovely white alcoved entry and curved stairway, presents a different kind of facade which nonetheless blends quite well with its neighbors.

Return to Madison Ave. The imposing brown-grey Marcel Breuer structure at 75th St. and Madison Ave., with its surrounding sunken sculpture garden, houses the **Whitney Museum of American Art**. Inside you will find contemporary masters on permanent exhibit, plus visiting displays of avant-garde works and experimental video exhibits often presented upstairs Tel. 570-3676. A lovely little café opens onto the sculpture garden. Open Wed. 11am-6pm, Thurs. 1pm-8pm; Fri.-Sun. 11am-6pm; closed Mon. and Tues. Admission charge, no admission for children under 12 years. Tel. 570-3600.

Continuing south on Madison Ave., we come upon an area devoted to European designer boutiques; the first to open was *Yves Saint Laurent* in 1968; others soon followed. The customers, too, are as often European as American, since the elegant

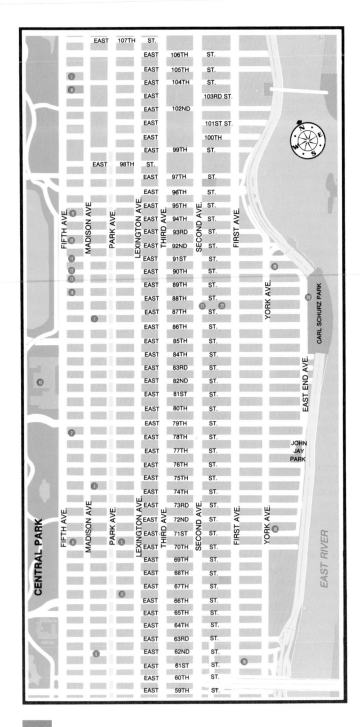

own houses on either side of Madison Ave. are home to many foreign embassies. The *Givenchy Boutique* is at Madison Ave. at 75th St., diagonally across from the Whitney Museum. *Chocolate Soup i*s at 946 Madison Ave., with its selection of children's clothing. *Fusen Usagi* is at 927 Madison Ave., with an extensive line of Japanese-designed children's clothing.

Further south on Madison Ave. is the beautifully ornate chateau, at the corner of 72nd St. The **Chateau** (1898) was once the home of NYC Police Commissioner Rhinelander Waldo, a character fictionalized and portrayed by James Cagney in the film version of E. L. Doctorow's *Ragtime*. Turn west on 72nd St. No. 9 is the **Lycée Français de New York**, designed by Carrere & Hastings, also architects of the NYC Public Library.

Return to Madison Ave., continue south and polish your French for the shopping to come: *Manon Chocolatier*, 872 Madison Ave., sells candies too beautiful to eat and too scrumptious not to. *Le Monde des Enfants*, 870 Madison Ave., offers French designer clothing for boys and girls, and *Saint Laurent Rive Gauche a*t 855 Madison Ave., grand-daddy of European boutiques, shows the French designer's ready-to-wear line for women.

A right turn onto 70th St., whose corner is enlivened by the jewels of *Cartier*, and the designs of *Mitsuhiro Matsuda*, brings us to several prime aesthetic diversions. We start at the *Knoedler*

UPPER EAST SIDE

Gallery (1846), 19 E 70th St., one of the major galleries in the area, Tel. 794-0550, and its neighbor *Hirschl and Adler*, Tel. 535-8810. Both galleries are closed Sun. and Mon.

At the corner of 5th Ave. is the **Frick Collection**, possibly the best-loved of all the city's museums and an absolute "must." Built in 1914 by a Carrere & Hastings design, the museum houses the private collection of Henry Clay Frick, chairman of Carnegie (the nucleus for *US Steel*, the first billion dollar company in the US), who was blessed by good taste as well as a lot of money. The collection contains many beautiful pictures, statues and artifacts. Open Tues.-Sat. 10am-6pm, Sun. 1-6pm, closed Mon. Admission charge. Children not admitted. Tel. 288-0700.

Returning to Madison Ave., you may want to continue east to Park Ave. for the **Asia Society**, 725 Park Ave., Tel. 288-6400. A large collection of Asian art, visiting exhibits and a well-stocked shop devoted to reading matter on Asia are here. The Rockefeller family, not the admission charge, keeps the Asia Society going.

Follow 69th St. back to Madison Ave. An expensive lunch or dinner is yours at the club-like, masculine *Polo Bar and Restaurant* in the *Westbury Hotel* on Madison Ave. just north of 69th St. It has been called the best hotel dining room in the city. The cuisine is classical-nouvelle. Open daily, Tel. 570-5590.

The Frick Collection – an absolute "must"

Back on Madison, we find some boutiques of world famous designers, names like *Kenzo* from Japan and *Armani* from Italy.

Again, a pause for art at the new **Center for African Art** in the cozy town house at 54 E 68th St. (admission charge, Tel. 966-1313); and the **Spanish Institute**, in the neo-Federal house farther east, at 684 Park Ave. (just north of 68th St., Tel. 628-0420). There are frequent exhibits of Spanish art and culture.

67th St. is a junior-grade Embassy Row; the Resident Consul of Japan at No. 4, Permanent Mission of the Czech Republic at No. 6 and Permanent Mission of Peru at No. 45 are only three examples. The **Park East Synagogue** at 163 E 67th St., (1890), houses Congregation Zichron Ephraim, consisting primarily of ex-Soviet Jews. The nearby intersection of 3rd Ave. and 67th St. is named "Sakharov/Bonner Corner" in honor of these notable Soviet dissidents.

Return to Madison Ave. *Chardon Chocolates of Switzerland* is at 24 E 66th St., offering delectable candies and membership to the *Chocolate of the Week Club*, Tel. 517-7383. Several worthwhile institutions follow. One is the **Lotos Club** (literature and the arts), newly located in the former William J. Schiefflin residence at 5 E 66th St. The French Renaissance-style house was designed by Richard Howland Hunt and built in 1900. Ulysses S. Grant, a great Civil War General and subse-

Temple Emanu-El – home of NYC's oldest Reform Jewish Congregation

quently the ineffective 18th President of the USA., spent his last years (1881-85) in the building at 3 E 66th St. Facing death as a very poor man, he wrote a set of memoirs here which, posthumously-published, brought $450,000 in royalties to his family. Grant is entombed in a mausoleum on the Upper West Side. Heading south on 5th Ave., note the massive **Temple Emanu-El**, home of NYC's oldest Reform Jewish Congregation, at E 65th St.

East on 65th St. just west of Park Ave. is *Le Cirque*, one of NYC's most elegant and expensive restaurants. The decor is slightly garish, but the appetizers, entrées and desserts are outstanding, Tel. 794-9292. Soaring over *Le Cirque* is the deluxe **Mayfair Regent Hotel**, 610 Park Ave., Tel. 288-0800. Continue east on 65th St. to No. 125, the former Henry R. Luce town house and now the **China Institute**, which presents occasional exhibits of Chinese art. It is an apt changeover, for Luce, co-founder of *Time Inc.*, was the son of Chinese missionaries, Tel. 744-8181.

Christatos & Koster, the florists at 201 E. 64th St., established in 1900, Tel. 838-0022. Just east at 28 E 63rd St. is the *Lowell Hotel* built in 1926 and faced with glazed terra-cotta at ground level. Note the Bertram Hartman mosaic above the entry and the octagon shape, common to the art deco style, Tel. 838-1400. Down 63rd St. at No. 128 is the *Society of Illustrators*. Its occasional exhibits highlight illustrators of books, stories and advertisements, open Mon.-Sat. 10am-5pm, till 8pm on Tues, Tel. 838-1400.

A beautifully adorned window of Temple Emanu-El

Back on Madison Ave., visit *Sherry-Lehmann Wine & Spirit Merchants,* 679 Madison Ave., arguably the world's best-known wine merchant in what is now regarded as the world's wine capital. Wine prices are now set in New York, where almost any wine will be given a try, and any wine that is accepted here, will be accepted everywhere. Sherry-Lehmann is indeed a king, with an all-inclusive catalogue, Tel. 838-7500.

Head west on 62nd St. to 5th Ave., noting the *Schiller-Wapner Gallery*; original book illustrations, Tel. 832-8231, and *Justin G. Schiller Ltd.*, vintage children's books, on the northeast corner. The telephone number is the same for both. The southeast corner belongs to the ultra-luxurious *Hotel Pierre* on 730 5th Ave., with world-renowned *Bulgari Jewelers* at ground level, Tel. 315-9000.

Walking south on 5th Ave., note the lovely *Sherry-Netherland Hotel* at No. 781 5th Ave., at the corner of Central Park.

The first building you will notice east on 60th St. is the *Metropolitan Club*, designed by McKim, Mead & White and built in 1893 for J.P. Morgan and cohorts, who were shunned by the more established clubs. When the great economic crash of that year bankrupted most of the country's largest railroads, Morgan came to their aid, accumulated massive clout and financed the merger resulting in *US Steel*. The "outcast", in short, wound up controlling much of the US economy.

Inside the Whitney Museum

82nd-104th Sts. — Museum Mile

We shall approach Museum Mile, along 5th Ave., from the north. Take Subway 4, 5 or 6 to 96th St. and follow 96th St. to 5th Ave. The best strategy is to forgo any idea of covering all the museums or every exhibit in any single museum. Check offerings, take in one or two per day and spend a couple of hours in each. Combine your museum visits with some Madison Ave. window-shopping and various culinary experiences. Note that most museums are closed Mon. and that several don't charge admission on Tues. from 5-8pm.

Several museums and cultural institutions lie north of 96th St. We will begin with these.

El Museo del Barrio, 1230 5th Ave. and 104th St., is devoted to Latin American, especially Puerto Rican, fine and performance art. The permanent collection includes pre-Columbian works. Open Wed.-Sun. 11am-5pm, Tel. 831-7272.

The *Heckscher Theater*, Tel. 534-2804 and the *AMAS Rep.*, Tel. 369-8000, just around the corner at 1 E 104th St., concentrate on the development of contemporary black musicals.

Inside the Metropolitan Museum of Art

The **Museum of the City of New York**, the red brick edifice on 5th Ave. and 103rd St., abounds in children's programs, among them puppet shows (Sat. 1:30pm), educational programs (Sun. 2:30pm), and "Please Touch" demonstrations (Sat. afternoon), where children are encouraged to handle antiques in a reproduced 17th-century Dutch room. There is no admission charge to the museum itself, only to the special programs. Open Wed.-Sat. 10am-5pm, Sun. and holidays 1-5pm, Tel. 534-1672. Subway 6 to 86th St.

Retracing our steps, we cross 96th St. and come to the **International Center of Photography**, 1130 5th Ave. at 94th St. The institution features an interesting exhibit for the photography enthusiast. A gift shop sells posters. Open Tues.-Sun. 11am-5pm. Admission charge. Tel. 860-1777.

The **Jewish Museum**, 1109 5th Ave. at 92nd St., is the largest such institution in the country. The upper levels house the permanent collection; the first floor is reserved for visiting exhibits, e.g., *The Jewish Heritage in American Folk Art*, including a walrus tusk from Nome, Alaska inscribed with Jewish New Year greetings. The new and abundant National Jewish Archive of Broadcasting gives public screenings. Special presentations and performances are offered throughout the museum during *Hanukkah*, the Festival of Lights. Open Sun. 11am-6pm, Mon., Wed., Thurs. 11am-5:45pm; Tues. 11am-8pm. Admission charge. Closed Fri., Sat., Tel. 423-3200.

The **Cooper-Hewitt Museum**, just off 5th Ave. at 2 E 91st St., resides in a mansion commissioned by Andrew Carnegie in 1901. Carnegie, known for his disdain of inherited privilege, independently developed a huge steel empire and is renowned as a generous philanthropist who believed in distributing his wealth during his lifetime.

The Jewish Museum, which is the largest museum of its kind in the United States

Designed by Babb, Cook & Willard, the house cost $1.5 million to build. Cooper-Hewitt is now home to the **Smithsonian Institution's National Museum of Design** (1906). The glassed-in conservatory where Mrs. Carnegie kept her plants during the winter is only one of the many lovely rooms inside. The art collection includes priceless ancient textiles and a wealth of architectural books and drawings. Note the rear gardens at 90th St. as you continue south on 5th Ave. Open Tues. 10am-9pm, Wed.-Sat. 10am-5pm, Sun. noon-5pm; closed Mon., New Year's Day, July 4th, Thanksgiving and Christmas. Admission charge. Tues. free 5-9pm, Tel. 860-6868.

Two good choices for lunch are located one block east: *Jackson Hole*, Madison and 91st St., offering excellent, inexpensive hamburgers, Tel. 427-2820, and the attractive *Summerhouse* at 50 E 86th St. with an affordable, limited menu that changes weekly, Tel. 289-9338.

Return to 5th Ave. and pause at the southeast corner of 90th St. The **Church of the Heavenly Rest**, 2 E 90th St., hosts the *Heavenly Jazz Series* and its heavyweight performers from the jazz world. Admission charge. Discounts for students and seniors, Tel. 369-8040. Here, too, is the *York*

*Outside the
Guggenheim Museum*

Theater Company, which specializes in revivals (Tel. 534-5366).

Follow 90th St. east to No. 15, the **Trevor House**. Built by Mott B. Schmidt in 1926, this house illustrates the popular architect's commitment to a balanced design with the door as centerpiece. The small residence features a Corinthian portico fronting a pedimented window; the facade is simple, delicate, yet strong. Other examples of Schmidt's work are found on Sutton Place (see "East 50s") and at 124 and 130 E 80th St.

Return to 5th Ave. The **National Academy of Design**, 1083 5th Ave. at 89th St., claims to be the first art gallery in NYC. Founded by inventor Samuel F. B. Morse, it originally opened near City Hall in 1825, moving to its present location in 1940. Both American and European works are shown. Open Wed.-Sun. noon-5pm, Tues. noon-8pm, tel. 369-4880.

Just east at 9 E 89th St. is **New York Roadrunners Club**, the place to register for major running events including the NYC Marathon and the race up the steps of the Empire State Building, Tel. 860-4455.

The unmistakable conical form of Frank Lloyd Wright's world-famous **Guggenheim Museum** (1959) unfolds between 88th and 89th Sts. Inside is a widening spiral of curved walls and ramps lined with exhibits. Take the elevator to the top floor.

*An exhibit at the
Metropolitan Museum
of Art*

Wind your way down, passing the sculptures and paintings exhibited. Permanent exhibits of modern art include works by Chagall, Klees, Delaunay and others. On the fourth floor find a display of over 20 pioneer abstractionists. On the second floor the Thannhauser Wing houses significant works of the past 100 years. Impressionist artists are represented by Renoir and some of Cezanne. Picasso's creations are also exhibited. Open Sun.-Wed. 10am-6pm; Fri., Sat. 10am-8pm. Closed Thurs. Admission charge, free for children under 12. Tel. 423-3500.

Glance eastward at 84th St. to No. 3, an art deco apartment house designed by Raymond Hood (responsible for the Daily News Building, the original

McGraw-Hill Building and much of Rockefeller Center) and built in 1928.

Goethe House, the German Cultural Center with a library, film hall and gallery, is located at 1014 5th Ave. at 82nd St. Open Tues. and Thurs. 11am-7pm, Wed., Fri. and Sat. noon-5pm. Admission free, Tel. 439-8700.

Directly across the street, embraced by Central Park, is the splendor of the **Metropolitan Museum of Art**. One of the most famous and largest museums in the world, the Metropolitan is a "must." Open Tues.-Thurs. and Sun. 9:30am-5:15pm; Fri.-Sat. 9:30am-8:45pm. Closed Wed. Tel. 879-5500. Subway 4, 5, 6 to 86th St. Note that besides the gift shop at the entrance, there is another shop specializing in beautiful reproduction posters. Ask for directions. The central block was designed by Richard M. Hunt in 1902, the north and south wings by McKim, Mead & White in 1908. Its permanent collection of more than three

The Guggenheim Museum

million items, recognized as one of the world's finest, is devoted in large part to Egyptian, Greek and Roman civilizations and still finds room for the most comprehensive compilation anywhere of American art, as well as European art from the Middle Ages to the present. Don't miss the Astor Chinese Garden Court, the Sackler Gallery (the newest addition) which houses the Far East collection, and the Costume Institute where former *Vogue* editor Diana Vreeland presents colorful,

imaginative displays of clothing designs throughout the ages.

The Metropolitan offers a wonderful series of
Young People's programs – different themes every
weekend (e.g., gallery talks, workshops, films, or
gallery hunts) for families with children ages 5-12.
Sessions begin at the **Uris Center for Education**,
with a separate museum entrance at 5th Ave. and
81st St. Suggested contribution. Admission to the
program allows you into the rest of the museum.

*The Metropolitan
Museum of Art – one
of the most famous and
largest museums in the
world*

East of the Park, 59th-79th Sts. – Fine Dining

We've reached the Upper East Side, the section below Yorkville and east of Park Ave. With its abundance of fine restaurants and ample selection of popular nightclubs, it's a good place to spend the evening after a day of museums, Madison Ave. boutiques and/or *Bloomingdale's*. The neighborhood also offers the shops along Lexington and 3rd aves. as a daylight diversion. Take Subway 4, 5, or 6 to 59th St. or R or N to Lexington Ave. and walk east on 60th St. to 3rd Ave.

For brunch, try *Yellowfingers* on 60th St. and 3rd Ave., Tel. 751-8615; recommended for people-watching. The rest of 60th St. between 3rd and 2nd Aves. is a cornucopia of small clothing boutiques, a junior league Madison Ave. Some of the names here include *Yves St. Tropez*, at 4 W 57th St., Tel. 765-5667, and the wild designs of *Betsey Johnson*, No. 251, Tel. 319-7699. The one "must" here is *Serendipity 3*, 225 E 60th St., a great little restaurant/boutique: buttons, dolls, souvenirs and jewellry up front, decent chilli and frozen moccaccino, served in a huge sundae glass, upstairs at the back, Tel. 838-3531.

Follow 60th St. eastward to *Tucano*, an expensive French restaurant at No. 333, Tel. 947-4090, and neighboring *Club A*, a private nightclub whose members are wealthy, famous or both. *Terrestris*, 409 E 60th, is the best place to shop for healthy, indoor jungle plants and trees, some at reasonable prices, Tel. 758-8181.

Walk north to 61st St. and turn west. No. 421 is the **Abigail Adams Smith Museum**, built on a site once owned by the daughter of John Quincy Adams (6th US President), though it was never her home. *The Colonial Dames of America* purchased and restored the house, filling it with period furnishings and details as if Abigail truly lived here. The house, facing warehouses and a parking lot, sits in an unusual spot of greenery. Open Mon.-Fri. noon-4pm, Sun. 1-5pm. Admission charge. Free for children under 13. Tel. 838-6878.

Next door is *Carriage House Motor Cars Ltd.*, a showroom of fine British cars. The largest fac-

Dining out in a cosy atmosphere

tory authorized dealership for Rolls-Royce and Bentley in the world, Tel. 688-4650. The *Vertical Club*, across the street at No. 330, Tel. 355-5100, is a trendy health club where the neighborhood's "beautiful people" come to work out and "hook up" with each other. Continue west. *Bowery Lighting*, at 148 Bowery, Tel. 941-8244, and *Light Inc.*, 1162 2nd Ave. and 61st St., Tel. 838-1130, are the two lighting shops most frequented by the city's interior designers.

Follow 61st west to Lexington and turn north. The *Antique Doll Hospital of New York*, 787 Lexington, stocks wigs and other replacement parts, restores antique dolls and appraises your pre-Barbie beauties, Tel. 838-7527.

Continue north, on Lexington Ave. the beautiful brick edifice at Lexington and 140 E 63rd (note the corner setbacks) is the excellent, relatively low-priced *Barbizon Hotel*, Tel. 838-5700. *Bravo Gianni* restaurant, east on 63rd at No. 230, is Italian, handsome, delicious and expensive, Tel. 752-7272.

Having a good time at one of the many places to hang out in the city

Pause at the corner of 65th St. A left turn takes you to *Old Denmark* at No. 133, Tel. 744-2533, a tiny shop bursting with spices, cookies and candies from the Netherlands up front and equipped with a luncheonette at the back. Open from 11am-4pm.

Return to Lexington and continue north. The cavernous, fort-like **7th Regiment Armory**, running from 66th to 67th and from Lexington west to Park Ave., hosts the annual *Winter Antiques Fair*.

The complex one block north belongs to **Hunter College**, founded in 1870 for working-class women. Now the largest City University school, its enrollment still consists mostly, though not exclusively, of women. Check its schedule of events; some are of public interest, Tel. 452-7000.

Note the apartment building at 210 E 68th St. and 3rd Ave. Designed by George and Edward Blum, this otherwise nondescript structure is adorned with an art deco band of terra-cotta ornamentation. The *68th St. Playhouse*, 68th St. and 1164 3rd Ave., generally presents first-run, special-interest or art films, Tel. 734-0302.

Return to Lexington Ave. and continue north. *An American Place*, No. 969 at 71st St., is a restaurant with a successfully innovative menu and an expensive, fixed-price dinner, Tel. 684-2122. Retrace your steps to *Garnet Wines and Liquors*, No. 929, for some of NYC's best bargains and perhaps its widest selection, Tel. 772-3211. Notice, too, that every block on Lexington Ave. seems to sprout a florist shop.

A less expensive lunch or dinner is yours one block away at *Fay and Allen's Catch of The Sea*, a small, affordable popular café at 71st St. and 3rd Ave., Tel. 472-9666. The *Marymount Manhattan Theater*, just east at 221 E 71St., features visiting modern and experimental dance companies, Tel. 737-9611. As you walk down 71st, notice the modernized façade of No. 251, with smoked oval windows, in the row of attractive town houses.

Mezzaluna, on 1295 3rd Ave., is one of the city's hottest pizza parlors. The young, trendy diners sit packed together but do not seem to mind at all. Pizza is served only at lunch and from 10:30pm-1am, Tel. 535-9600. *Jim McMullen's*, 1341 3rd Ave., north of 76th St., is a favorite lunch spot for business people, as well as a popular evening spot for well-heeled singles and local professional athletes, Tel. 988-7676.

As you head east on 78th St., notice the eight-story house at No. 266 and the high-rise "sliver" looming above. Land values in Manhattan are such that builders often find it profitable to erect narrow high-rises on tiny plots such as this. New zoning restrictions enacted after this addition was built have curtailed "slivers" on the lower pattern of the side-streets.

Continue east to 1st Ave. and turn south. David Brenner, Robin Williams and Pat Benatar are only some of the famous alumni of *Catch a Rising Star*, the famed comedy cabaret at 1487 1st Ave. Week night shows continuous from 9pm, two shows Fri. and Sat., 8:30pm and midnight. Cover charge, two-drinks minimum. Reservations are highly advisable, Tel. 794-1906.

The *Foul Play* book shop specializing in mystery books is on 1465B 2nd Ave, between 76-77 Sts.

For excellent Eastern European/ Hungarian dining, your choices in this area are three: *Csarda*, 1477 2nd Ave. at 77th St. – recommended for large, hearty servings and very reasonable prices, Tel. 472-2892, the *Red Tulip*, 439 E 75th St., Tel. 650-0537, and *Ruc*, 312 E 72nd St., Tel. 650-1611. The latter has a lovely outdoor patio for warm-weather dining.

Other inexpensive dining possibilities are the tiny *Szechuan Kitchen* at 76st and 1st Ave. – spicy and delicious. On 74th St. at No. 354 you will find *Andrée's Méditerranée*, an attractive, homey restaurant serving delicious Middle Eastern food, Tel. 249-6619.

Nearby is *Chicago City Limits*, the improvisational comedy troupe offering some of the best entertainment of its kind, is at 351 E 74th St., Tel. 772-8707.

Head east to York Ave. for the fine *Sotheby's* art auction house at 1334 York Ave at 72nd St. The inventory is on public display Tues. 9:30am-7:30pm, Wed.-Sat. 9:30am-5pm. Sometimes open only by appointment Sun.-Mon., Tel. 606-7000.

Return to 1st Ave. and continue south. *Zucchini*, 1336 1st Ave. south of 72nd St., serves delicious health food in a setting replete with antiques, Tel. 249-0559. Look east at 66th for a glimpse of the entrance to **Rockefeller University**. Visit the lovely grounds during the day with the guard's permission.

Return to 1st Ave. at 66th St. and enjoy an ice cream cone at *Peppermint Park*. The rest of the walk south is all restaurants and nightclubs. A few examples: the *Manhattan Café* is a spacious, classy establishment, Tel. 888-6556; *Friday's*, in the red, white and mostly blue building at 63rd St. and 1st Ave. is a pub/restaurant popular with singles, Tel. 832-8512, and *Il Vagabondo*, 351 E 62nd St., a homey Italian restaurant more affordable than its nearby competitors, Tel. 832-9221.

At *Chippendale's*, just south at 1110 1st Ave., male dancers in skimpy bikinis perform erotic routines for appreciative audiences, open Wed.-Sat., doors open at 6:30pm; showtime at 8pm, Tel. 935-6060.

Finally, the area is home to several movie theaters with first-run offerings. They include the previously mentioned *68th St. Playhouse, Leows 1 and 2*, 2nd Ave. and 66th St., Tel. 737-2622; *Beekman*, 2nd Ave. and 62th St., Tel. 832-2720 and *Gemini 1 and 2*, 2nd Ave. and 64th St., Tel. 832-1670.

For information on movies shown in the city call Tel. 777-Film, 777-3456 – a *New York Times* service.

Yorkville – A Little Taste of Europe

Yorkville is bounded by 79th-96th Sts. and Lexington Ave. to the East River – just off Museum Mile and not far from Madison Ave. Apart from some worthwhile shopping on the avenues, a few terrific restaurants and nightclubs and the *"92nd St. Y"* with its concerts and lectures, the largely residential area has little to see during the day. Yorkville began as New York's second residential area (the first being the Lower East Side), as host to large numbers of German-Hungarian immigrants in the late 19th century. The neighborhood has retained its middle-class ethnic character ever since. The dramatic rise in land values in recent years, however, has obfuscated the boundary between Yorkville and the true "Upper East Side" to its immediate south. Since the latter is more "chic," developers of the border area are likely to ignore the Yorkville appellation. Today Yorkville's casual German, Greek and Hungarian restaurants share the scene with apartment towers and fancy Italian restaurants.

Upper East Side

A daytime visit to Yorkville begins at Subway Station 6, at 77th St. and Lexington Ave. Head north on Lexington, noting some worthwhile clothing shops, and turn west at 80th St. Notice Nos. 124 and 130, brick and stone structures respectively. Both were designed by architect Mott B. Schmidt; No. 124 for Clarence Dillon and No. 130 for Vincent Astor, son of hotel tycoon John Jacob Astor II. Vincent, who managed the family real estate business after his father's demise on the *Titanic*, favored social reform and sold much of his property to the city at a low price for the construction of housing projects.

Return to Lexington Ave. and head north. *Jenny B. Goode*, 1194 Lexington Ave. north of 81st St. is an

excellent place to pick up innovative gift housewares products, Tel. 794-2492. Across the street at 1201 Lexington Ave. is *Go Fly a Kite*: over 100 different designs for the novice or experienced kite-flyer, Tel. 472-2623. At 86th St. and Lexington Ave. is *Gimbel's Uptown*, a large branch of the Herald Square department store, Tel. 348-2300.

A special restaurant called *Luncheonette* is on 1226 Lexington, at the corner of 83rd St. Established in 1925, it caters especially for youngsters.

Northward at 1395 Lexington is the **92nd St. YM/YWHA** or the "*92nd St.* Y," a predominantly Jewish athletic and cultural center where famous authors, accomplished musicians and noted critics give a variety of concerts, readings and lectures. Box office and program schedules are available in the lobby. Every program is worthwhile and tickets are usually quite affordable, Tel. 996-1100.

Capped dummies on display

Follow 92nd St. east to 3rd Ave., noticing the wood-frame house at No. 160, unusual for Manhattan. Turn north on 3rd Ave. *Mumbles*, 1622 3rd. Ave., Tel. 427-4355, and *Ruppert's*, 1662 3rd. Ave., Tel. 831-1900, are reasonably-priced and good places to eat. Now head south on 3rd Ave., crossing 91st St. Here is *Gran Gelato*, repository of Italian ice cream, denser and richer than the American species. *Gran Gelato*, owned by an ex-lawyer who went to Italy to study the process and purchase the equipment, features music, murals and, of course, a menu which immediately transports you to Rome. For American ice cream proceed to *Agora*, a combination ice cream parlor and clothing boutique at the corner of 3rd Ave. and 87th St. Just south, at 1543 3rd Ave., is *Gotham Liquors*: wines at excellent prices.

Walk east to 2nd Ave. and head north. *Elaine's*, 1703 2nd Ave., is a favorite among entertainment celebrities. Woody Allen, for example, has his own table here. Don't come to gawk, however – the stars feel comfortable here precisely because they are not hassled by their fans. Elaine herself oversees the over-priced Italian offerings. Come

for a drink; spend your dinner money elsewhere. Tel. 534-8103.

Continuing east to York Ave., note the concrete parabolic arch known as **Asphalt Green** at 555 E 90th St. at York Ave. Designed by Kahn & Jacobs in 1944 as an asphalt plant and subsequently recycled into a community center and athletic facility, this is considered NYC's greatest piece of 20th-century industrial architecture. The arch, 90 ft. (approx. 27 m) high, houses two gymnasiums, a theater, classrooms, locker rooms, offices and the *Mazur Theater* with its drama and reading performances, some free. Tel. 206-7004.

Turn east on 88th St. Between East End Ave. and the East River are Carl Schurz Park and its main attraction, **Gracie Mansion**. Now the official residence of the Mayor of New York, the mansion, built in 1799 as the private country home of Archibald Gracie, was renovated and enlarged according to a Mott B. Schmidt design in time for the tenure of Fiorello La Guardia (1941). Tour information, Tel. 570-4751. The surrounding Carl Schurz Park, a lovely plot of greenery, offers an enjoyable view across the East River. Students and children free of charge.

Follow exclusive residential East End Ave. south to 84th St. and take 84th west to York Ave. We can recommend a casual restaurant on this corner. The small, intimate *Wilkinson's 1573 Seafood Café*, 1573 York, has a nouvelle-cuisine menu which goes beyond fish, Tel. 535-5454.

For your appetite and evening entertainment we shall complete the litany of Yorkville restaurants, theaters and clubs: At 270 W 89th St., next door to the **Church of the Holy Trinity**, in buildings donated by Serena Rhinelander, is the *Theater of the Open*

Eye. Most *Open Eye* performances, often put on by experimental dance companies, involve aspects of myth or ritual. Note the attractive grounds and the beautifully carved doorway, where saints and angels curve in ascent toward the center of the arch, Tel. 860-7244, 769-4141.

Choose among several good, reasonably-priced restaurants two blocks south on 86th St.: *Estia* at No. 308 for simple, authentic Greek food and live late-evening music, Tel. 628-9100, or *Kleine Konditorei* between 2nd and 3rd Aves., for a family restaurant with a hearty Germanic kitchen, Tel. 675-7418.

Three Italian restaurants are in this neighborhood – *Trastevere*, 309 E 83rd St., Tel. 734-6343, *Erminia*, 250 E 83rd St., Tel. 879-4284, and *Trastevere 84* (Italian glatt kosher), 155 E 84th, Tel. 744-0210, serve excellent food. They are all owned by the same family.

Informal, cozy *Mocca Hungarian* at 1588 2nd Ave., north of 82nd St., offers delicious and extremely affordable Hungarian food, Tel. 734-6470. *Red Blazer Too*, across the street at No. 1571, presents live jazz every evening, Tel. 262-3112. *The Comic Strip*, 1568 2nd Ave., is where the city's young comedians come to pay their dues and hone their routines. The continuous show begins at 9:30pm Sun.-Thurs., Sat. 9pm and midnight. Cover charge and minimum, Tel. 861-9386.

Another rather homely restaurant is *Frankie's* on 1546 2nd Ave. between 80-81 Sts. Good, cheap Italian-Greek food.

A final Yorkville entertainment stop: the *New Media Repertory Company* at 1463 3rd Ave. near 83rd St. Performances Thurs.-Sat. plus Sun. matinee. The theater is also home to the *Children's Improvisation Co.* – after midnight children's theater. For tickets and schedule, call Tel. 734-5195.

Central Park –
The Country in the City

The 843 acres of today's Central Park were home to pigsties, swamps, stone quarries and thousands of squatters until 1858. Then Frederick Law Olmstead and Calvert Vaux submitted the winning entry in a design competition for the verdant, natural-looking landscape they called *Greensward*. Yes, those gentle slopes, rocky terraces and beautiful forests look natural but they are not!

The park, envisioned by the designers as a tranquil refuge where all social classes could intermingle, took 15 years and $14 million to build. After the squatters were evacuated and their shacks levelled, workers relocated tons of stone and soil, drained stagnant swamps, laid 114 miles (180 km) of drainage tile to channel rainfall to the new lakes and planted half a million trees and shrubs. The sunken transverse roads allow east-west traffic through the Park so as not to affect Park users. Olmstead and Vaux placed entrances all along the park perimeter for maximum public access.

Instead of attempting to walk you through the 58 miles (90 km) of paths, we shall survey the park's "natural" beauty and the more organized diversions that dot the landscape.

Perhaps the best place to start is **The Dairy**, located midway through the Park opposite 64th St. Take Subway R or N to 5th Ave.; enter the Park at 59th St. and head north. The Dairy, an 1870 Victorian Gothic house designed by Vaux, truly began as a milk dispensary for mothers and nurses and is

The world famous Central Park

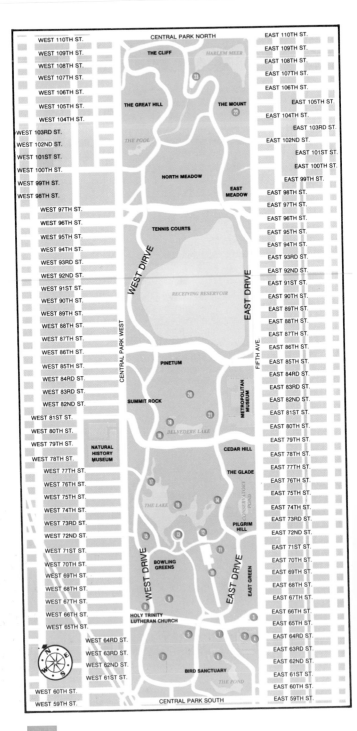

now the Park's Visitor Information Center and Exhibit Hall. Tel. 794-6565. A map of the Park informs you of special seasonal events. The Dairy, in addition to occasional special exhibits, offers "The Heart of the City" slide show chronicling Central Park's history. It starts on the half hour.

The famous **Zoo** is just east of the Dairy at 5th Ave. and 64th St. Open daily 10am-5pm; weekends 10:30am-5:30pm, children under 16 must be accompanied by an adult. Admission charge. Tel. 439-6500. The

Winter at the Central Park Zoo

facilities are now ultra-modern and sparkling new after renovations. The **Children's Zoo** at 67th St. and 5th Ave. is open daily 10am-4:30pm. Children may pet the animals and hold the smaller ones.

Between the two zoos is the **Delacorte Clock**, above the archway at 65th St. Mechanical animals perform at the toll of every half hour.

The Arsenal, 64th St. and 5th Ave., predates the Park. Built in 1848 to house the National Guard and used for the quartering of troops during the Civil War, the Arsenal now operates an art gallery; open Mon.-Fri. 9:30am-4:30pm.

The Carousel, just west of the Dairy, is open 10:30am-4:45pm, only on weekends during the winter, weather permitting. Every day the rest of the year.

The **Wollman Memorial Ice-Skating Rink** is located just south of the Dairy.

Just west is the *Hecksher Playground and Puppet*

CENTRAL PARK

1. The Dairy
2. The Zoo
3. Delacorte Clock
4. The Arsenal
5. The Carousel
6. Wollman Memorial Ice-skating Rink
7. Hecksher Playground and Puppet House
8. Tavern on the Green
9. Sheep Meadow
10. The Mall
11. Naumburg Bandshell
12. Bethesda Fountain
13. Cherry Hill Fountain and Concourse
14. Loeb Boathouse
15. Strawberry Fields
16. The Ramble
17. Ladies Pavilion
18. Belvedere Castle
19. Delacorte Theater
20. The Great Lawn
21. Cleopatra's Needle
22. Conservatory Garden
23. Lasker Skating Rink and Pool

The Carousel at Central Park

The Wollman Skating Rink

House. Enter the Park at 59th St. and 7th Ave., and head north to the equivalent of 62nd St. Puppet shows: Mon.-Fri. 10:30am, noon. Admission charge, reservations required, Tel. 371-7775.

Glass-walled *Tavern on the Green* is the lovely restaurant just inside the Park at Central Park West and 67th St. There are several dining rooms, one with crystal chandeliers, Tel. 873-3200.

Just east is **Sheep Meadow**, an expanse of greenery named for its original use. The meadow has been resodded and transformed into a gorgeous stretch of lush lawn. It is now open for passive play, limited by weather and official determination to keep it healthy.

East of the meadow is **The Mall**, whose promenade, lined with giant elm trees, runs north to the **Naumburg Bandshell** (1923). Impromptu concerts are offered when weather permits. Just north of the Bandshell are the lakeside **Bethesda Fountain** and **The Terrace** – beautiful if somewhat run-down.

The **Cherry Hill Fountain** and **Concourse** lie just west of the Bethesda Fountain. Looking north, we see the **lake** and **Bow Bridge**. The lake is open for boating in warmer weather. Boat rentals are available at the **Loeb Boathouse** on the lake's east side, just north of Bethesda Fountain.

Strawberry Fields, Central Park West and 72nd St., bears the name of a 1967 song by the late ex-Beatle John Lennon, who lived nearby.

North of the Lake is **the Ramble**, a twisting, twining pathway through dense foliage. This is the place for bird-watching. Don't come alone; join one of the Park's frequent bird-watching tours. Inquire at the Dairy, Tel. 794-6565.

The **Ladies Pavilion**, 75th St. at the

northwest tip of the lake, is the last of six delicate wrought-iron shelters at various lake shore landings.

Visit the lovely **Conservatory Water**, just inside the east end of the Park at 74th St., to behold the model boat marina. Sail your own or watch the masters, who sometimes bring entire fleets. The *Kerbs Memorial Boathouse* has refreshments.

The Conservatory Water with its model boat marina

The **Swedish Cottage**, north-west of the lake at approximately 79th St., houses the *Marionette Theater*. Shows are scheduled Tues.-Fri. for school groups and Sat. for the general public. Admission charge, reservations required, Tel. 683-5740.

Just east is **Belvedere Castle**. Looming above the rest of the Park atop Vista Rock, the 1869 structure now serves as a weather station and a learning center, offering weekend workshop programs and performances. The workshops, most scheduled on Sat., are free for kids ages 5-11 and their families; Sun. shows are free for all. Open Tues.-Sun. 11am-5pm, mid Oct.- mid Feb. until 4pm, Tel. 772-0210.

The Belvedere serves as a magnificent distant backdrop for the popular Summer Shakespeare Festival at the *Delacorte Theater*. The free-admission "Theater in the Park" program, the "baby" of producer Joseph Papp and the *Public Theater*, stages two productions per summer season – one of which is Shakespeare. Obtain tickets, free, on the day of performance, but be prepared for a long wait.

The lush **Great Lawn**, just north of the Delacorte, is used for free summer concerts – opera, jazz, pop – and ball games. It is hard to imagine the Depression-era shantytown of destitute citizens which once stood here.

East of the Great Lawn is the backyard of the Met-

Manhattan's skyline sets a lovely background for sunning on the Sheep Meadow at Central Park

ropolitan Museum of Art, punctuated by the obelisk known as **Cleopatra's Needle**. A gift of the Khedive of Egypt to NYC on Feb. 22, 1881, it was transported at the expense of William H. Vanderbilt. The Needle is misnamed: it was built for Thutmose III, whose reign (1490-1436 BC) predated Cleopatra's by about 1,400 years.

The **Reservoir** claims 106 acres just north of the Great Lawn. Its 1.5 mile circumferential jogging track is a local favorite.

The **Conservatory Garden**, 5th Ave. and 105th St., embraces three formal gardens which you can tour.

The northeast corner of the park is dominated by The Meer lake. The *Lasker Skating Rink* and Pool, at the Meer's southwestern tip, is open for skating Wed.-Sun. between Nov.-Feb. Admission charge, Tel. 996-1184.

The elevated north end of the Park afforded US Forces a good view of the East and Hudson Rivers during the Revolution and the War of 1812. George Washington's troops used **McGown's Pass** as a retreat route. Of the various forts in the area, only the Blockhouse remains.

The 110th St. *Boathouse i*s a restaurant and boat-rental facility.

Recreation

The park offers a vast selection of sport and recreation facilities. Garden tour information, Tel. 860-1382. Some of the most popular facilities are described below:

BOATING

During warm weather, row-boats can be rented at the *Loeb Boathouse, located* on the lake at E 74th/75th Sts.

Sailing of model boats: the **Conservatory Water**, 5th Ave. and 74th St.

ICE SKATING
Lasker Rink, mid-Park at 106th St. Open Wed.-Sun., Nov.-Feb. Admission charge, Tel. 996-1184.

Wollman Rink, at East 68 and East Drive, Tel. 517-4800.

JOGGING
The most popular spot is the track around the Reservoir. The *NY Road Runners Club* organizes group runs every Sat. at 10am, 90th St. and 5th Ave., Tel. 860-4455.

WALKING TOURS
Urban Park Rangers lead 90-minute tours every Sunday at 2pm, rain or shine, Tel. 427-4040.

BALL GAMES
Permits are required for the use of designated fields. For information call Tel. 794-6565.

Locker rooms are available at the **North Meadow Center**, mid-Park north of 97th St. Open 8am-5pm. Bring your own lock.

HORSEBACK RIDING
Rental at *Claremont Riding Academy*, 175 W 89th St., open 6:30am till one hour before dusk on week-

Have a ball at Central Park in the winter snow

The NYC Marathon

days, until 4pm on weekends. Only for riders experienced in the English saddle. Riding only on the Park's bridle paths, Tel. 724-5100.

HORSE-DRAWN CARRIAGES
59th St. at 5th and 6th Aves. Charge is for the first hour, with an additional charge for every quarter of the hour. Maximum of four people per carriage.

CYCLING
Restricted to the designated recreation lane when the Park drives are open to motor traffic. When drives are closed to motorists, use the outside right lane throughout the park. Never ride on pedestrian paths; always travel counter-clockwise around the Park.

Park drives are closed to motorists weekends from 7pm Fri. to 6am Mon., May 1-Nov. 1, and weekdays 10am-3pm and 7pm-1am. To rent a bike, Tel. 861-4137.

Annual Events
"You Gotta Have Park," takes place on a May weekend during which volunteers try to elicit contributions from each person entering the park, chiefly for its conservation. The occasion is usually sweetened with special events and concerts to attract crowds. While NYC spends approx. $6 million per year on the park, recent years' volun-

eer promotions raised sums of more than $3 million.

The 26.2 mile (42 km) NYC Marathon, organized by the NY Road Runners Club, has taken place every fall since 1970. Originally confined to Central Park the race was re-routed in 1976 to include all five boroughs, beginning in Staten Island and finishing at Tavern on the Green in the Park. The thousands of participants – almost 15,000 in recent years – are cheered on by millions of spectators lining the course.

Three Final Reminders:
- Remember to keep the park clean!
- Do not walk alone at night!
- If you get lost, do not panic. Most park lamp-posts have four ID numbers. The first two indicate parallel cross streets outside the park; the second two denote East Side (even) or West Side (odd).

Central Park at fall

UPPER WEST SIDE – CLASSICAL MUSIC, TRENDY LIFE STYLES

Rejuvenated, renovated, and increasingly upwardly-mobile, the Upper West Side is "hot." Originally developed in the late 1800's, this neighborhood possesses some of the city's most charming row-houses and most elegant apartment buildings, especially those lining Central Park West (CPW).

While Riverside Drive, with its view of the Hudson River, and Central Park West with its view of the Park, have never lost their exclusivity as residential quarters, the blocks in between had lapsed into decay. The first step toward revival came in 1962, with the opening, at the neighborhood's southern border, of Lincoln Center, the nerve-center of NYC high culture and home to the Metropolitan Opera, the NYC Opera, the City Ballet and the NY Philharmonic Orchestra. But the more important change began to occur only several years ago when the young and affluent, especially single professionals, reconsidered the Upper West Side as a place to live, creating a demand for good restaurants and boutiques. Though reminiscent of the Upper East Side, its counterpart across Central Park, the West Side is younger and much more informal. We have divided the neighborhood in two, north and south of 77th St.

We shall first head north on Columbus Ave., *the* place to be seen, and south again on Broadway to Lincoln Center. The route is lined with landmark buildings, shops, restaurants, clubs and theaters, plus several places ideal for "people-watching." Remember that many of the concerts and performances we shall mention require advance booking.

59th-77th Sts.

Here is a perfect place for a stroll, combined with shopping by day or dining by night. Day and night are quite different here; neither is ever boring. Saturday afternoon or evening is best.

We begin at **Columbus Circle** at the southwestern corner of Central Park. Take Subway 1 to 59th St. Begin carefully though. Merging traffic from all directions makes the Circle a pedestrian's nightmare.

First, the Circle itself. Its center is graced by Gaetano Russo's monument to Christopher Columbus, erected in 1892; the fountain at its base was donated by George T. Delacorte in 1965. The odd-shaped white marble building with circular cut-outs at the southern end, at No. 2, is the **NYC Department of Cultural Affairs**. A ground-floor information center displays NY Subway, bus and street maps and free hand out on cultural activities, sites and attractions, Tel. 841-4100.

The **NY Coliseum**, used mostly for trade shows and large exhibitions, is located at the Circle's western fringe.

The Christopher Columbus Monument on Columbus Circle, erected in 1892

At the Circle's northern edge, Broadway and 60th-61st Sts., is the **Gulf and Western Tower**. At its base is the *Paramount movie theatre*, which screens mostly new movies. Head north on Broadway, turn west on 61st St. and follow 61st St. to Columbus Ave. The **Sofia**, a brick art deco masterpiece which had been a warehouse, is a luxury residential condominium.

Continue north on Columbus Ave., noting **Fordham University** across the way. **Lincoln Center** begins on your left at 62nd St. and Columbus Ave. Climb the stairs and face the **Fountain**; reflected sunlight off the surrounding travertine walls creates a gleaming plaza cooled by the fountain's spray. Night time center-pieces are the two spotlit **Chagall murals** suspended just inside the **Metropolitan Opera Guild Inc.** directly behind the fountain. The Metropolitan Opera performs during a 30-week season ending in April. In summer, many shows are brought to this stage from abroad. The box office is open Mon.-Sat. 10am-8pm, Sun. noon-6pm. Tickets available four weeks prior to week of performance. Lincoln Center Plaza information Tel. 769-7000.

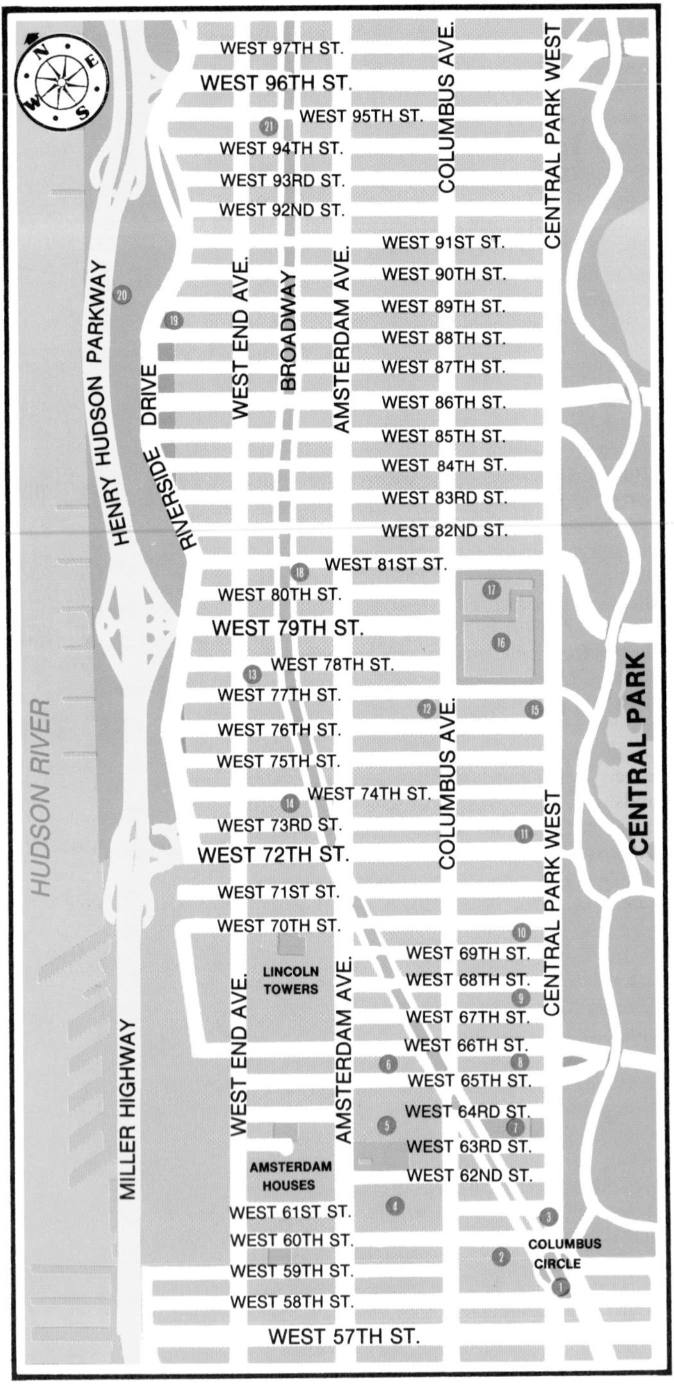
N
E
S
W
WEST 97TH ST.
WEST 96TH ST.
WEST 95TH ST.
WEST 94TH ST.
WEST 93RD ST.
WEST 92ND ST.
WEST 91ST ST.
WEST 90TH ST.
WEST 89TH ST.
WEST 88TH ST.
WEST 87TH ST.
WEST 86TH ST.
WEST 85TH ST.
WEST 84TH ST.
WEST 83RD ST.
WEST 82ND ST.
WEST 81ST ST.
WEST 80TH ST.
WEST 79TH ST.
WEST 78TH ST.
WEST 77TH ST.
WEST 76TH ST.
WEST 75TH ST.
WEST 74TH ST.
WEST 73RD ST.
WEST 72TH ST.
WEST 71ST ST.
WEST 70TH ST.
WEST 69TH ST.
WEST 68TH ST.
WEST 67TH ST.
WEST 66TH ST.
WEST 65TH ST.
WEST 64RD ST.
WEST 63RD ST.
WEST 62ND ST.
WEST 61ST ST.
WEST 60TH ST.
WEST 59TH ST.
WEST 58TH ST.
WEST 57TH ST.
COLUMBUS AVE.
CENTRAL PARK WEST
HENRY HUDSON PARKWAY
RIVERSIDE DRIVE
WEST END AVE.
BROADWAY
AMSTERDAM AVE.
HUDSON RIVER
CENTRAL PARK
LINCOLN TOWERS
AMSTERDAM HOUSES
MILLER HIGHWAY
COLUMBUS CIRCLE
1
2
3
4
5
6
7
8
9
10
11
12
13
14
15
16
17
18
19
20
21

Left of the fountain is the **New York State Theater**, home of the late George Balanchine's *NYC Ballet* and the *NYC Opera*. The NYC Opera season runs from early July to mid-Nov. All foreign-language operas are simultaneously subtitled in English on a screen above the stage. State Theater box office is open Mon. 10am-8pm, Tues.-Sat. 10am-9pm, Sun. 11:30am-7:30pm, Tel. 870-5570 for information, Tel. 944-9300 to reserve tickets.

A right turn at the fountain brings us to **Avery Fisher Hall**, home of the New York Philharmonic, guest orchestras and visiting soloists. In addition to its regular schedule, the Philharmonic presents reduced-price young people's concerts and holds public rehearsals with an admission charge. Thurs., Sept.-May at 9:35am. Box office is open Mon.-Sat. 10am-6pm, Sun. noon-6pm, and some nights until 9pm depending upon performance schedules, Tel. 875-5035 for information and to reserve tickets.

The Avery Fisher Hall in Lincoln Center

Left of the Metropolitan Opera is the serene greenery of **Damrosch Park** and the **Guggenheim Bandshell**. Free outdoor concerts held here on summer evenings rank among NYC's best, least-utilized offerings. Performance schedules, printed in the *New York Times*, may vary according to the weather.

The *Vivian Beaumont Theater*, Broadway at 65th St., a right turn from the "Met," is the most con-

UPPER WEST SIDE

1. NYC Department of Cultural Affairs
2. NY Coliseum
3. Gulf and Western Tower
4. Fordham University
5. Lincoln Center
6. Juilliard Music School
7. YMCA
8. Holy Trinity Lutheran Church
9. Second Church of Christ Scientist
10. Congregation Shearith Israel
11. Dakota apartment-house
12. Columbus Ave. Flea Market
13. West End Collegiate Church and School
14. Ansonia
15. NY Historical Society
16. American Museum of Natural History
17. Hayden Planetarium
18. Zabar's
19. Rice Mansion
20. Soldiers' and Sailors' Monument
21. Symphony Space

Columbus Circle

troversial space in Lincoln Center. Built for the staging of drama, the Beaumont is usually closed and has lost money even when open. The lower-level *Mitzi Newhouse Theater* is also closed at present, Tel. 239-6200.

A pedestrian bridge across 65th St. links the Center to the famous **Juilliard Music School**. Students perform all year round, Tel. 799-5000.

Below Juilliard, at street level on 65th St. and Broadway, is **Alice Tully Hall**. The Lincoln Center Chamber Music Society performs here, as do a great number of guest artists. The Chamber Music Society offers students and senior citizens discount "rush tickets" 30 minutes prior to any performance which is not sold out. The box office is open Mon.-Sat. 11am-7pm, Sun. noon-6pm, Tel. 721-6500 for information, Tel. 875-5030 to reserve tickets.

Lincoln Center offers several guided tours. One option, taking you through the Met, NY State Theater and Avery Fisher Hall, begins on the lower (Concourse) level and takes about an hour, 10am-5pm daily. Reservations recommended, Tel. 877-1800, ext. 512. Another fascinating possibility is the "Backstage Tour of the Metropolitan Opera House", Tel. 582-7500. Finally, the Center runs a "Meet the Artist" program, arranging full-day events for groups of 20 or more, Tel. 877-1800, ext. 547, or write to "Meet the Artist," Lincoln Center, New York, NY 10023.

Advertizing posters at Lincoln Center entice you to a performance at Alice Tully Hall

The new **Museum of American Folk Art** at 2 Lincoln Square, (near Lincoln Center), recently moved from 125 W 55th St. exhibitions for public viewing. Open Tues.-Sun. 11:30am-7:30pm. Free of charge. Tel. 977-7298.

One of Lincoln Center's hidden treasures is the **Library of the Performing Arts**. Walk down the Columbus Ave. stairway from the fountain, turn left and then left again onto 65th St.; walk under the span and turn left on Amsterdam Ave. to No. 111, between 64th and 65th. You will see performing artists availing themselves of the library's copious collection of study and exhibition material in music, drama and dance. The dance collection is unique. Its film and video archive is open to visitors; watch your favorite dancers perform on private hand-viewers. The library houses several galleries and puts on free recitals in its Bruno Walter Auditorium. Obtain tickets in person after 3pm on day of performance, noon for Sat. performances. Free tours of the library: Thurs. 11am-noon, Tel. 879-1670 for reservations. The library is open Mon. and Thurs. 10am-8pm, Tues. and Sat. 10am-6pm, Wed. and Fri. noon-6pm.

At Lincoln Center

Lincoln Center houses four gift shops. The *Performing Arts Shop a*nd *The Gallery* are on Concourse level; exit the Library, turn left and enter the enclosed walkway beneath the "Met". *The Performing Arts Shop* carries books, recordings, musical games, stuffed toys, etc. Open Mon. 4-8pm, Tues.-Sat. 11am-8pm, Sun. 2-7pm. Tel. 875-5000. Upstairs next to the box office at 835 Madison Ave. is the *Metropolitan Opera Shop*: recordings, books, posters, clothing and souvenirs. Open Mon.-Sat. 10am through last intermission, Sun. noon-6pm. Tel. 734-8406. *The Avery Fisher Hall Boutique* (main lobby) stocks unique musical items. Open Mon-Thurs. and Sat. 6pm through first intermission, Fri. 1pm through first intermission. All proceeds from the shops benefit the Center; many of the staff are performers.

Return to Broadway and head south; our day-long tour will double back to the Center in time for an evening performance. Head one block east on 62nd St. to Central Park West and note the **Century Building**, Central Park West between 62nd St. and 63rd St., a twin-tower apartment building with an art deco edifice designed by Irwin Chanin, built in 1932.

By the fountain of the Valiant Seamen at Columbus Circle

Just off Central Park West at 5 W 63rd St. is the **YMCA**. Of all its interesting lectures and discussions, the *Writer's Voice* series is one of the best. Call Tel. 787-1301 or step inside to the box office.

Continue north on Central Park West. At 64th St. is the **NY Society for Ethical Culture**, housed in an Art Nouveau building designed by Robert D. Kohn, Tel. 874-5210. Walk one block west on 64th St. to Columbus Ave. and head north. The *Lincoln Square Coffee Shop*, between 65th and 66th Sts., specializes in salads, home-baked bread and muffins, Tel. 799-4000.

Across the street at No. 37 is the *First Act Theater*, where the young (10-22 years old) cast of the first all children's theater performs musicals specifically written for them. Inexpensive., Tel. 873-6400. A performance of a different kind is yours at the **Holy Trinity Lutheran Church**, northwest corner of Central Park West and 65th St.: a weekly series of Bach cantatas in Lutheran Vespers, Sun. 5pm from Oct. to Apr. The church opens 30 minutes before each service.

Heading north on Central Park West, notice the apartment house at No. 55. Viewed from the park side of the street, the brick changes from a dark, purple tone at bottom to a light, blondish hue at the top. The effect is one of greater height. The 1930 building also appears sunlit even on cloudy days.

The next stop on Central Park West is the **Second Church of Christ Scientist** at 68th, a neo-Classical structure – rare on this block – designed by Fredrick R. Comstock. Walk south to 67th St. and turn west. The **Hotel des Artistes** at 1 W 67th St. was truly built for the artist, with extra-high ceilings to accommodate large paintings and sculptures. One of its tenants, Howard Chandler Christy, produced the murals which grace the ground-level *Café des Artistes*, the most romantic place imaginable for brunch or pre-theater dinner, Tel. 877-3500.

We're now heading north on Columbus Ave., the Upper West Side's once-dilapidated shopping-dining promenade. The street now abounds with popular restaurants and trendy boutiques; on summer evenings the cafés open their doors wide, and their patrons happily crowd onto the sidewalks.

Congregation Shearith Israel is at the southeast corner of 70th St. and Central Park West. This Spanish/Portuguese neo-Classical synagogue is the fifth home of the city's oldest Jewish congregation (1654).

Return to Columbus and continue north. *Charivari 257*, southeast corner of Columbus Ave. and 72nd St., one of several Charivari boutiques in the area, featuring top designers including Matsuda and Yamamoto, for men and women, Tel. 496-8700. Across Columbus at No. 256 is *To Boot* arguably NYC's best men's shoe and boot shop. High prices, quality ware Tel. 724-8249.

Heading toward the Park on 72nd St. we come to *Dallas BBQ*, No. 27, one of the best dining bargains in town. Its delicious barbecued chicken and ribs are always in demand, though you will never wait too long for a table and take-out picnic baskets are available for an afternoon in the park. The price is incredibly right, Tel. 873-2004. *Dallas BBQ* is situated in Hotel Olcott, which also houses the Manhattan and Gotham Bridge Clubs. The Penthouse Manhattan Club is well-known for duplicate  bridge. Afternoons belong to retired people, evenings to young professionals. It is open daily, Tel. 799-4242. The Gotham, featuring rubber bridge, is a more serious, high-stake establishment, Tel. 874-2180.

Across the street is the *Oliver Cromwell Residen-*

The exclusive Dakota apartment house

tial Hotel (1928), the personal favorite of designer Emery Roth, Tel. 362-2000. Roth architecture dots the Upper West Side. Examples: the San Remo at 145 Central Park West, the Beresford at 211 Central Park West, the Belleclaire at 77th St. and Broadway. Though Roth's firm is now famous for glass and steel skyscrapers, his own taste leaned to masonry structures like the Cromwell.

Henry J. Hardenbergh's **Dakota apartment house** (named for its one-time distance from the city's heart), at the northwest corner of Central Park West and 72nd St., predates the *Cromwell* by more than 40 years. Developed by Edward S. Clark, heir to the Singer (Sewing Machine) fortune, the *Dakota* is one of Manhattan's most exclusive apartment houses, favored by stars of the entertainment world. It was here that John Lennon, resident of the building, was shot down in 1980.

Walk north on Central Park West; turn west on 73rd St. and head for Columbus Ave. On the way, note the *TOMI Park Royal Theater* at No. 23, another quality neighborhood theater at affordable prices. Box office, Tel. 787-3980. *La Tablita* restaurant at No. 65 offers moderately-priced Italian and Argentinian food and wine; Argentinian is recommended, Tel. 838-7275.

Turn north again on Columbus Ave. The *Kenneth Cole Shoe Boutique* at 76th St. sells this designer's avant-garde footwear. The **Columbus Avenue Flea Market**, located in the playground and indoors of Intermediate School 44, between 76th and 77th Sts., displays the wares of up to 200 dealers – everything from Fiesta ware and Depression-era glass to clothing and junk jewellry. Sun. only, 10am-6pm. Tel. 721-0900.

Proceed to museum territory: the **American Museum of Natural History**, located on Central Park West between 77th and 79th Sts., the **New-York Historical Society** on Central Park West and 77th St. and the **Hayden Planetarium**, on Central

Park West and 81st St. We shall explore these in the next section, "79th to 96th Sts."; for now let's turn west to 77th St. Take 77th St. west to Broadway, a wide, two-way divided boulevard.

Note the **Belleclaire**, southwest corner of Broadway and 77th St. Architect Emery Roth was in his 20s when he designed the *Belleclaire*, one of his first apartment houses; the result shows his lack of a clearly-defined style. Ignore the ugly, tacked-on entrance and the dirt; notice instead the rounded corners, bay windows and ornamental arches. Roth's later works better exemplify his gift of creating large buildings elegantly punctuated with subtle ornamentation.

The **West End Collegiate Church and School**, one block west at the northeast corner of 77th St. and West End Ave., presents architecture buffs with a rare example of Flemish style. Built in 1892 for the Collegiate Reformed Protestant Church, established by the Dutch colonists in 1628, the school, founded ten years later, is thought to be the oldest independent secondary school in the country. Observe the building from across West End Ave. and note the red-tiled, steep-angled roof with its tall dormer windows.

Return to Broadway and head south. The newly-renovated *Promenade Theater*, 2162 Broadway, is nevertheless "off-Broadway" due to its size and distance from the Theater District. Box office, Tel. 580-1313. The *Second Stage Theater Company* shares the same address, Tel. 873-6103.

At the Columbus Ave. Flea Market

Ernie's Café, 2150 Broadway, occupies a cavernous and unadorned hall in which a hot singles crowd can observe one another without distraction. In summer the huge front doors swing open and the party spills into the street, Tel. 496-1588.

The *Beacon Theater*, 3021 Broadway 74th St., attracts big-name pop, rock and soul musicians and singers. Its concert hall is a work of art in its own right, Tel. 787-1477.

Continue south on Broadway, passing the **Ansonia** at 73rd St. The most ornate of all apartment buildings in the area, the 1904 chateau-like *Ansonia* has been a favorite home and studio for many famous performers and musicians, including Caruso, Toscanini and Stravinsky.

At No. 1987 Broadway is the *Regency Theater*, a revival house with double-feature old movies, Tel. 724-3700. The **Merkin Concert Hall**, half a block west of Broadway at 129 W 67th St., offers excellent acoustics and enjoyable, affordable programs of classical music, Tel. 362-8719.

The West End Collegiate Church and School

No spot could be better than this music-filled neighborhood for the newly-opened *Tower Records/Video* – uptown branches of the huge Village establishment – at the corners of Broadway

and 66th and 67th Sts. respectively, just north of Juilliard and Lincoln Center. Both stores, with their orange neon signs and bright interiors, are considered happenings. Tel. 799-2500 (Across from Lincoln Centre) and Tel. 505-1500 (On 4th and Broadway), are unsurpassed in a huge selection of music, they also rent and sell video films.

The **Richard Allen Center**, just west of Broadway at 36 W 62nd St., is devoted to Black theater and culture, Tel. 316-1200. Next door is *Tovarisch*, specializing in traditional Russian cuisine, Tel. 757-0168. The *Lincoln Plaza Cinemas*, across Broadway between 62nd and 63rd Sts., screen the newest foreign films.

79th-96th Sts.

The following tour takes you through the northern Upper West Side, 79th to 96th Sts. west of Central Park. To get there, take Subway 1 to 79th St.

We shall begin with a visit to several museums, but not before breakfast. A wonderful choice is virtually at your feet as you exit the subway. A few steps east on 79th St. and a turn north on Amsterdam Ave. bring you to *Sarabeth's Kitchen*, open 9am-7pm, Tel. 496-6280.

Visiting the dinosaurs at the American Museum of Natural History

Now follow 79th St. east to Columbus Ave., head two blocks south and turn east on 77th St. to the Park. The **New-York Historical Society**, founded over 190 years ago when people spelled New York with a hyphen, occupies the southwest corner of 77th St. and Central Park West. In its museum and historical archives, devoted primarily to New York history, are Napoleon's signed authorization for the Louisiana Purchase, John James Audubon's bird watercolors, and the coach that may have brought George Washington to his first inauguration. All that, plus the city's largest collection of Tiffany lamps. Tel. 873-3400.

On the northwest corner of 77th St. and Central Park West is the Society's more famous neighbor, the **American Museum of Natural History**. Notice the reddish-brown 77th St. facade and then enter on the 79th St. side where an equestrian statue of Theodore Roosevelt greets you at the front

steps. Inside, the museum is a treat for young and old alike – 40 exhibition halls, over 34 million artifacts and specimens. Explore on your own or take a free tour. All sorts of animals are depicted in their natural habitat: African mammals, ocean birds, reptiles, amphibians and ocean creatures. You can also behold a 1,300-year-old giant sequoia tree, see the *Star of India* sapphire and the largest meteorite ever retrieved. There are special see-and-touch exhibits for children; guest lectures and performances for adults. Don't miss the 94-ft. (30-m) long blue whale – a children's favorite although it's not real. The *Naturemax Theater* presents spectacular films on giant screens, for an additional charge: *To Fly*, a simulation of balloon, glider and jet fighter flight, and *Living Planet*, around-the-world tour and a film about the Grand Canyon – not to be missed. The museum operates several restaurants and two gift shops: adults' shop on 1st floor, children's shop on basement level. The Museum is open Mon-Thurs. and Sun. 10am-5:45pm, Fri. and Sat. 10am-8:45pm. Tel. 769-5100, 873-6380. Contribution suggested.

The **Hayden Planetarium**, corner of 81st St. and Central Park West, is immediately recognizable by its copper dome. Inside, the comfortable *Sky Theater* takes you for a show of the heavens. Call Tel. 769-5920 for the schedule. Calculate your weight on other planets; view exhibits on the history of astronomy, a solar system mobile and an Aztec calendar. Special shows for pre-schoolers. It is open Mon.-Fri. 12:30-4:45pm, Sat. 10am-5:45pm, Sun. noon-5:45pm. Admission also covers the Museum of Natural History.

The Planetarium presents *Laserock* shows which include a star projector and an array of over 150 special effects. – Fri. and Sat. evenings, 7:30pm, 9pm and 10:30pm. Admission charge, Tel. 769-5100.

The east side of Central Park

At the Hayden Planetarium

Shopping at Zabar's

West affords a relaxing stroll north along the park and a look at some of the beautiful architecture which faces it. The **Beresford**, at No. 211 between 81st and 82nd Sts., is another Emery Roth building, one year older (1929) than the San Remo. Its contemporary is **El Dorado** at No. 300, between 90th and 91st Sts., a Margon & Holder design featuring twin art deco towers. At 92nd St. is the **Ardsley**, yet another Emery Roth creation (1931), this one decorated at its base with bands of sandstone and colored concrete skirting. Farther north at 96th St. is the **First Church of Christian Scientists**, designed by Carrere & Hastings (1903), the same team responsible for the NY Public Library.

Turn south, cross to the west side of Central Park West, retrace your steps to 86th St. and follow 86th St. west, past the *Riverside Shakespeare Company* at No. 165 (check the schedule, Tel. 877-6810) to Amsterdam Ave. Head south. Amsterdam Ave. in the low 80s is dotted with antique shops and offers a couple of good choices for a reasonably-priced dinner. Turn north onto Broadway for the best Sunday brunch fixings (as well as several excellent clubs and performance spaces).

For bagels try *H & H Bagels*, southwest corner of Broadway and 80th St.; try *Zabar's*, on the northeast corner, for just about everything else. Never mind the crowds, *Zabar's* is a landmark, an ever-expanding institution when it comes to smoked fish, prepared foods, fresh pasta, fresh-baked bread, dried fruits and candies, even housewares and cookware. *Zabar's* typifies the crowded yet homey city, as it is stocked with the best of everything... it essentially gained its fame for the enormous selection of cheeses, perhaps the largest you will find. Open Mon.-Thurs. 8am-7:30pm, Fri.-Sat. 8am-midnight, Sun. 9am-6pm, Tel. 787-2000.

For a great combination of Chinese and Cuban food try *La Caridad Restaurant* on 2199 Broadway, Tel. 874-2780, 874-8001. The food here is cheap and tasty, especially recommended is a dish of fried bananas and vegetables.

On the corner of 81st St. is *Shakespeare and Co.*, Tel. 580-7800, and its tremendous paperback inventory. A boutique in the Charivari chain, *Charivari Men's Store*, Tel. 362-1212, occupies a corner of Broadway and 85th St., with additional outlets on Columbus Ave. and 81st and 72nd Sts. This chain of high-fashion designer clothing has colonized the West Side.

A small detour west on 89th St. to its end on Riverside Dr. affords you a glimpse of one of Manhattan's last free-standing mansions: the **Rice Mansion** on the southeast corner, a 1901 beaux-arts neo-Georgian hybrid. Notice the distinctive *porte-cochere* on the 89th St. side. Designed by Herts & Tallent for railroad magnate Isaac L. Rice, the mansion now houses **Yeshiva Chofetz Chaim**, a rabbinical school.

The **Yeshiva University Museum** is open for visitation Tues.-Thurs. 10:30am-5pm, Sun. noon-6pm.Tel. 960-5390.

Across Riverside Dr. is the beautiful, columned **Soldiers' and Sailors' Monument,** erected in Riverside Park in 1902. Riverside Park was designed by Frederick Law Olmstead (more famous for Central Park). His attention to grand planning and detail is apparent in the sloping embankment and terraces. The park, running from 72nd to 145th Sts., separates the drive from the Hudson River and is dotted with basketball and tennis courts, playgrounds, benches and jogging tracks.

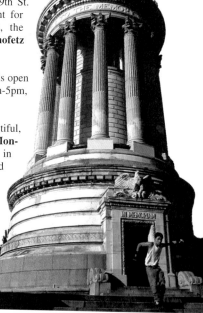

At the Soldiers' and Sailors' Monument, on Riverside Drive

The 79th St. **Boat Basin** is used by sailing enthusiasts and the tenants of houseboats.

Return to Broadway and walk slightly east. Here are the **Claremont Stables**, the only riding stables still existent in Manhattan. This is where you get your mount to ride in Central Park, Tel. 724-5100.

Continue north on Broadway. No. 2537 is *Symphony Space*, a performance center of the highest caliber. Call Tel. 864-1414 to check the schedule, which might include classical, modern or experimental music, dance or children's programs. The *Metro Cinema*, slightly farther north, is a serious revival house that screens old, classic films, Tel. 222-1200.

Head north on Columbus Ave. and west on 103rd St. to Riverside Dr. for the *Equity Library Theater*, well-known for its high-quality revivals, Tel. 678-9505. Alternative theater entertainment: *West End Theater* at 302 W 91st St. or *West Side Rep.* at 252 W 81st St., Tel. 874-7290. One may, of course, forgo them all and spend the evening just strolling up Columbus Ave. from 67th to 86th Sts.

A note of caution: you will be more comfortable and safe taking a taxi, rather than walking along the northern streets of this neighborhood, particularly during the evening.

At Riverside Park

UPPER MANHATTAN AND HARLEM –
THE NORTHERN BOUNDARY

Upper Manhattan is dotted with pockets of culture, history and learning, some conveniently clustered together. Because these enclaves border potentially unsafe neighborhoods, we do not recommend strolling the streets. Go directly to the worthwhile spots; if you plan to attend a performance, call ahead to reserve seats. We recommend several nearby restaurants. Yes, be a little more cautious in this area, but don't be scared off, there are some wonderful things to see, during the day and the evening.

It's worthwhile taking a guided tour around Harlem (some tours include the Bronx). Tours leave from Victors Sportsworld, 489 5th Ave. between 41-42 Sts. on Tues.-Sun. Tours are available in English, French and Spanish. For reservations call Tel. 855-1544.

We shall begin at the cluster which includes Columbia University, the Cathedral of St. John the Divine, Riverside Church and Grant's Tomb. First, Columbia: take Subway 1 to the 116th St. station at the western edge of the campus. The campus proper stretches from 114th to 120th Sts. Guided tours: Mon.-Fri., beginning at 201 Dodge Hall, Tel. 280-2845. The information desk is at the Broadway/116th St. corner of the campus.

Columbia University, one of the best universities in the world

The history of **Columbia University** dates back to 1754, when Samuel Johnson taught eight students at Trinity Church near Wall St. Chartered as King's College that year, NYC's first institute of higher learning was renamed Columbia in 1784 and moved to its present site in 1897. This respected

Ivy League school spearheaded the 1960s movement against US involvement in Vietnam.

The oldest buildings on campus were designed by McKim, Mead & White. Especially noteworthy is the centrally-located, domed, **Low Library**, now

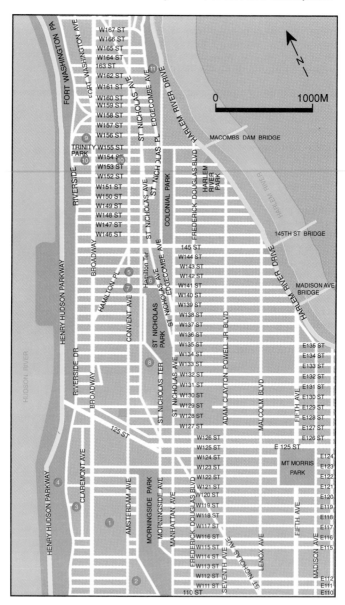

he home of campus administration. **Butler Library**, facing Low, is worth a visit for its Rare Book and Manuscript Room; archives are displayed on the sixth floor. Open Mon.-Fri. 9am-5pm, admission free.

The **Cathedral of St. John the Divine** is just south of Columbia on 1047 Amsterdam Ave. and 112th St. Walk south from the 116th St. Subway Station to 114 St., east to Amsterdam Ave. and south to 112th St. Construction of the Byzantine-Romanesque cathedral by the firm of Heins & La Farge, who won a competition for the original design, began in 1892, and still continues. Heins & La Farge lived to see only the apse, choir and crossing completed. Architect Ralph Adams Cram, took over in 1911 and changed the overall design to Gothic; the façade and the nave, 601 ft. (183 m) by 320 ft. (97.5 m), reflect Cram's design, as will the spire when completed. Construction halted in 1941 due to US involvement in World War II and did not resume because the NY Episcopal Diocese gave higher priority to the alleviation of neighborhood poverty than the erection of an ornate cathedral. Under a 1982 program with both goals in mind, the Cathedral hired youths from Morningside Heights, Harlem and Newark, New Jersey and trained them in stone-cutting. The new artisans, following Cram's blueprints, continued the building but the work hasn't yet been finished. *St. John*, larger than any Gothic cathedral in Europe, hosts many concerts, plays, dance performances and art exhibits. Open 7am-5pm. Gift shop and tours, Tel. 316-7540, box office, Tel. 662-2133.

Hard at work on the steps of the Columbia University

Head north on Broadway and turn west on 120th St. The **Riverside Church**, built in 1930 through a donation by John D. Rockefeller, stands on Riverside dr. between 120th and 122nd Sts. The **observation deck** atop its 21-story tower affords you a great view of the Hudson River. Open Mon.-Sat. 11am-3pm, Sun. 12:30-4pm, small admission charge; its 74-bell carillon, the world's largest,

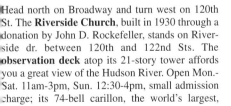

UPPER MANHATTAN AND HARLEM
1. Columbia University
2. Cathedral of St. John the Divine
3. Riverside Church
4. Grant's Tomb
5. Hamilton Grange National
   Memorial
6. Harlem School of the Arts
7. City College of NY – North Campus
8. City College of NY – South Campus
9. Audubon Terrace Museum Complex
10. Trinity Cemetery
11. Morris-Jumel Mansion

performs Sat. at noon and Sun. at 3pm. Tel
222-5900.

Like St. John the Divine, Riverside Church is
involved in supporting culture. The *Riverside
Church Theater*, most famous for its Dance
Festival, presents concerts and drama as well. Ruth
St. Denis, a modern dance pioneer, performed here
in 1934. Admission charge is always reasonable
with discounts for students and senior citizens.
Box office, Tel. 222-5900.

Across Riverside Drive, in the park at 122nd St., is
Grant's Tomb, the solid white granite mausoleum
erected in 1897 for Ulysses S. Grant (18th President) and his wife. Grant, a great Civil War
General, but an ineffective President, died a very
poor man; the sales of his posthumously-published
memoirs, however, brought $450,000 to his
family. The tomb's $600,000 construction cost was
raised by popular subscription. His words, "Let us
have peace," are carved over the tomb's entrance.
The crypt is open; two side rooms exhibit famous
memorabilia. Open Wed.-Sun. 9am-5pm, admission free, Tel. 666-1640.

Harlem harbors a second cultural enclave, with
two theaters, two museums, an important library
and a designated historic district. A brief history of
Harlem: settled by the Dutch in 1658 and urban-
ized in the late 1800s, Harlem has been inhabited
largely by Blacks since the early 1900's, excluding
the eastern area, which was settled more recently
by a largely Hispanic population and is known as

Spanish Harlem. Authors Langston Hughes, Richard Wright, Ralph Ellison and James Baldwin are Harlem-born. Take Subway 2 or 3 to 125th St. and Lenox Ave.; for safety's sake, however, you may prefer a taxi.

The *New Heritage Repertory Theater* is on the third floor of 290 Lenox Ave., at 125th St. Call the box office for information, Tel. 876-3272. The **Studio Museum of Harlem**, slightly west at 144 W 125th St., exhibits paintings and photography on themes of Africa and the Black experience in America. Open Wed.-Fri. 10am-5pm, Sat.-Sun. 1-6pm. Admission charge, Tel. 864-4500.

The *National Black Theater* is at 9 E 125th St., just east of 5th Ave., box office, Tel. 234-2469. As you cross 5th Ave., look south toward **Marcus Garvey Park**. In its center stands NYC's last surviving fire watchtower (1856). The park is bounded to the west by the **Mount Morris Park Historic District** (designated in 1971), which runs from 124th-120th Sts. and from the park west, to Lenox Ave. The houses near the Lenox Ave. end are especially beautiful.

The famous *Cotton Club* is located on 125th St. and still features great blues, jazz and gospel music in memory of the hey days. Tel. 663-7980.

Follow 125th St. to its eastern extremity. We have reached the end of this enclave; enjoy a view of the **Triborough Bridge** (1936) linking Manhattan, the Bronx and Queens.

Head north on Lenox Ave. to 126th St. The **Black Fashion Museum**, just west at 155 W 126th, exhibits theater, films and TV costumes as well as changing exhibits from foreign lands. Donations requested. Open Mon.-Fri. 12:30-7:30pm. Call for an appointment before visiting, Tel. 666-1320.

Continue north to the **Arthur Schomburg Center**, 515 Lenox Ave. near 134 St., home of America's largest collection of Black history and literature along with occasional art exhibits, Tel. 491-2200.

The next area worthy of our attention is the former country

245

estate of Alexander Hamilton, now the **Hamilton Heights Historic District**. Take Subway 2 to 145th St., head west to Convent Ave. and follow Convent Ave. south to 141st street. The historic district encompasses those blocks you passed on Convent Ave. (145th-141st Sts.) plus Hamilton Terrace, one block east and accessible from 141st or 144th Sts.

First stop is **Hamilton Grange National Memorial**, 287 Convent Ave. at 141st St., home of Alexander Hamilton, first US Secretary of the Treasury, slain by Aaron Burr in a pistol duel in 1804. A national memorial and artifacts of Hamilton's life are on display. Open Wed.-Sun. 9am-5pm, admission free, Tel. 283-5154.

The **Harlem School of the Arts**, slightly east at 645 Saint Nicholas Ave., near 141st St., has become one of America's most important schools for the performing arts – dance, theater, visual arts and music. There's a theater too, Tel. 926-4100.

A few blocks south on Convent Ave. is **City College of NY** (CUNY). **North Campus**: 138th-140th St.; **South Campus**: 131st-136th Sts., bordering Saint Nicholas Park. The **Aaron Davis Hall**, at 134th St. on the south campus, offers live performances, films and lectures, Tel. 690-8166.

Playing basketball at Harlem

Our next stop consists of the **Audubon Terrace**

Museum Complex. Take Subway 1 to 157th St. Audubon Terrace, just south on Broadway between 155th and 156th Sts. The complex comprises the following museums, most are beaux-arts style structures dating from the early 1900s.

The **American Numismatic Society** on Broadway and 156th St. has coin exhibits, numismatic library and a curator on duty to answer questions or help trace a particular coin. Open Tues.-Sat. 9am-4:30pm, Sun. 1-4pm, admission free, Tel. 234-3130.

At the Fort Tryon Park, with the George Washington Bridge in the background

The **American Academy and National Institute of Arts and Letters**, the honor society's exhibition hall exhibits writings, music scores and miscellaneous artwork. Open Mon.-Sat. 9:30am-4:30pm, Sun. 1-5pm, admission free, Tel. 368-5900.

The **Hispanic Museum**, Broadway and 155th St., offers paintings of Spanish masters and other Iberian artwork. Open Tues.-Sat. 10am-4:30pm, Sun. 1-4pm, admission free, Tel. 926-2234.

Just south of the Audubon Terrace complex is **Trinity Cemetery**, 153rd-155th Sts. from Riverside Dr., east to Amsterdam Ave., cut in two by Broadway, Tel. 283-6200. The cemetery, open only by special arrangement, is the final resting place of several Astors and Van Burens, members of families instrumental in building the city. Other luminaries buried here include John James Audubon (the land was part of his estate) and Clement Moore, author of *The Night Before*

Christmas. The lovely **Church of the Intercession** (1914) sits within the cemetery grounds at 550 W 155th St.

EXCURSIONS

The following Upper Manhattan attractions do not belong to any area mentioned thus far:

The **Morris-Jumel Mansion**, built in 1765, which was once part of the country estate of Roger Morris. General George Washington made his headquarters here in 1776, during the Revolutionary War. The home is beautiful, decorated with period furnishings and visitors are welcome to relax on the grounds. Head north on Audubon Terrace, then turn east on 160th St. It is located at 65 Jumel Terrace. Open Wed.-Sun. 10am-4pm, Admission charge, free for children under 10. Tel. 923-8008.

The Cloisters in a monastic setting

The beautiful **George Washington Bridge** at 178th St., spanning the Hudson River from Upper Manhattan to New Jersey: 3,500 ft. (1,066 m) span, gleaming 600 ft. (183 m) towers soar above the river. It was built in 1931.

Fort Tryon Park is home of **the Cloisters**. Situated close to Manhattan's northern tip, from 190th St. to Dyckman St. between Riverside Drive and Broadway. Take Bus 4 from anywhere on Madison Ave. to the last stop or Subway A. The grounds, designed by Fredrick Law Olmstead Jr., are beautiful, as is the view of the Hudson River. John D. Rockefeller Jr. donated the land to the city in 1930, and was the guiding influence in building the Cloisters (1934-1938). A mock monastery in authentic European medieval architectural style, the Cloisters houses the Metropolitan Museum of Art medieval collection. The hilltop museum overlooks the Hudson River to an undeveloped stretch of the New Jersey Palisades on the western side. It is undeveloped because Rockefeller bought it precisely to preserve the museum's unspoiled view forever. The Cloisers furnishings include exquisite tapestries, stained glass, sculptures and manuscripts. The monastic setting provides the perfect atmosphere for occaional concerts. Free tours Tues.-Thurs. at 3pm; Wed. only during the winter. Usually open Tues.-Sun. 9:30am-5:15pm. Call Tel. 923-3700 to confirm. No set entrance fee but donation suggested.

The George
Washington Bridge

BROOKLYN

Brooklyn, derived from the Dutch "Breukelen," is NYC's most populous
borough. First settled in 1636 in the area known as Flatlands, called New
Amersfoort by the Dutch, the town soon grew to include other Dutch
outposts – Midwout (now Flatbush), Boswyk (Bushwick) and New Utrecht
plus the English settlement of Gravesend. The English, taking control of the
colony in 1664, renamed Breukelen "Kings County." During the American
Revolution, Brooklyn was divided between American patriots and Tories
(British loyalists).

Brooklyn Bridge

Incorporated as a city in 1834, Brooklyn retains many aspects of its independence despite its subsequent union with the four other boroughs. The
downtown area – Borough Hall – boasts an extensive court system as well as
major financial and commercial headquarters. Brooklyn Museum houses
world-famous collections of Egyptian, pre-Columbian and primitive art. The
Botanic Gardens are famous for the Japanese cherry blossom gardens and the
Garden of Fragrance. Brooklyn once even had its own baseball team, the
Dodgers. "The Bums", as they were affectionately called, left their Ebbets
Field Stadium for Los Angeles, California in 1958; the loss is still mourned.

Brooklyn has much to be proud of, as its residents – past and present – will
gladly tell you. Some of its more famous sons and daughters are George
Gershwin, Norman Mailer, Jackie Robinson, Woody Allen, Lena Horne,
Barbara Streisand, W.E.B. Du Bois and Beverly Sills. Brooklyn's ambience
is not Manhattan's: it is traditional rather than trendy, middle-class rather
than up-scale.

Each section of Brooklyn maintains a distinct character. The heart of commerce is the port, which handles 40% of all NYC imports. With over 200 miles (320 km) of waterfront, Brooklyn is renowned for its Navy Yard. During the Civil War, the famous warship *Monitor* was launched from Williamsburg (1862). Williamsburg is largely ethnic, inhabited by Italians, Poles, Blacks, Puerto Ricans and Orthodox Jews. Bay Ridge has a sizeable Scandinavian population. Coney Island, though not as splendid as it once was, has a playground, a beach and is home to the marvellous New York Aquarium. **Brooklyn Heights** was originally the home of affluent merchants and ship owners. This neighborhood of brownstone town houses has been designated a city landmark.

Note: Before we start our tour, remember, all telephone numbers require a 718 area code if calling from Manhattan (for more details see "Introduction"). Now, let us begin.

Take Subway 2 or 3 to Clark St., and then follow Clark St. several blocks to the water. You've reached the **Brooklyn Heights Promenade**, with the most breathtaking view of the lower Manhattan skyline – Wall Street, the harbor, Brooklyn Bridge and the Statue of Liberty. While here, walk up and down a few streets and notice the homes, a sampling of Italian brownstones, wood-frame houses and apartment buildings, all extremely well-maintained. You are also within walking distance of several fine restaurants, a Mideast enclave and an antique market. If you are here on Independence Day or New Year's Eve, you will enjoy the fabulous show of fireworks.

A left turn from Clark St. takes us to **Columbia Heights**, a secluded street of brownstones and apartments parallel to the Promenade, which resembles sections of London and Paris. The homes are in demand for their view. Another left turn from Columbia Heights brings us to

Brooklyn Heights Promenade with a view of Manhattan

Montague St., the main shopping street of Brooklyn Heights: clothing boutiques, small shops, galleries and several restaurants – an impressive variety for such a small neighborhood.

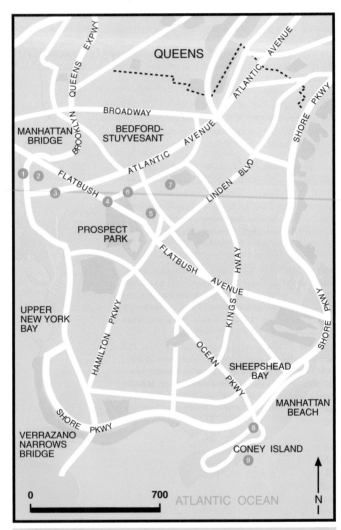

BROOKLYN

1. Brooklyn Heights Promenade
2. Borough Hall
3. Brooklyn Academy of Music
4. Grand Army Plaza
5. Botanic Garden
6. Brooklyn Museum
7. Brooklyn Children's Museum
8. Astroland
9. New York Aquarium

From here it's a short walk to Borough Hall or Atlantic Ave., the latter a stretch of Mideast restaurants and antique shops. To get to Borough Hall, turn right from Montague St. onto Henry St., then left onto Joralemon St.; Sidney Place, just off Joralemon St. to your right, is even prettier. Follow Joralemon to Court St., where we come upon the stately government buildings and courthouses of downtown Brooklyn. **Borough Hall** itself (1851) on your left at 209 Joralemon St., bears a strong resemblance to City Hall in lower Manhattan.

A house in Brooklyn Heights

From Borough Hall turn to Boerum Place and walk southwards to Atlantic Ave. – a rich hunting ground for antiques. *Horseman, Inc.*, No. 351 and *Dan's Antiques*, No. 363 are two examples. A final "must" here is *Sahadi Importing Co.*, 187 Atlantic Ave., with its wonderful aroma of spices, coffee, nuts and grains, Tel. 624-4550.

Complete the evening with a performance at the **Brooklyn Academy of Music** (BAM), 30 Lafayette Ave. (Subways 2, 3, 4, 5, D, or Q to Atlantic Ave.-Flatbush Ave.). This legendary cultural center (est. 1859) is home of the Brooklyn Philharmonic and Twyla Tharp's Dance Company; Sarah Bernhardt, Edwin Booth, Anna Pavlova and Caruso all performed here. Besides the classics, BAM is at the forefront of innovative music, dance and theater with its Next Wave Festival. BAM's season runs Sept.-June, Tel. 636-4100, credit card reservations: *Chargit*, Tel. 944-9300. Open for visits, Mon.-Fri. 10am-6pm.

The Prospect Park area offers daytime fun. Take Subway 2 or 3 to Grand Army Plaza or the D, M, QB or S Subway to **Prospect Park**. The park itself, bordered by the Grand Army Plaza, the Botanic Gardens and exclusive Prospect Park West, was designed by Frederick Law Olmstead and Calvert Vaux, better-known for Central Park but more pleased with the results of Prospect Park. **Grand Army Plaza** is the designers' conception of a majestic entrance to the park. The **Soldiers' and Sailors' Memorial Arch**, crowned by a Frederick MacMonnies sculpture, and the fountains are spectacular. No streets run through the grounds. Rent a boat at the beaux arts boathouse for a cruise

At Prospect Park

on the lake; play croquet at the park's southern end in a shelter designed by Stanford White. Free concerts are offered in the bandstand periodically throughout the summer. Ice skate from early Nov. through mid-March. For further details on all park activities, Tel. 965-8954.

North of Prospect Park across Flatbush Ave. is **Institute Park** – the Brooklyn Botanic Garden, Brooklyn Museum and the Brooklyn Public Library's main branch. The **Botanic Garden**, 1000 Washington Ave., founded in 1910 on the site of an ash dump, embraces a fragrance garden for the blind, known as the **Garden of Fragrance**, and a 90-variety rose garden. The Conservatory is a McKim, Mead & White design. Admission to the grounds is free; nominal fee on weekends and holidays for the Conservatory and specialized gardens. Tel. (718) 220-8777.

Take Subway 2 or 3 to Eastern Parkway-Brooklyn Museum for the **Brooklyn Museum**, 200 Eastern Parkway. Designed by McKim, Mead & White in 1895, the Museum houses the best Egyptian collection in the country as well as marvellous collections of African and pre-Columbian art together with important American paintings. A gift shop sells books, jewelry, antiques and reproductions. Open Wed.-Sun. 10am-5pm, closed Mon., Tues., Tel. 638-5000.

The **Brooklyn Children's Museum**, 200 Brooklyn Ave., the first of its kind in the world, is another recommended stop, especially, of course, for the kids. It's packed with terrific natural and technological environmental exhibits to wander through and touch. The neighborhood, however, is questionable; call for directions. Open Wed.-Fri. 2-5pm, Sat., Sun. noon-5pm. closed Mon., Tues., admission charge, Tel. 735-4400.

For a tour of exclusive Brooklyn architecture, take Subway 2 or 3 to Grand Army Plaza. The residential streets along Prospect Park bear much in common with those fronting Central Park. Prospect Park West and the streets of Park Slope between Union and 14th Sts. are symbolic of urban elegance: gaslights, ornate carvings and rolling stone stairways. From the subway station, walk along Plaza St. West away from

Flatbush Ave. Turn right on Lincoln Place, then left onto 8th Ave. This is a beautiful thoroughfare, lined with trees and immaculately maintained bay-fronted brownstones. Turn left onto Carroll St. On your left is **117 8th Ave.**, designed by C. P. H. Gilbert for Thomas Adams, Jr., the *Chiclets* chewing-gum millionaire. Gilbert designed much of this block, including Nos. 838, 842 and 846. The intersection of Carroll St. and Prospect Park West affords a terrific view of the **Arch** to your left. Take a right on Prospect Park West and another right onto Montgomery Place. Gilbert collaborated with real estate developer Harvey Murdock on most of this street. Turn right on 8th Ave. and then left onto Carroll St. This section of Carroll St. displays a remarkable architectural sight: a continuum of three-story brownstones with unbroken stoops. Follow Carroll St. to 7th Ave., the main shopping and dining street of Park Slope. Two of the better restaurants here are friendly *Charlie's,* 348 Flatbush Ave. (at 8th Ave. and Sterling St.) – simple American food, Tel. 857-4585, and small, romantic *Raintree's*, 142 Prospect Park West at 9th St., Tel. 768-33723.

Prospect Park

Coney Island

A full day's pleasurable if somewhat tacky entertainment is yours at **Coney Island**. Take Subway B, D, F, M, N or QB to Stillwell Ave. – Coney Island. Come for the cotton candy, corn on the cob and hot dogs, the rides of Astroland and the atmosphere. **Astroland** is a lot of fun, the most famous attraction being the Cyclone – a scary roller-coast-

er built on a lattice of white wood and iron supports. *Nathan's Famous* is indeed famous for its hot dogs, french fries, corn on the cob and the long queue, Tel. 266-3161. Astroland is open in the summer from noon to midnight, Tel. 372-0275.

Next door at W 8th St. and the Boardwalk is the **New York Aquarium**, home to whales, sharks, eels, sea turtles, penguins and other species of sea life. Open Mon.-Fri. 10am-5pm. The dolphin shows and the Children's Cove see-and-touch exhibits, however, are seasonal pleasures, closed in the winter. Admission charge, Tel. 265-3474. Parking is available.

The best nearby dinner possibilities feature Italian cuisine. *Gargiulo's*, 2911 W 15th St., serves what many consider NY's finest Italian food. Prices are reasonable. Open daily noon-10pm, Tel. 266-4891. *Carolina*, 1409 Mermaid Ave., is a very popular spot offering generous portions at affordable

prices. Reservations are not accepted; be prepared to wait for a table, Tel. 714-1294.

East of Coney Island are **Manhattan Beach** and **Brighton Beach**, two sections of a former resort for the wealthy, who lounged at the fancy hotels and gambled at the racetracks. When the masses moved in, the rich moved on. While Manhattan Beach remains exclusive,

Brighton Beach has been a solid middle-class Jewish neighborhood for 50 years. Large numbers of Russian Jewish immigrants have taken the place of older residents who, having prospered, have moved to Long Island. This neighborhood has been the inspiration for many movies and plays, among them Neil Simon's *Brighton Beach Diary* and Woody Allen's *Radio Days*. The neighborhood now features many Russian restaurants and nightclubs, most along Brighton Beach Ave.

Sheepshead Bay is another solid, middle-class seaside neighborhood. Take Subway D, M, or QB to Sheepshead Bay Station; the largely aboveground ride gives you a good view of Brooklyn. Once in Sheepshead Bay, visit the docks with their proliferation of fishing boats – some for hire, others selling their fresh catch. Along the promenade many restaurants offer these fresh fish and shellfish, but generally they are not better than other seafood restaurants in other parts of New York.

Every year the **Celebrate Brooklyn Festival** takes place, including a series of shows in the theaters and public parks at Brooklyn. All shows are free of charge. For information about the festival, which takes place in July and Aug., Tel. 783-4469, 768-0611.

Grand Army Plaza

QUEENS

Queens is the largest of NYC's five boroughs: approx. 115 sq. miles (300 sq. km). The first Dutch settlement here, Maspeth, dates back to 1642. The name Queens came later; the English captured Nieuw Amsterdam in 1664 and called the area "Queens" in honor of Catherine of Braganza, Queen Consort to King Charles II. Queens adopted the British county system of government in 1683, setting up village sub-divisions which, in a sense, still exist: the locals refer to their neighborhoods - Flushing, Forest Hills, Astoria, etc. – rather than Queens, as their homes.

Each section supplies its own historic sites, cultural activities and sporting events. Astoria offers a film studio, once used by the Marx Brothers and W.C. Fields, among others, where major motion pictures are still filmed. The annual US Open Tennis Tournament is held at Flushing Meadow Park, the site of two World's Fairs. With more park land than any other borough, Queens even maintains a stretch of public beach on the Atlantic Ocean. If you arrived by plane you probably landed in Queens at La Guardia or Kennedy Airport.

Two bridges and a tunnel, in addition to the subway, link Queens to Manhattan. The Triborough Bridge (1936) runs from Astoria in northwestern Queens to Manhattan and the Bronx. The Queensborough Bridge (1903) and the Queens Midtown Tunnel join Queens with midtown Manhattan; the former was designated a city landmark in 1973 and was commemorated in Simon & Garfunkel's pop classic, *The 59th Street Bridge Song (Feelin' Groovy)*. These arteries go to Long Island City and Astoria, two sections well worth a visit.

Note: All telephone calls to Queens require a 718 area code.

Long Island City, an industrial area on the East River shore opposite the UN,

Long Island City on the East River shore

is reached via Subway E or F. Close to Manhattan and far less expensive in rent, it has developed a sizeable artist community.

Long Island City's waterfront, slated for revitalization as a recreation area, boasts several seafood restaurants. Among them, *Water's Edge*, 44th Dr. at the River, offers the most breathtaking view of Manhattan, though the food is expensive and not up to the setting. Open daily, noon-1am, Tel. 482-0033. Nearby *Manducatis*, 13-37 Jackson Ave. at 47th St.., is a family-style Italian restaurant with delicious and less expensive offerings made of fresh ingredients. Open Mon.-Sat. 11:30am-3pm, 5-10pm, Tel. 729-4602.

The **Hunters Point Historic District** at 45th Ave. between 21st. and 23rd Sts., designated a city landmark in 1968, is a showcase of 19th-century Italian and French-style architecture.

Northeast of Long Island City is **Astoria**, an early Colonial settlement known, until 1839, as "Sunwick" named after a local Indian tribe. Now home to a large Greek population, the area around Ditmars Blvd. and Broadway abounds with Greek restaurants, coffee shops and late-night clubs. The best reason to visit Astoria by day, however, is the **Kaufman Astoria Film Studio** at 36th St.. 34th Ave. Tel. 392-5600. Used by Paramount through the 1920s and into the 1930s for Marx Brothers, W. C. Fields and Gloria Swanson films, the long-run-down facility has been revived. New York is currently a hot site for on-location filming; the Astoria Studio, for example, is a favorite of director Sidney Lumet, who made such movies as *The Wiz*, *The Verdict* and *Prince of the City*. While you visit, stop in at the **American Museum of the Moving Image**, 36th St.. and 35th Ave. for the history of motion pictures in NYC from 1896-1982, including photographs, costumes, posters, props, set designs and occasional screenings of old films. A great attraction are the computer games with movie-motifs. Open Tues.-Fri. noon-4pm, Sat., Sun. noon-6pm. For information and reservations, Tel. 784-0077. The museum gallery is open to the public by appointment only, Tel. 784-4520.

Further east along the East River is **La Guardia**

Airport, opened in 1939 on a 650-acre site and renamed in 1947 for NYC Mayor Fiorello La Guardia. The Central Terminal Building has an observation deck; observe take offs and landings

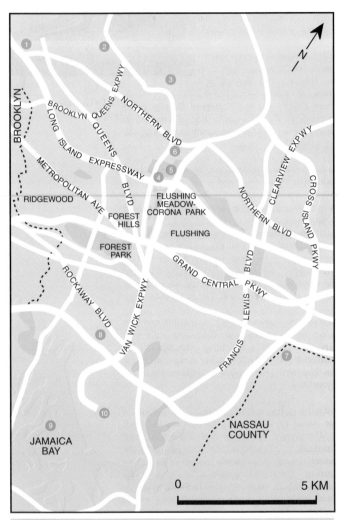

QUEENS

1. Water's Edge
2. Kaufman Astoria Film Studio
3. La Guardia Airport
4. Queens Museum
5. US Tennis Association, National Tennis Center
6. Shea Stadium
7. Belmont Park
8. Aqueduct Racetrack
9. Jamaica Bay Wildlife Refuge
10. John F. Kennedy International Airport

for a small admission fee. For general airport information, Tel. 476-5072.

Ridgewood, a solid middle-class community listed in the National Register of Historic Places, abounds with beautifully maintained turn-of-the-century rowhouses and churches. Don't miss the 200-year old **Onderdonk House** at 1-20 Flushing Ave., where the *Ridgewood Historical Society* offers programs on Colonial crafts. For information on these activities and the community as a whole, call Tel. 456-1776.

La Guardia Airport

Kew Gardens, a pastoral neighborhood of large Tudor-style homes on tree-lined streets, just half-an-hour from Manhattan, was developed in the early 1900s by Manhattan lawyer Albon Platt Man as an alternative to hectic city life, attracting mainly the affluent. The main shopping avenue, Lefferts Blvd., offers two worthwhile restaurants: *Pastrami King*, a good Jewish deli at 124-24 Queens blvd. and 82nd St.., Tel. 225-3636, and *The Garden*, 120-20 Queens Blvd., which favors the local rich singles crowd, Tel. 846-9464.

West of Kew Gardens at Park Lane South and 89th St. are the picnic areas and riding stables of *Forest Park*, Tel. 261-7674 for riding information. The **Seuffert Bandshell** offering free band concerts on Sun. June-Sept., is nearby at Woodhaven Blvd. and Myrtle Ave.

Just north of Forest Park is Forest Hills Gardens, a fine suburban residential neighborhood designed by Grosvenor Atterbury and Frederick Law Olmstead, Jr. following a 1909 commission by the Russell Sage Foundation for working-class housing. The resulting 175-acre Forest Hills Gardens suburb, built around a Tudor-style square – with brick paving, archways and tower – was so lovely that it became one of NYC's most desirable neighborhoods. The Greenway, a central park area, leads from the square through the winding residential blocks. Most homes are Tudor; quaint street lamps and sundial signposts add to the overall unity of design. The *West Side Tennis Club* is nearby, bounded by Burns and Dartmouth Sts. and 69th and 70th Aves. The "lawn tennis capital of the Western hemisphere," predecessor of

Flushing Meadow Park as home of the US Open, offers the public 46 courts in season for an admission charge. For information, Tel. 268-2300.

Flushing, now densely populated, began life as a Quaker village in the late 1600's. The **Friends' Meeting House** at 137-16 Northern Blvd. (1694) is open 2-4pm the first Sunday of every month except Jan., Feb. and Aug., Tel. 358-9636.

Shea Stadium

Flushing's main attraction may well be the **Flushing Meadow-Corona Park**. To get there, take Subway 7 to Shea Stadium. Once a swamp, Flushing Meadow Park, stretching from Jewel Ave. to Roosevelt Ave., hosted the World Fairs of 1939 and 1964, and some of the buildings still remain. The park is still used for boating, picnicking and skating. There is also a wild life conservatory here, featuring animals from North America, Tel. 760-6600. The **Queens Museum**, in the north wing of the New York City Building, presents changing exhibits as well as a permanent collection which includes a 15,000 sq. ft. model of New York City, an attraction at the 1964 Fair. Open Tues.-Fri. 10am-5pm, Sun. noon-5pm, admission charge, Tel. 592-5555.

Theater in the Park, housed in the centrally-located New York State Pavilion (another lasting benefit of the 1964 Fair) stages plays, musicals, concerts and dance, Tel. 592-5700. Children may hand-feed small animals at the Children's Zoo, 111th St.. and 54th Ave. Open daily 9:30am-4:30pm, admission free.

At Flushing Meadow Park

A highlight of the Park is the **US Tennis Association, National Tennis Center**, host to the US Open Tennis Championships since 1978. The facility maintains 27 outdoor (lighted) courts and 9 indoor courts. Open 8am-midnight. Tel. 271-5100. An alternative to tennis, ice skating, is available in the south wing of the NYC

Building beside the spectacular Unisphere. Open Nov.-Mar. Wed.-Sun., admission charge, Tel. 271-1996.

Just north of Flushing Meadow Park at 126th St.. and Roosevelt Ave. is **Shea Stadium** (capacity 55,300), where the New York Mets baseball team plays from mid-Apr. to early Oct., Tel. 507-TIXX. Take Subway 7 to Willets Point Shea Stadium. For day-of-game ticket information see the section on Yankee Stadium ("The Bronx").

The **Queens Botanical Garden** at Flushing Meadow Park's eastern edge, 43-50 Main St., maintains 15 acres of outdoor gardens and a 23-acre Arboretum, including the Bird and Bee Gardens, with active beehives, and an award-winning Wedding Garden. Open daily, 9am to dusk, admission free, Tel. 886-3800.

Contact the Queens Historical Society, Tel. 445-0021 for a walk along Flushing's Freedom Mile, tracing the area's Colonial past.

Queens College is east of Flushing Meadow Park, just off the Long Island Expressway at Kissena Blvd. Exit No. 24. The main reason to visit the College is the *Golden Center for the Performing Arts* with its weekly schedule of classical, pop and jazz concerts, theater, opera and children's events. Free parking. For information and reservations, Tel. 793-8080.

The World's Fairs' Globe at Flushing Meadow Park

The eastern extremity of Queens borders the suburban communities of Nassau County. In Douglaston, on the Queen's side, the **Alley Pond Park and Environmental Center** at 228-06 Northern Blvd., offers the naturalist a variety of interests – live animals, natural history museum, gift shop and recycling center. Among its attractions: *Cattail Pond*, a freshwater pond and wetlands, home to aquatic birds; the two-mile *Pitobik Trail* through an original Mattinecock Indian camp site; and *Turtle Pond Trail*, former site of a continental glacier, now full of vegetation, wildlife and kettle ponds. Parking and admission

free; schedule and trail maps available at the Center. Opening hours and information, Tel. 229-4000.

The **Queens County Farm Museum** is east of the Alley Pond Park at 73-50 Little Neck Parkway, Floral Park. The 52-acre farm, dating back to 1772, is still in operation. Open Sat. 11am-4pm, Sun. 1-4pm, admission free, Tel. (718) 347-3276.

Belmont Park with its picnic grounds, lake and racetrack is due south, just over the border in Nassau County. Have lunch at the racetrack clubhouse; chat with jockeys and trainers. Open 9:30am-4:30pm, Tel. (516) 488-6000, for directions and information.

Larger than Belmont is the **Aqueduct Racetrack** (capacity 80,000) at Rockaway Blvd. and 108th St.. in Ozone Park. Not only is Aqueduct the largest thoroughbred racing track in the US, it is also more accessible by public transit: the subway takes you right there. Racing season is Jan.-May and Oct.-Dec., Tel. 641-4700.

We have now reached a section of Queens which occupies a peninsula fronting the Atlantic Ocean. Jacob Riis Park, at the western end, is a beautiful public beach equipped not only with sand and surf but with boardwalk, pool and miniature golf. Open daily till dusk, admission free. Packed on summer weekends.

Eastward on the peninsula is **Rockaway Playland Amusement Park**, located at Beach 97th-98th Sts., on the ocean. Its 65 rides, games and attractions open daily at noon. Two sessions: noon-6pm, 4pm to closing. One admission ticket allows unlimited access to all adult rides; kiddie rides are not included, Tel. (914) 967-2040, for directions and information.

The **Jamaica Bay Wildlife Refuge**, home to over 300 species of birds, water fowl and small animals, lies between the peninsula and the "mainland." The park opens every day at dawn, the perfect time for bird-watching, and closes at dusk. An environmental slide show and tour are offered on weekends. Admission free. For directions and information, Tel. 474-0613. Just past the Refuge, occupying most of Queens' southern waterfront is **John F. Kennedy International Airport**.

Shea Stadium

THE BRONX

The Bronx, NYC's northernmost borough and the only one connected to the mainland, bears the name of Johannes Bronck, a Dane who settled here in 1641. With its territory distributed among a very few landowners, the Bronx grew slowly during the Colonial period. Three Bronx communities were annexed to NYC in 1874; the remainder joined by 1898.

The Bronx, from the sloping hills of exclusive Riverdale to some of the city's worst slums, is largely residential. In its eastern district we find Parkchester, NYC's best large-scale housing complex, built 1938-1942 to house a population of 40,000. The Hunter College Campus, Fordham University, and the Albert Einstein College of Medicine are only some of the Bronx's institutes of higher education. For recreation the Bronx offers several beautiful parks, the world-famous Bronx Zoo, which is the largest urban zoo in the US, and **Yankee Stadium**.

The latter – the "House that Ruth Built" – (at 161 St. and River Ave.) is home to the most successful baseball team ever. In addition to Babe Ruth, other immortal alumni include Lou Gehrig, Joe DiMaggio, Casey Stengel and Mickey Mantle. The Stadium itself, remodelled several years ago for more than $100 million, is one of the best baseball facilities in the nation. The baseball season runs from mid-April to early Oct. For advance ticket information, schedules and reservations, call *Charit*, Tel. 307-4100, or *Telecharge*, Tel. 239-6200. The

Yankee Stadium

Stadium box office is open Mon.-Fri. 9am-5pm, Tel. 293-6000. If you decide to attend a game without reservations, **avoid street scalpers** and buy your tickets at one of the many box offices around the Stadium. Bleacher seating is cheapest, though disadvantageous in two ways: it's the area most distant from the infield where things are busiest and you will be totally exposed to the elements, whatever they may be, for three hours. Better alternatives would be reserved seats between first or third base and home plate at the field or mezzanine level.

At the Bronx Zoo – the largest urban zoo in the US

Next stop is the **Hall of Fame for Great Americans**, at Bronx Community College's University Heights Center. The Hall contains the busts of almost 100 famed American statesmen, artists, authors and scientists. Open daily 10am-5pm, admission free, Tel. 220-6003.

The **Edgar Allan Poe Cottage** at Grand Concourse and East Kingsbridge Rd. was the author's home from 1846-48 and serves now as a museum of his works such as *The Raven*, *The Telltale Heart* and *Annabel Lee*. Open Mon.-Fri. 9am-5pm, Sat. 10am-4pm and Sun. 1-5pm. Admission charge, Tel. 881-8900.

The **Bronx Zoo** is an absolute must. The largest urban zoo in the US, home to over 3,600 wild animals from around the world, it can be reached by taking Subway 2 to Pelham Parkway and walking east to the Bronxdale entrance. Another option is the *Liberty Lines* express bus service from Madison Ave. at 28th, 32th, 40th, 47th, 54th, 63rd and 84th Sts. Tel. 652-8400, 367-1010. for schedule and information.

The Zoo opens Mon.-Fri. 10am-5pm, weekends until 5:30pm. Admission charge Fri.-Mon.; free the rest of the week; contribution recommended. Children under 16 must be accompanied by an adult. To reserve a free guided walking tour, available only Sat. and Sun., Tel. 220-5141.

The Zoo's tenants, living in natural habitats in the 265-acre expanse, hail from around the globe:

Wild Asia: a monorail takes you through Asian

forests populated with free roaming elephants, rhinoceroses, antelopes and tigers.

African Plains: giraffes, zebras, gazelles and lions live without bars, though the paths are separated by moats.

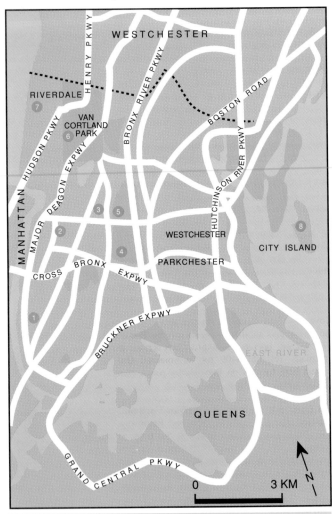

THE BRONX

1. Yankee Stadium
2. Hall of Fame of Great Americans
3. Edgar Allan Poe Cottage
4. Bronx Zoo
5. New York Botanical Garden
6. Van Cortlandt Museum and Park
7. Wave Hill
8. City Island Historical Nautical Museum

World of Birds: a wide variety of exotic birds soar freely above you in this enclosed rain-forest; a simulated thunderstorm occurs every day at 2pm.

De Jur Aviary: a colony of cliff and beach-dwelling South American penguins.

World of Darkness: the Zoo has turned day into night, enabling you to observe nocturnal animals when they are awake.

Children's Zoo: climb a spider's web; try on a turtle shell; pet and feed the farm animals. Small entrance fee requested.

One of the Bronx Zoo's tenants

Cross Pelham Parkway for the Zoo's neighbor, the **NY Botanical Gardens**: 250 acres of outdoor flora including rose garden, rock garden and 40 acres of uncut hemlock. Open April-Oct., Mon.-Sun. 10am-6pm; Nov.-March until 4pm. Don't miss the **Enid A. Haupt Conservatory**, a Victorian Crystal Palace of 11 glass pavilions including desert houses, sub-tropical groupings and a palm court. The Conservatory also operates *Greenworld,* a teaching center for young visitors. Advance registration for courses and tours, Tel. 220-8748. The *Snuff Mill*, an 18th-century stone building where snuff was once ground, is now a snack bar with an outdoor dining terrace and a gorgeous view. Tel. 817-8700.

Move on to Riverdale, an exclusive area of estates and apartments in the northwest of the Bronx. *Liberty Lines* operates an express bus service to Riverdale, Tel. 652-8400 for information. Our interest here focuses on two nearby parks, Van Cortlandt Park and Wave Hill.

Van Cortlandt Park houses the **Van Cortlandt Museum**, just north of 242nd St. and Broadway. The 1748 mansion, which served at one point as George Washington's military headquarters, has been restored with furnishings from the Dutch and English Colonial periods. Tours and occasional concerts are offered. Open Tues.-Sat. 10am-4:45pm, Sun. 2-4:45pm, admission charge, Tel. (718) 543-3344.

Wave Hill, nearby at Independence Ave. and 249th St., is a beautiful 280-acre estate overlooking the Hudson River. Previously occupied by Theodore Roosevelt, Mark Twain, Arturo Toscanini, among others, Wave Hill and its lush grounds host an annual outdoor sculpture show and free concerts in the stately Armor Hall. Some of these concerts are live; others are recordings from Wave Hill's music collection, which includes all of Toscanini's commercial concerts. Wave Hill is open daily 10am-4:30pm, closed Mon.; guided tour of the garden daily at 2:15pm. Weekday admission free, Tel. 549-3200.

Off the Bronx's eastern shore is **City Island**, linked to the mainland by a narrow bridge which may be the only indication that you are still in NYC. City Island resembles a small New England town, complete with sailboats and yacht clubs. The Island has one main boulevard; streets are lined with farmhouses, quaint bungalows and gingerbread houses. Seafood restaurants abound. Visit the crafts center; rent a fishing boat or sailboat. The **City Island Historical Nautical Museum**, 190 Fordham St., exhibits the island's history from pre-Colonial days to its present role as a yachting center. Open Sun. 2-4pm, admission free, Tel. 885-1616 .

Winter in City Island

STATEN ISLAND

The westernmost of NYC's five boroughs, Staten Island – officially Richmond County – was the last to be founded (1661), the last to join the city (1898) and the least well-known. The reason probably lies in its geography: separated by water from the other boroughs and closer to New Jersey than New York, Staten Island is not connected to the rest of the city by subway. Take Subway R to Whitehall St. or Subway 1 to South Ferry, the last stop in Manhattan. The ferry ride is inexpensive and quite romantic, especially on the return leg to Manhattan. From St. George on the Staten Island side, reach your destinations by cab or bus, but call each location first for directions or public transit information.

All telephone calls from Staten Island require a 718 area code.

Staten Island and the ferry connecting it with Manhattan

A row of antique shops await you on Bay St., within walking distance of the ferry dock. One of which is *The Edgewater Hall Antique Center* at 691 Bay St. – a large collection of boutiques, Tel. 720-0900. Most of the shops are open Wed.-Sun. noon-5pm, closed Mon. and Tues.

A five-minute ride from the dock on the No. 2 Bus brings you to the **Staten Island Children's Museum** at 15 Beach St. The Museum is worth-while for its daily young people's programs. Participation is based on a first-come/first-served basis; membership in the museum is included with the admission fee. Open Tues.-Fri., Sun. and holidays noon-5pm, Sat. 11am-5pm. Most programs begin at 1:30pm, Tel. (718) 448-6557.

The short trip to Richmondtown brings us to

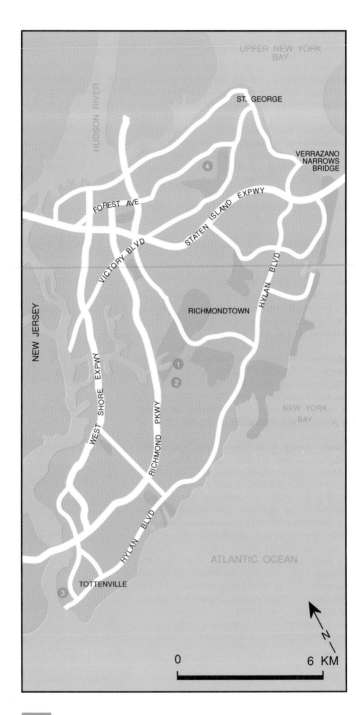

another worthy museum, the **Jacques Marchais Center of Tibetan Art** at 338 Lighthouse Ave. Set atop a hill, the museum's two buildings house America's largest private Tibetan art collection plus work from other Asian cultures. Open Sat.-Sun. 1-5pm Apr.-Nov.; Thurs.-Sun. 1-5pm June-Aug.; closed Dec.-Mar., Tel. (718) 987-3478.

While in Richmondtown visit the **Richmondtown Restoration**, 441 Clarke Ave., a re-creation of 17th-19th century village life. Several buildings are open to the public, some still located on their original sites. Open Wed.-Sun. 1-5pm. Tel. 351-1611. Take part in period craft-making and baking; learn all about methods of historic preservation. The Restoration's two museums, the **Transportation Museum** and the **Staten Island Historical Society Museum**, display exhibits of local period life. Museum gift shop, snack bar and picnic grounds available. Open Wed.-Sun. 1-5pm. Admission charge, Tel. 351-1611.

On the Staten Island Ferry

Following Hylan Blvd. to its end in Tottenville, we come to the **Conference House** (1670). Here in 1776, British Admiral Lord Howe and colonists Benjamin Franklin and John Adams convened in the only peace conference devoted to preventing the American Revolution. Enjoy exhibits of period craft-making and cooking; have a picnic on the grounds. Open Wed.-Sun. 1-5pm April-Sept.; Wed.-Sun. 1-4pm Oct.-Mar.; closed Mon., Tues. and holidays. Admission charge, Tel. 984-2086.

Staten Island's best restaurant is *Framboise*, a short bus or cab ride from the ferry at 585 Forest Ave., New West Brighton. Its interesting nouvelle-cuisine menu, which changes monthly, is prepared by chef-owner Frank Puleo. The decor is lovely: five cozy dining rooms graced with raspberry-hued upholstery and antiques. The ferry ride and *Framboise* add up to a romantic evening. Open Tues.-Sat. 6-11pm, Sun. 3:30-8:30pm, Tel. 448-4252.

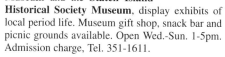
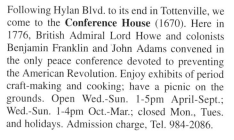

STATEN ISLAND

1. *Jacques Marchais Center of Tibetan Art*
2. *Richmondtown Restoration*
3. *Conference House*
4. *Framboise*

A few words on the island's bridges: The **Goethals Bridge** (1928) is named for the builder of the Panama Canal and spans Arthur Kill to New Jersey. **Outerbridge Crossing** was opened the same year and serves the same purpose. **Bayonne Bridge**, the world's longest steel arch bridge upon construction (1931), also connects Staten Island with New Jersey. The only bridge between Staten Island and another NYC borough (Brooklyn) is the **Verrazano-Narrows Bridge**. The graceful steel bridge, built in 1964, seems at night to be illuminated by twinkling diamonds. It is the world's longest suspension bridge at 4,260 ft. (1,300 m), and named after Giovanni da Verrazano, the first European known to have entered New York Harbor and explored the area.

Verrazano-Narrows Bridge, the world's longest suspension bridge

"MUSTS"

As we suggested in our introduction, the following is a list of not-to-be-missed-places. The selection, organized more-or-less in order of importance, includes some of New York's most famous buildings, museums and sites, without which no visit to the Big Apple can be considered complete.

Statue of Liberty: Take the ferry from Gangway No. 1 at Battery Park. Take Subway 1, 9 to South Ferry, Subway 4 or 5 to Bowling Green or R to Whitehall St. The ferry operates every day from 9am-4pm, Tel. 363-3200 (see "Lower Manhattan", p. 55).

Empire State Building: 5th Ave. and 34th St. Take Subway B, D, F, N, Q, or R to 34th St. or the Subway 6 to 33rd St. Observatories open: 9:30am-midnight, 7 days a week. Tel. 736-3100. Admission charge (see "Herald Square", p. 129).

Times Square: Intersection of 42nd St., Broadway and 7th Ave. NYC's busiest, flashiest and most decadent locale. Take Subway 1, 2, 3, 7, N or R to 42nd St./Times Square (see "The Theater District", p. 148).

Rockefeller Center: extends from 48th to 52nd Sts. and from 5th Ave. to midway between 6th and 7th aves. Attraction: the RCA Building, the Plaza, Radio City Music Hall, shops, exhibits and restaurants. Take Subway N or R to 49th St., the Subway 6 to 51st St., or Subway B, D, F or Q to 47th-50th Sts. (see "Fifth Ave.", p. 159).

St. Patrick's Cathedral: 5th Ave. and 51st St., the most beautiful church in the city. For travel directions see Rockefeller Center (see "Fifth Ave.", p. 163).

Broadcasting from the United Nations Headquarters

United Nations: 1st Ave. at 46th St. Admission charge. Children under five not admitted. Guided tours begin every 30 minutes every day from 9:15am-4:45pm. To arrange for tours in other languages, Tel. 963-1834 (see "East Side, 42nd-51st Sts", p. 179).

Metropolitan Museum of Art: 5th Ave. and 82nd St., one of

An exhibit at the American Museum of Natural History

the world's greatest museums. It is open Tues.-Thur. and Sun. 9:30am-5:15pm, Fri.-Sat. 9:30am-8:45pm, closed Mon. Tel. 535-7710. Take the Subway 4, 5, or 6 to 86th St. (see "Museum Mile", p. 203).

Guggenheim Museum: 5th Ave. and 89th St. Open Sun.-Wed. 10am-6pm, Fri., Sat. 10am-8pm. Closed Thur. Admission charge, free on Tues. 5-8pm and for children under 12. Tel. 423-3500. Take Subway 4, 5, or 6 to 86th St. (see "museum mile", p. 202).

American Museum of Natural History: 79th St. and Central Park West. Affiliated with the Hayden Planetarium and home to the world's finest dinosaur collections and archives. Open Mon.-Sun. 10am-5:45pm; Fri., Sat. 10am-8:45pm, admission charge. Tel. 769-5100. Take Subway 1 to 79th St. or Subway B or C to 81 St. (see "79th-96th Sts.", p. 236).

World Trade Center: Cortlandt and Church Sts.; six buildings and an underground concourse of shops and restaurants, of which the Twin Towers (One and Two WTC) are the most famous. Visit the Commodities Trading Observation deck Mon.-Fri. 9:30am-3pm, admission free. The Observation Deck on the 107th floor of Two WTC is open 7

The World Trade Center

days a week, 9:30am-9:30pm. Admission charge except for children under 6, Tel. 435-4170. Take Subway 1, R or N to Cortlandt St. or A, C or E to Chambers St. (see "Lower Manhattan", p. 66).

New York Stock Exchange: 20 Broad St. Admission to Visitor's Center and Trading Floor Observation Deck free. Open Mon.-Fri. 10am-4pm, Tel. 656-5167. Take Subway A, M or Z to Broad St., Subway 1, R or N to Rector St., or 2, 3, 4, or 5 to Wall Street (see "Lower Manhattan", p. 64).

South Street Seaport: 19 Fulton St. A complex combining restored 19th-century buildings and shops, restaurants, bars, museums and entertainment. Open 10am-10pm 7 days a week; restaurant and bars are open later. Sunday hours: retail stores noon-8pm, food shops 10am-10pm. Museum opens Mon.-Sat. 10am-7pm, Sun. 10am-6pm. Admission charge, Tel. 732-7678, **Sea-Port**. Take Subway J, M, Z, 2, 3, 4 or 5 (see "Lower Manhattan", p. 70).

A street in Chinatown

Chinatown: the area south of Canal St. between Mulberry St. and the Bowery, with Mott St. at its heart. Take Subway J, M, N, R, Z or 6 to Canal St. (See "Chinatown", p. 77).

Intrepid Sea Air And Space Museum: Pier 86, Hudson River at W 46th St. Open Wed.-Sun. 10am-5pm, during summer 7 days. Tel. 245-0072. Take Bus M27 or M42 to last stop (see "The Theater District", p. 154).

Museum of Modern Art (**MOMA**): 11 W 53rd St., exhibits post- Impressionism through Contemporary art, including films and furniture design. Open Sat.-Tues. 11am-6pm, Thur., Fri., noon-8:30pm. Closed Wed. Admission charge, free under 16 accompanied by adult. Take Subway 6 to 51st St. or Subway E or F to 5th Ave, Tel. 708-9750 (see "Fifth Ave.", p. 165).

Frick Collection: 1st E 70th St., a superb collection of art, antiquities and artifacts. Open Tues.-Sat. 10am-6pm, Sun. and holidays 1-6pm. Closed Mon. Admission charge. Children under 10 not admitted, Tel. 288-0700. Take Subway 6 to 68th St. (see "Madison Ave.", p. 196).

Lincoln Center: Broadway and 62nd-65th Sts. –

home to the Metropolitan Opera House, New York State Theater, Avery Fisher Hall, Damrosch Park, Alice Tully Hall and the Julliard Music School. Take Subway 1 to 66th St. (see "59th-77th Sts.", p. 225).

Bloomingdale's: Lexington and 3rd Aves., from 59th-60th Sts. – the department store with class. Take Subway 4, 5, 6, R or N to 59th St., Tel. 705-2000 (see "The East 50s", p. 184).

Macy's: one of the world's largest department stores, occupying the square block from Broadway-7th Ave. and 34th-35th Sts. Take Subway B, D, F, N, Q or R to 34th St., Tel. 695-4400 (see "Herald Square", p. 132).

Tiffany's: exclusive jewelry store, 5th Ave. and 57th St., next to Trump Tower, Tel. 755-8000 (see "Fifth Ave.", p. 169).

Trump Tower: 5th Ave. between 56th-57th Sts., the most eagerly anticipated Midtown building. Attractions: exclusive shops, restaurants and apartments (see "Fifth Ave.", p. 168).

Chrysler Building: 42nd St. and Lexington Ave., the most glorious of NYC's art-deco skyscrapers. Visit the lobby. Take Subway 4, 5, 6, or 7 to 42nd St. (see "East Side, 42nd-51st Sts.", p. 176).

Inside the Metropolitan Museum of Art

Central Park: an oasis in the middle of the city. Zoo, recreational lake, sport fields, etc. Entrance to the park is free. Do not walk around after dark.

Many lines reach the park, including those which go to the Museum of Natural History (see "Central Park", p. 215).

Washington Square Park: in the center of Greenwich Village. A living museum of New Yorkers. Colorful and "hip" street musicians, comedians, students and drug dealers all live together in harmony. Take Subway A, B, C, D, E, F or K to W 47th St. (see "Greenwich Village", p. 98).

Central Park – right in the middle of the city

MAKING THE MOST OF YOUR STAY

Wining and Dining

Culinary pleasures are a serious matter in the Big Apple, if you take into consideration the amounts of time and money spent by locals on dining out. The quality and character of the restaurants are fervently discussed and rated, and establishments flourish or wane depending on local favor. A wide variety of eating pleasures await the visitor to New York, with restaurants galore to suit both palate and pocket.

At Central Park

Generally, people dine in restaurants in the evening, for their main meal of the day. Most restaurants are quiet during the day hours as New Yorkers prefer to grab a bite for lunch from street vendors – such as hot dogs or pretzels. Restaurateurs try to encourage breakfast and lunchtime dining by lowering prices (see "Thrifty Spending", p. 43).

The human tapestry of the city, a consequence of the many waves of immigrants that reached its shores, is reflected in the culinary variety of New York. In some cases the geographical remoteness from the homeland has tended to improve the fare, and many Chinese restaurants in Manhattan offer dishes more delicious than can be found in Shanghai or Peking! The range of restaurants, the food and the prices in New York are constantly being reappraised according to what fads are currently "in" or "out." In the middle of the 80's, the city was swept by a wave of Japanese eateries. In the late 80's this wave subsided somewhat in favor of macrobiotic and organic eating places, and other health food restaurants which adhere to different philosophies of life.

Be aware that better restaurants usually require jacket and tie for men. The women's dress code is less restrictive but dresses are better received than slacks. With regard to reservations, some restaurants don't accept them at all; others, though booked weeks in advance, just might have a last-minute cancellation. It's always a good idea to call ahead of time.

Most restaurants accept credit cards, but to avoid unpleasant surprises it is always better to find this out in advance. The standard rate for tipping is 15%, which rises to 20% at better restaurants (5% for the captain and 15% for the waiter). The 15% can easily be calculated as it is approximately double the 8% municipal tax which appears on the bill. Doormen and coat check attendants should be tipped.

The following is a restaurant guide arranged first by those establishments which are typical of the city, followed by those arranged according to ethnic cuisine, such as Chinese, Italian, Japanese, etc.

TOP OF THE TOWN

In pampered New York a number of restaurants have transformed into social institutions for the wealthy elite. These restaurants are extremely elegant, and one has to dress accordingly. They are all very expensive, but this does not seem to be of any importance to those who dine here. Advance booking is essential.

Lutece: 249 E 50th St., Tel. 752-2225. French cuisine, regarded as one the city's most exclusive restaurants.

Le Cirque: 58 E 65th St., Tel. 794-9292. French cuisine, with classical dishes as well as nouvelle cuisine.

Four Seasons: 99 E 52nd St., Tel. 754-9494. Here the decor and menu change with the season. Magnificent art works, some by Picasso, adorn the walls.

Le Bernardin: 155 W 51st St., Tel. 489-1515. A superb French restaurant, particularly recommended for its seafood.

La Grenouille: 3 E 52nd St., Tel.

Checking the menu at Lincoln Center

752-1495. French kitchen, both traditional and nouvelle cuisine.

Petrossian: 182 W 58th St., Tel. 245-2215. New restaurant near Carnegie Hall. Pink-granite floors, Erte-designed mirrors, caviar with champagne or vodka. Very expensive.

FOOD WITH A VIEW

Atop some of New York's skyscrapers are restaurants and bars which offer magnificent views of the city. These are usually popular cocktail spots with visitors who wish to see the city from another angle after a busy day of touring and shopping. These establishments are more of an attraction for their views rather than their menus.

Top of the Sixes: 666 5th Ave., Tel. 757-6662. American menu at moderate prices, with a dramatic 38th floor view.

Top of the Tower: Atop Beekman Tower, corner 1st Ave. and 49th St., Tel. 355-7300. A wonderful view of the eastern side of the city. Different floor shows. Expensive.

Nirvana: On a rooftop at 30 Central Park Square. Offers Indian-Bangladesh and Pakistani gourmet. Tel. 486-5700.

Windows of the World: Located on the 107th floor of the Twin Towers, this is the highest and most famous

restaurant in the city. Actually it is a number of restaurants and cocktail lounges offering French and American cuisine at moderate to expensive prices. The experience of eating 1,300 ft. above the ground is perhaps more impressive than the food itself. Advance booking and formal attire. Tel. 938-1100.

SIMPLY NEW YORK

There are a number of typically New York restaurants which have become popular with tourists. They gained popularity either for their pleasant atmosphere, or for a famous chef who once worked there or even for appearing in a movie.

Union Square Café: 21 E 16th St., Tel. 243-4020. Modern and original.

Brother Jimmy's BBQ: 76th St. and 1st Ave., Tel. 545-7427. A well known establishment, most popular among the younger folk (after 11pm) serves a southern, moderately priced cuisine.

Carnegie Deli: 854 7th Ave., Tel. 757-2245. Always crowded, huge sandwiches, good fun, moderately priced.

Gallagher's Steak House: 228 W 52nd St., between 8th Ave. and Broadway, Tel. 245-5336. Has served American cuisine for 50 years in old NY atmosphere. Over 600 steaks are displayed in a chilled glass case. Open noon-midnight. Expensive.

Sparks Steak House at 210 East 46th St., Tel. 687-4855, has the best steaks in the city and a wonderful wine cellar.

Tavern on the Green: Corner of Central Park and W 67th St., Tel. 873-3200. This crystal palace offers European and American fare at moderate to expensive prices. Advance booking and jacket and tie required.

Russian Tea Room: 150 W 57th St., Tel. 265-0947. Situated near Carnegie Hall, the atmosphere here is nostalgic old Russian, reminiscent of Czarist splendor. Russian and American kitchen. Book ahead for dinner, formal dress. Moderately priced.

Sardi's: 234 W 44th St., Tel. 221-8440. Theatrical restaurant, haunt of actors and their directors, offering Italian and American menus. Preferably jacket and tie, advanced booking required. Moderate to expensive prices.

"Club 21": 21 W 52nd St., Tel. 582-7200. This famous club has undergone extensive renovations. New and traditional American cuisine prepared by the top American chef of nouvelle cuisine, Alain Sailhal. Formal dress and advance booking recommended. Moderate to expensive.

Teacher's Too: 81 Broadway Ave. (Upper West Side). A fine restaurant with an enormous selection of salads, seafood and pasta in high quality.

Gotham Bar and Grill, 12 East 12th St., Tel. 620-4020 offers a selection of Italian, French and NY cuisine and... it's "in"!

GOURMET STORES AND DELIS

Scattered throughout the city, these delicatessens are distinctly New York. They serve everything from salads, to cheese platters to sausages, specializing mainly in "home-cooked" meals. One can sit down to a full meal, or just order a sandwich. The sandwiches are made to order and are generally enormous and very filling. Most delis are small establishments, but some have developed into real gourmet establishments. One is *Zabar's*, 2245 Broadway, Tel. 787-2000, famous for its bagel and lox. *Balducci's* between 9th and 10th Sts. in Greenwich Village serves delicious cheeses and sausages from the all over the world. At *Mad 61*, located in the basement storey of *Barney's*, one can also sample superb cheeses,

lots of salads and other wonderful food on 10 East 61, Tel. 833-2200.

ITALIAN

Many Italian restaurants can be found in greater New York, starting from the inexpensive family restaurants in Brooklyn to deluxe establishments in Manhattan. Note that in Little Italy there are more Italian coffee shops and confectioners than exclusive restaurants.

Parioli Romanissimo: 24 E 81st St., Tel. 288-2391. A prestigious and very expensive restaurant, one of the best the city has to offer. Reserve a table in advance, formal dress required.

Lello: 65 E 54th St., Tel. 751-1555. Excellent food in a subdued but elegant setting. The Spaghetti Primavera is particularly recommended. Book in advance. Expensive.

Il Nido: 251 E 53rd St., Tel. 753-8450. Superb restaurant, specializing in northern Italian dishes. Expensive. Book in advance.

Tre Scalini: 230 E 58th St., Tel. 688-6888. Decor reminiscent of restaurants in Rome. Northern Italian fare. Expensive. Book in advance.

Trastevere: 309 E 83rd St., Tel. 734-6343. A popular restaurant which has a glatt kosher branch

called *Trastevere 84* at 155 E 84th St., Tel. 744-0210. Moderate prices.

Patsy's: 236 W 56th St., Tel. 247-3491. Excellent Neapolitan cuisine. Advance booking recommended. Despite simple decor, formal dress is required. Moderately priced.

Grand Ticino: 228 Thompson St., Tel. 777-5922. Beautiful location in the heart of the Village, one block from Washington Square. The restaurant has been open since 1919; a lovely place to spend the evening after wandering around the Village all day. Tasty and moderately priced.

In Little Italy
Paesano: 135 Mulberry St., Tel. 966-3337. Authentic atmosphere in a spacious restaurant. True Italian fare. A must for those who enjoy Italian atmosphere; music sometimes played live by old Italian musicians. Inexpensive.

Luna's: 112 Mulberry St., Tel. 226-8657. Popular food, the mussels are particularly good. The gimmick which originally attracted people to the restaurant was the rustic rudeness of the waiters. Today, the service is more polite and the establishment is less popular. Inexpensive.

INDIAN
Lovers of Indian cooking can have their fill in any of the abundant Indian restaurants to be found in East Village. It is not advisable, however, to walk around here after dark. There are also a proliferation of Indian restaurants between 20th and 30th Sts. on the East Side.

Dawat Haute: 210 E 58th St., Tel. 355-7555. "New York's Best Indian Restaurant" (NY Magazine 5/92). Reserve a table in advance.

Taste of India: 181 Bleecker St., Tel. 982-0810. A small and quaint restaurant in the center of Greenwich Village, next to Washington Square. The food has a definite moderate American influence. Inexpensive. Suitable for a break while touring the area.

Village Maha Rajah: corner of 7th Ave. South and Bleecker St., Tel. 243-4362. Nice selection of breads. Moderate prices.

CHINESE
The seemingly endless number of Chinese restaurants throughout New York can be very daunting for the uninitiated. In Chinatown, for instance, there are dozens of restaurants, one next to the other. This is in addition to all those found in other parts of town. Before setting out, remember that there are different kinds of Chinese food: Schezuan and Hunan are spicy and hot; Cantonese and Mandarin are much milder.

Take note that the most Chinese restaurants serve lunches from 11:30am-2:30pm at greatly reduced prices. For only a few dollars you can enjoy a tasty and filling meal. This is particularly convenient for tourists who want to walk into any such restaurant unplanned and have a satisfying and inexpensive lunch.

Tse Yang: 34 E 51st St., Tel. 688-5447. Like its sister restaurant in Paris, this establishment serves excellent French-Chinese fare. An intimate atmosphere and expensive prices. Advance reservations and formal dress required.

Shun Lee: 155 E 55th St. (opposite Lincoln Center), Tel. 371-8844. First rate Chinese food. Expensive and suitable for special occasions. It has another branch:
Shun Lee West: at 43 W 65th St., Tel. 595-8895. This is worth visiting just for the excellent

A restaurant in Chinatown

selection of Dim Sun. Reserve tables in advance.

Peking Duck House: 22 Mott St., Tel. 227-1810. An excellent restaurant in Chinatown. It is recommended to order the specialty of the house, Peking Duck, in advance, and come when very hungry! Moderately priced.

There are a number of simpler and cheaper Chinese restaurants near *Peking Duck House*:

HSF: 578 2nd Ave., Tel. 689-6969. Hong Kong-style kitchen. Pleasant atmosphere. The owners boast a menu with over 60 types of Dim Sun. Moderately priced. Book in advance.

The Cottage: 33 Irving Place (on Union Square between 15th and 16th Sts.), Tel. 505-8600. Good Chinese cuisine.

JAPANESE

Like mushrooms after the rain, dozens of Japanese restaurants have sprung up all over New York in the last decade. With the change in fad and fashion, a number of these subsequently closed down but there is still an impressive number of Japanese restaurants to enjoy throughout the city.

Takesushi: 71 Vanderbilt Ave., Tel. 867-5120. As the name of the restaurant testifies, the specialty here is *sushi*. Excellent food at moderate prices.

Hatsuhana: 17 E 48th St., Tel. 355-3345. An established Japanese restaurant. Excellent *sashimi*, possibly the best in town. It has another branch at 237 Park Ave., Tel. 661-3400.

Mitsukoshi: 461 Park Ave., Tel.

935-6444. An elegant restaurant, with completely authentic Japanese cuisine. Moderate prices. Book in advance.

Nobo: A restaurant and Sushi-bar, 105 Hudson St., Tribeca, Tel. 219-0500.

Benihana: Japanese food prepared American style. Goes under the name of a "Japanese Steak House". The waiters and chefs take advantage of every opportunity to prepare the food next to the table with an impressive display of swords and fire. Suitable for those uninitiated in Japanese food, or for those who feel like a fun evening. Moderately priced, there are branches with the identical menu in several locations: 15 W 44th St., Tel. 682-7120, 120 E 56th St., Tel. 593-1627 and 47 W 56th St., Tel. 581-0930.

A table for two at a restaurant in Lincoln Center

MEXICAN
Mexican Village: A very quiet restaurant with a large menu. Moderate prices. Advance reservations recommended, Tel. 475-9805.

Cantina: 221 Columbus Ave., Tel. 873-2606. A delightful old restaurant which serves food that is not quite so spicy. Inexpensive.

Rosa Mexicana: 1063 1 Ave., Tel. 753-7407. Specializes in stuffed peppers, fish in an oriental herb and other delightful Mexican dishes.

Rosa's place: 303 W 48th St., Tel. 586-4853. The finest Mexican restaurant in the Theater District.

KOSHER
Levana: 141 W 69th St., Tel. 877-8457. Glatt Kosher. Superb meat. Moderately priced.

Trastevere 84: 155 E 84th St. Glatt kosher Italian cuisine, Tel. 744-0210.

UKRAINIAN
Kiev: 117 St. and 6th Ave. Tel. 727-0144. Open 24 hours a day. This is definitely the place to visit for an excellent Ukrainian palate.

FRENCH
Bouley, 165 Duane St., Tel. 608-3852. Excellent, exclusive.

CHAIN RESTAURANTS
Fast food chains are very characteristic of American culture. The food is mass produced and the standard plastic furnishings of these restaurants are well suited to the fare. Hamburgers, fries and coke are the most popular, and are served up to you almost immediately. A whole "meal" can cost you less than $5. The popularity of these joints is undisputed, particularly among children.

McDonalds and *Burger King* are the two main chains for hamburgers. There is a *McDonalds* branch at 160 Broadway, Tel. 385-2063. Another place for superb hamburgers is *Jackson Hole Hamburgers* at 517 Columbus Ave. Tel. 962-5177. *Kentucky Fried Chicken*, as its name states, specializes in fried chicken in a rich batter. The *Sizzler* chain offers better food at reasonable prices, specializing in steaks. They have an impressive salad bar which is sufficient as a meal on its own.

Entertainment

New York City has it all. In spite of rumors that it is no longer the hub of international art and culture, New York is still the culture capital of the world – offering the best in every form of entertainment.

Local newspapers and magazines print details about what is on all around New York. "Arts and Leisure", the *New York Times* Sunday supplement is a comprehensive and invaluable source of up-to-date information on all cultural events taking place in the city. Another excellent weekly guide is the *New York Magazine*, which has details on everything that goes on in the city. It includes performance times and prices. For those who enjoy alternative culture, the *Village Voice*, which comes out each Wednesday, is filled with information about not-so-mainstream happenings. The city's *Critic Center* publishes an excellent booklet every season which has details about forthcoming shows, within the next few months (see their "Information for Tourists").

Evening performance hours are Mon.-Sat. 3pm-8pm; for matinees Wed.-Sat. 10am-2pm, Sun. 12-7pm.

THEATERS

What would New York be without glittering **Broadway** and the spectacular musicals which are staged each evening in the different theaters? And which visitor to the city can resist the temptation of those beckoning neon lights of Times Square on his way to a show? In addition to the glitter of Broadway, there are also the **off-Broadway** shows and the experimental **off-off-Broadway** productions. The most expensive shows are, naturally, on Broadway, but many successful Broadway shows started out off-Broadway in the smaller experimental theaters.

Another excellent weekly guide is the *New York Magazine*, which has details on exhibitions and whatever is going on in the city. It also includes performance times and prices.

Here is a list of 42nd St. theaters:
Actors and Directors Theater: 410 W 42nd St., Tel. 697-0707.
Harold Clurman Theater: 412 W 42nd St., Tel. 749-7959.
Samuel Beckett Theater: 412 W 42nd St., Tel. 594-2826.
Playwrights Horizons: 416 W 42nd St., the most prestigious of the lot, Tel. 564-1235.
Intar Theater: 420 W 42nd St., Spanish-language productions, Tel. 695-6134.

Douglas Fairbanks Theater: 432 W 42nd St., Tel. 239-4321.

The following, nearby though off Theater Row, are considered off-Broadway:

American Place: 111 W 46th St. between Broadway and 6th Ave., Tel. 840-2960.

Ensemble Studio Theater: 549 W 52nd at 11th Ave., Tel. 247-3405.

Irish Arts Center: 553 W 51st at 11th Ave., Tel. 757-3318.

Negro Ensemble Co./Theater 4: 424 W 55th between 9th and 10th Aves., Tel. 582-5860.

Puerto Rican Traveling Theater: 276 W 43rd at 8th Ave., Tel. 354-1293.

The Lambs: 130 W 44th between Broadway and 6th Ave., Tel. 997-1780.

The Quigh: 108 W 43rd between Broadway and 6th Ave., Tel. 382-0618.

Westside Arts Theater: 407 W 43rd at 9th Ave., Tel. 315-2244.

**Let's move on to the "genuine" Broadway theaters.
A brief list:**

Barrymore: 243 W 47th St.

between Broadway and 8th Ave., Tel. 239-6200.

Booth: 222 W 45th St. between 8th and Broadway, Tel. 239-6200.

Broadway: 1681 Broadway, Tel. 239-6200.

Brooks Atkinson: 810 7th Ave., Tel. 719-4099.

Circle in the Square: 1633 Broadway at 50th St., Tel. 307-2700.

Cort: 138 W 48th St. between 6th and 7th Aves, Tel. 239-6200.

Edison: 240 W 47th St. between Broadway and 8th Ave., Tel. 239-6200.

Eugene O'Neill: 230 W 49th between 8th Ave. and Broadway, Tel. 382-2790.

Gershwin: 1633 Broadway at 50th St., Tel. 586-6510.

Golden: 252 W 45th St. between 8th Ave. and Broadway, Tel. 246-6740.

Helen Hayes: 240 W 44th St. between 8th Ave. and Broadway, Tel. 944-9450.

Imperial: 249 W 45th St. between 8th Ave. and Broadway, Tel. 239-6200.

Longacre: 230 W 48th St. between Broadway and 8th Ave., Tel. 239-6200.

Lunt Fontanne: 205 W 46th St. between Broadway and 6th Ave., Tel. 575-9200.

Lyceum: 149 W 45th St. between Broadway and 6th Ave., Tel. 239-6200.

Minskoff: 1515 Broadway between 44th-45th Sts., Tel. 869-0550.

Music Box: 239 W 45th St. between 8th Ave., and Broadway, Tel. 239-6200.

Nederlander: 208 W 41st St. at 7th Ave., Tel. 921-8000.

Neil Simon: 250 W 52nd St. between 8th Ave. and Broadway, Tel. 307-4100.

Palace: 1564 Broadway, Tel. 730-8200.

Plymouth: 236 W 45th St. between

8th Ave. and Broadway, Tel. 239-6200.

Princess: 200 W 48th St. between Broadway and 7th Ave., Tel. 586-3903.

Royale: 242 W 45th St. between 8th Ave. and Broadway, Tel. 239-6200.

Shubert: 225 W 44th St. between 8th Ave. and Broadway, Tel. 239-6200.

St. James: 246 W 44th St. between 8th Ave. and Broadway, Tel. 239-6200.

The Ritz: 225 W 48th St. between Broadway and 8th Ave., Tel. 239-6200.

Virginia: 245 W 52nd St. between 8th Ave. and Broadway, Tel. 239-6200.

Winter Garden: 1634 Broadway at 50th St., Tel. 239-6200.

Other performance spaces which deserve special mention:

Carnegie Hall: 57th St. and 7th Ave. (see "57th St."), classical concerts and recitals, Tel. 247-7800.

City Center: 130 W 56th St. between 6th and 7th Aves., performances of the Alvin-Ailey Dance Co. and occasional cabaret-style shows, Tel. 247-0430.

St. Clement's: 423 W 46th St., occasional music concerts, Tel. 246-7277.

Ziegfeld: 141 W 54th St. between 6th and 7th Aves., one of the city's largest, most ornate movie theaters. All screenings first-run, Tel. 765-7600.

Tickets

There are several ways to purchase tickets. You can almost always purchase tickets through the theater's box office. This is convenient, but not always the least expensive method.

For Broadway shows, if you have a particular show in mind, call *Telecharge*, Tel. 239-6200, or *Ticketmaster*, Tel. 307-7171, and reserve tickets by credit card as much ahead of time as you possibly can. A service charge is added to the price of the ticket and one sometimes has to wait for quite a long time on the line. The tickets, kept at the box office under your name, can be picked up on the day of the show or before. Mail reservations, though possible, are not recommended.

The *Broadway Theater Guide* is available at the Broadway Theater ticket-stands. It includes theater maps as well as information on the shows to be performed.

If you're already in NYC, same-day or advance-sale full-price tickets for the show of your choice can be purchased at the given theater's box office. Or, tickets for many off-Broadway shows are concentrated at *Ticket Central*, 406 W 42nd St., open 7 days a week 1-8pm, Tel. 279-4200.

TKTS is still the best source of reduced-price tickets. Listings often include last year's hits which, though no longer "new in town," are still running strong. Open Mon.-Sat. 3-8pm for evening performances, (which almost always begin at 8pm), Wed.- Sat. 10am-2pm, and Sun. noon-7pm, for

matinee tickets. Matinees are usually Wed. 2pm, Sun. 3pm, and less frequently Sat. 2pm or 3pm. The line at *TKTS* begins forming before the booth opens, so get there early. Tel. 768-1818.

The ticket booth is at Times Square, in the part officially known as Father Duffy Square, at the intersection of Broadway, 7th Ave. and 47th St. It sells half-price day-of-performance tickets for certain shows. Take Subway 1, 2 or 3 to Times Square/42nd St. and walk north on Broadway or 7th Ave. to 47th St., or take Subway R to 49th St. and Broadway, walking south to 47th St. There is also a branch at the World Trade Center.

Another booth can be found at The World Trade Center; and in Brooklyn, at Court and Montague Sts. Both are open 11am-5:30pm, Sat. 11am-3:30pm. Travelers' Checks are accepted.

Ask for central mezzanine seats, which may be better, though farther away from the stage. Evening-performance Broadway tickets are available on the day before the performance. Use cash or travelers' checks. Add a service charge to each ticket; no refunds or exchanges.

The *TKTS* method, however, entails certain disadvantages:

The precise selection of shows, though almost always numerous, is posted only at the booth itself. The very latest "hits" are usually unavailable, since they've been sold out in advance; the ticket seller "determines" the best available seats for you. There are no seating charts; the line moves too quickly for lengthy decisions on your part. Most such tickets are for orchestra seats toward the ends of the rows. Ask for centrally-located mezzanine seats, which are preferable to off-center orchestra seats; the theaters generally give *TKTS* their higher-priced seats which, regardless of price, have not been sold at the box office because their viewing angle is not the best. Your half-price ticket – half of $60 – is still expensive, especially as you pay a service charge too. Sometimes, of course, you can relocate to better seats after the show begins or at intermission.

The *Public Theater* at 425 Lafayette, also offers a discount system, *Quiktix*, for half-price tickets on the day of performance. They are available two hours before curtain time. Full price tickets are available at the box office, Tel. 598-7150.

TICKETS FOR OPERA, DANCE AND MUSIC

The *Bryant Park Music and Dance Ticket Booths* are the place for half-price same-day tickets, or for full-price advance-sale tickets. Located at 1180 Avenue of the Americas. Open Tues., Thurs. and Fri. 12pm-9pm; Wed. and Sat. 11am-7pm, Sun. 12pm-6pm. Closed Mon. and every day between 2-3pm. Tel. 782-4390.

The Broadway Line Tel. 563-2929, offers information on Broadway and off-Broadway, tickets, locations and schedules.

Opera

Lincoln Center is home to the **Metropolitan Opera**, arguably the most prestigious and elegant opera house in the world. For information about forthcoming performances, Tel. 875-5000. The **New York City Opera** is also located in the Lincoln Center, Tel. 870-5570. During the summer, several operas are performed in the city's larger parks. Those of the Metropolitan are particularly recommended. For details, Tel. 362-6000.

It's usually possible to purchase tickets for an opera up to the last minute and, of course, the price then is much lower.

Dance

Several varieties of dance companies regularly perform in New York. The range is enormous, from classical ballet to avant-garde modern dance. Of the many prominent companies in the city, a few are particularly noteworthy, such as the **New York City Ballet**, a highly esteemed corps which performs at the Lincoln Center, Tel. 870-5660. The **Alvin Ailey Dance Company** is the resident dance company of the City Center but other modern

Night life at Greenwich Village

dance companies also make use of this venue, Tel. 767-0590. The **Dance Theater of Harlem** also dances here, as well as at other locations in and out of the city.

Classical Music

The **New York Philharmonic Orchestra** is only one of the many musical treats which this city has to offer classical music lovers. The world's top musicians regularly perform at the Avery Fisher Hall in the Lincoln Center, Tel. 875-5030, and at Carnegie Hall, Tel. 247-7800. During the summer, **Pier 84** hosts several outdoor concerts, Tel. 632-4001, and many free concerts of the Philharmonic are performed in the city's parks, often accompanied by impressive firework displays. For information, Tel. 580-8700.

Hard Rock Café

Jazz

Jazz was born in America's south and found its way to New York where it matured and blossomed. Today, this music is an indivisible part of New York. Strains of jazz can be heard emanating from concert halls and clubs throughout the city. Street musicians confirm this link between the pulsating city and soulful rhythm music. Jazz concerts are held in big concert halls as part of the Jazz Festival, but for a more intimate experience visit one or more of the several special jazz clubs around the city. Here you can enjoy the best of jazz while you sip a drink or enjoy a meal. Among New York's best clubs are:

The Blue Note: 131 W 3rd St., Tel. 475-8592.
Fat Tuesdays: 190 3rd Ave., Tel. 533-7900.
Sweet Basil's: 88 7th Ave., Tel. 242-1785.
Village Gate: corner Bleecker and Thompson Sts., Tel. 475-5120.
Village Vanguard: 178 7th Ave., Tel. 255-4037.
Duplex Jazz Club: 55 Grover St., Tel. 255-5438.
Michael's Pub: 55th St. between 2nd-3rd Ave. Tel. 758-2272. Reservations must be made.

Jazz line: Tel. (718) 465-7500.

Pop Concerts

Huge pop concerts are held in the city's biggest concert halls, such as **Carnegie Hall**, Tel. 247-7800, **Radio City Music Hall**, Tel. 247-4777 and the biggest of them all, **Madison Square Garden**, Tel. 563-8300. If an artist or group can command even a greater audience than can be housed in any of these halls, performances are held in one of the large sport stadiums (see "Sport").

Dance Clubs

New comers and old-timers appear in small clubs, some trying to work their way up the ladder while others cling tenaciously to the lower rungs on the way down from the top. Either way, the talent is still of a high standard. The clubs either have a cover charge or minimum order, some have both. The best known clubs are:

The Bottom Line: 15 W 4th St., Tel. 228-7880. For pop-rock and folk rock.
The Other End: 147 Bleecker St., Tel. 673-0730. For different types of music.
Sounds of Brazil (S.O.B.'s): 204 Varick St., Tel. 924-5221. South American, mainly Brazilian.

Comedy

If they cannot make you laugh in New York they'll never make you laugh. Try:

The Comic Strip : 81st St. and 2nd Ave. A showcase for stand-up comics and singers, Tel. 861-9386.
Chicago City Limits: 351 E 74th St. NY's longest-running comedy group. Tel. 772-8707.
Carolines Comedy Club: 1626 Broadway at 49th St., Tel. 757-4100.
Improvisation: 358 W 44th St., Tel. 279-3446. Comedy club founded in 1963.

Movie Theatres

In New York there is no lack of movie theaters. At every corner you will find one, and they screen the newest features hot from the editors table.

Sony-Imax: A unique attraction, this theater houses an 8 storey , 3-dimensional screen, with specially suited eye-ware for the viewer, this

The notable "Blue Note" jazz club

apart from ten ordinary screening halls, and a theater-props shop. 1990 Broadway Ave., Tel. 336-5600, for ticket reservations call Tel. 595-6297.

Shopping – What and Where?

A first-time visitor to New York will probably be overwhelmed by the huge variety of shopping possibilities before him. He is faced with seemingly endless stores, and piles of merchandise at an incredible range of prices.

Shopping in New York has become an end in itself, and tourists and locals alike visit the huge stores as if they were historical or natural sites of interest.

For bargains and curios read the chapter on "The Lower East Side and Little Italy." For high-quality

gifts and brand names, see "57th St."

The visitor to the city is limited, perhaps to his regret, as to the quantity of goods and chattels he can purchase and transport home. An excess of luggage makes travel cumbersome and it can be costly to pay excess baggage on flights. Sometimes one even has to pay high taxes on imported goods when returning home.

It is impossible, however, to return empty-handed and most tourists regard themselves as that part of the human species with a highly developed shopping sense. There are some basic rules which are well worth remembering: compile a detailed shopping list before setting out on your shopping spree; take note of sales which take place in the majority of stores and which offer significant reductions on the

Bargains for all

price of goods; special sales usually coincide with holidays; remember that you are limited by the airlines as to how much baggage you may take; take note of the customs regulations in your country regarding what you can bring in and how much customs you will have to pay; try and estimate how much you intend spending before entering a store and then try not to exceed this amount by more than 30%. If in spite of all this advice, you still over-bought, never mind, you won't be the first nor the last, so just relax and enjoy your purchases!

Street vendors sell a variety of merchandise, some legitimate, some "hot" (stolen), and some not quite what it appears to be – when rayon is described as cashmere, for example! The vendors are supposed to have licenses, but many do not. Despite this, you can get excellent prices on certain items. It is recommended not to purchase anything electronic – if it doesn't work when you get home, you can't return it. However, certain items are perfect street-fare, including umbrellas, scarves, earrings and other "junk" jewelry.

Uniquely New York: huge stores with a wide selection of merchandise.

Macy's: Herald Square, Tel. 695-4400. One of the biggest department stores in the world. Located in a building which stretches across the corner of 34th St. and Broadway. Take Subway B, D, F, N, Q or R. Open Mon., Thurs. and Fri. 9:45am-8:30pm, Tues. and Wed. 9:45am-6:45pm and Sun. 10am-6pm.

Bloomingdale's: 1000 3rd Ave., Tel. 777-0000. Size-wise comparable to *Macy's*, but more up-market with a classy and expensive range of just about everything. Located on the corner of 3rd Ave. and 59th St. Take Subway 4, 5, 6, N or R. Open Mon. and Sat. 10am-6:30pm, Tues. and Thurs. 10am-9pm and Sun. 12-6.30pm.

Saks Fifth Avenue: 611 5th Ave., Tel. 753-4000. Renowned worldwide for its designer clothing, this store is now one of a chain. Take Subway E or F. Open Mon.- Sat. 10am-6pm, Tues. until 10pm. Closed Sun.

Alexander's: 731 Lexington Ave., Tel. 593-0880. A wide selection of clothes and shoes. Quality goods and affordable prices. Located opposite the department store *Bloomingdale's*.

Century 21: This somewhat smaller department store is on 22 Cortland St., opposite the World Trade Center. Prices here are very reasonable.

In next-door New Jersey one can find the same stores as in the city, and without the taxes. The bus ride costs about $10.

What to Buy and Where

Lower East Side: Clothes, linen and electrical equipment using 220 volt.

Chinatown: Housewares, inexpensive electronic equipment.

47th Street: (between 5th and 6th Aves.) Jewelry and precious stones.

5th Ave.: (between 50th and 59th Sts.) Electrical equipment, cameras, designer clothes.

42nd St. and Times Square: Electrical equipment.

14th St. East: Textiles, cosmetics and photographic equipment at bargain prices.

57th St.: (between 3rd and 7th aves.) Exclusive clothing.

W. 8th St.: (between 4th and 6th Aves.) Shoes.

Shopping by Category

BOOKS
Scribner's: 597 5th Ave., Tel. 486-4070. A wonderful bookstore,

Shopping for Christmas

worth visiting even if you don't intend making any purchases.

The Strand: 828 Broadway, Tel. 473-1452. The largest collection of used editions in the city. Excellent prices and a knowledgeable staff.

Barnes and Noble: Jr. 128 5th Ave., Tel. 633-3500. There are a number of branches in the city. It is the largest bookstore in town and its Sales Annex offers the best bargains on new books.

The French and Spanish Bookstore: 115 5th Ave., Tel. 581-8810. The best bookstore for foreign language volumes.

Rizzoli: 31 W 57th St., Tel. 759-2424. A comprehensive selection of fine art books. There are a number of branches throughout the city.

Books of Wonder: 464 Hudson St., Tel. 645-8006. Great children's books, new and old.

Many stalls selling new books at bargain prices line Broadway.

RECORDS

Tower Records: Two large branches of this all-American chain with an incredible inventory of all styles of music, with a particularly vast

At Tower Records

Watch out for enormous-sized boxing gloves at "Think Big!"

selection of jazz. The Village branch is at 692 Broadway, Tel. 505-1500 and the other is next to the Lincoln Center, corner Broadway and 66th St., Tel. 496-2500.

J and R Music World: 23 Park Row Brooklyn, Tel. 238-9000. A wide selection to answer to all your musical requirements, electronic equipment and computers. The record store is divided into three separate stores for classical, jazz and pop. The cheapest prices in town, but no cash refunds after purchases have been made.

For lovers of vintage records and other oldies, Greenwich Village offers a few shops specializing in second-hand and old records. The most popular among them are:

Vinylmania, Tel. 924-7223; *House of Oldies*, Tel. 243-0500; and *Bleecker Bob's Golden Oldies*, Tel. 475-9677. These stores can all be phoned to first check that they have the records you're looking for.

TOYS

FOA Schwartz: 767 5th Ave., Tel. 644-9400. The most famous toy chain-store in the city and among the most famous in the world. An overwhelming selection, but prices are high.

Forbidden Planet: 821 Broadway, Tel. 473-1576. A marvellous collection of robots, science-fiction toys and literature.

San Francisco Ship Model Gallery: 1089 Madison Ave. at 82nd St., Tel. 570-6767. Toys for grown-ups. Scaled models of famous ships.

Kids'R US: Many branches of this huge store are scattered around the city.

SPORTS AND CAMPING

Paragon: 867 Broadway, Tel. 249-3178. Probably offers everything you'll ever need for a variety of sports or for camping. A sports person's paradise.

Herman's: 845 3rd Ave., Tel. 688-4603. An impressive variety at reasonable prices.

COSMETICS, JEWELRY AND ACCESSORIES

Tiffany's: 727 5th Ave., Tel. 755-8000. A movie star in its own right, it now carries more than jewelry. Very exclusive and expensive.

Van Cleef & Arpels: In *Bergdorf's*, 744 5th Ave., Tel. 644-9500. Very nice.

Louis Vuitton: 51 E 57th St., Tel. 371-6111. For the famous ostentatious luggage.

Hermes: 11 E 57th St. For "the" scarf. Nice leather goods.

Fortunoff's: 681 5th Ave., Tel. 758-6660. An abundance of merchandise at excellent prices.

Georgette Klinger: 501 Madison Ave., Tel 838-3200. Several "make-over" programs are available to you.

Bordels: 3rd Ave on the corner of E 56th St. The store is in a black building behind a bank and has a vast collection of perfume at bargain prices.

MEN'S CLOTHING

Barney's: 106 7th Ave., Tel. 929-9000. Every designer line is represented here. There is another branch for businessmen in the Twin Towers.

Paul Stuart: Madison Ave. and 45th St., Tel. 682-0320. Good quality, conservative and expensive fashion.

Moe Ginsburg: 162 5th Ave. Suits, tuxedos and shoes at reasonable prices. Tel. 242-3482.

Guy Laroche: 36 E 57th St., Tel. 759-2301. French. Sauve. Ready-to-wear.

Today's Man: 6th Ave. between 18th-19th Sts. Sells fashionable clothes, coats and suits at very reasonable prices.

WOMEN'S CLOTHING

For women's clothes, *Bloomingdale's* and *Saks Fifth Avenue*, which have already been mentioned, are both recommended. Other stores definitely worth visiting include:

Bergdorf Goodman: 754 5th Ave., Tel. 753-7300. Offers the height of fashion with equally high prices.

Henri Bendel: 712 5th Ave., Tel. 247-1100. An "in" store that is considered typically New York. Up-market fashions and relatively inexpensive.

Gap: Sells "cool" unisex clothes, also from the *Banana Republic* trademark. There are branches all over the city.

Forgotten Woman: 888 Lexington Ave., Tel. 247-888. Larger sizes, located near the Lincoln Center.

Maud Frizon: 49 E 57th St., Tel. 980-1460. For "the" French shoe.

ELECTRONICS AND PHOTOGRAPHIC EQUIPMENT

These goods are available in the large department stores as well as in little shops scattered throughout the city. The selection is infinite and the prices low.

47th Street Photo: 67 W 47th St., Tel. 921-1287. A huge selection, and one can bargain down the price. Make your selection *before*

Football – an American symbol

entering the store as the steady flow of customers makes browsing impossible.

Olden Camera: 1265 Broadway, Tel. 725-1234. Lots of bargains, antiquities, and junk. The mecca for photography afficionados.

ABC: 31 Canal St., Tel. 582-9334. In Lower East Side, specializing in 220v equipment.

Sport

The most popular sports in New York are baseball, football and basketball. The city's basketball team, the *Knickerbockers (the Knicks)*, plays at Madison Square Garden, Tel. 563-8300. The local football team, the *New York Giants,* plays at the Giants Stadium in neighboring New Jersey, Tel. (201) 935-8222. Baseball lovers divide their support between the two local teams, the *Mets*, whose home field is Shea Stadium in Queens (which also hosts pop and rock concerts), Tel. (718) 507-8499, and the *Yankees* who play at the famous stadium in the Bronx which bears the name of the team, Tel. 293-6000.

The US Open Tennis Championships attract thousands of spectators and is held at Flushing Meadow, Tel. (718) 271-5100. Spectators and others who enjoy a flutter at the races gather at the Aqueduct Racetrack and Belmont Park, Tel. (718) 641-4700, both in Queens. Madison Square Gardens also hosts major boxing matches, which usually attract huge crowds. For details of sporting events in the city it is recommended to consult the sports section of the *New York Times* and ticket offices such as *Ticketron*, Tel. 399-4444.

SPORT'S INFORMATION

The NY Marathon: information at NY Runner's Club, Tel. 860-4455. US Tennis center box office: Tel. 696-7284.
Mets – tickets and information: Tel. 507-TIXX.
The Knicks Hotline: Tel. 465-JUMP.
The Rangers Hotline: Tel. 463-6741.

Horse Racing at Belmont Park: Tel. 641-4700.
Horseback Riding: Jamaica Bay Riding Academy, Tel. (718) 531-8949.
Rock Climbing: Recreation Center, W 59th, Tel. 397-3166.
Cycling: Central Park Bicycle Rentals, Tel. 210-0201.
Skating: Rockefeller Center Ice Skating Rink, Tel. 757-5730.

Playing baseball at Yankee Stadium

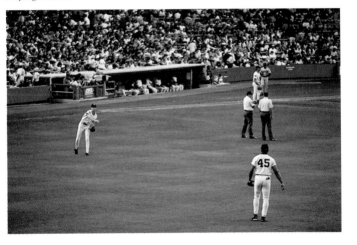

Important Phone Numbers

EMERGENCIES
Ambulance, Fire and Police: Tel. 911 or 0; 693-9911.
Bus and Subway Information: Tel. 718-330-1234.
Car Trouble: Tel. 411 (Information) for nearest police precinct for local towing listings.
Police Hotline: Tel. 340-2723.
Lost and Found: Tel. 435-2611.
24hr. Pharmacy: *Kaufman Pharmacy*, Lexington Ave. and 50th St. Tel. 755-2266.
Weather: Tel. 976-1212.
Emergency Dentist: Tel. 972-9299.
Crime Victims Help: Tel. 577-777.
Mt. Sinai Hospital: 101 St. and 5th Ave., Tel. 241-6500.

AIRLINES
American Airlines: Tel. 800-223-5436.
Continental Airlines: Tel. 800-231-0856.
Delta: Tel. 239-0700.
T.W.A.: Tel. 290-2121.
United: Tel. 800-241-6522.
US Air: Tel. 800-428-4322.
NorthWest: Tel. 800-441-1818.
America West: Tel. 800-235-9292.
Virgin: Tel. 800-862-8621.
Air France: Tel. 247-0100.
Alitalia: Tel. 582-8900.
El Al: Tel. 800-223-6700.
KLM: Tel. 800-374-7747.
British Airways: Tel. 800-247-9297.
Sabena: Tel. 800-955-2000.
Tower Air: Tel. 553-4300.
Lufthansa: Tel. 800-645-3880.

American Flag Airlines has a terminal in Manhattan. It is located at 100 E 42nd St. (across from Grand Central Terminal). The ticket offices are on the 2nd floor, Tel. 986-0888.

TOURIST INFORMATION
The New York Convention and Tourist Bureau has two offices, one at 2 Columbus Circle and the other at 1465 Broadway (in Times Sq.).

All lined up and ready to go – the New York Police Department

For both locations, call Tel.
397-8222. Open Mon.-Fri., 9am-
6pm. Sat., Sun. and holidays,
10am-6pm.
Brooklyn's – BACA, is at 200
Eastern Parkway. Tel. 397-8222;
Travelers Aid Society: Tel.
944-0013.

MISCELLANEOUS
Mayor of NY, office: Tel. 788-7585.
US Post Office: Tel. 967-8585.
Immigration: Immigration Informa-
tion Service, 2 Park Ave., Tel.
206-6500.
Parks and Recreation (24 hours.
hotline service): Tel. 360-1333.

QUESTIONNAIRE

In our efforts to keep up with the pace and pulse of New York, we kindly ask your cooperation in sharing with us any information which you may have as well as your comments. We would greatly appreciate your completing and returning the following question-naire. Feel free to add additional pages.

Our many thanks!

To: Inbal Travel Information (1983) Ltd.
18 Hayetzira St.
Ramat Gan 52521
Israel

Name: _____

Address: _____

Occupation: _____

Date of visit: _____

Purpose of trip (vacation, business, etc.): _____

Comments/Information: _____

_____

_____

_____

_____

_____

_____

INBAL Travel Information Ltd.
P.O.B 1870 Ramat Gan
ISRAEL 52117